The African Novel in English

STUDIES IN AFRICAN LITERATURE

▼▼▼▼▼▼▼▼▼▼▼▼▼▼▼▼▼▼▼▼▼▼▼▼▼

▼▼▼▼▼▼▼▼▼▼▼▼▼▼▼▼▼▼▼▼▼▼▼▼▼▼▼▼▼▼▼

The African Novel in English

An Introduction

M. KEITH BOOKER
University of Arkansas

HEINEMANN
Portsmouth, NH

JAMES CURREY
Oxford

Heinemann
A division of Reed Elsevier Inc.
361 Hanover Street
Portsmouth, NH 03801-3912

Offices and agents throughout the world

James Currey Ltd.
73 Botley Road
Oxford OX2 0BS

Heinemann ISBN 0-325-00030-1
James Currey ISBN 0-85255-552-0

British Library Cataloguing-in-Publication Data
Booker, M. Keith
    The African novel in English : an introduction.— (Studies in African literature)
    1. African fiction (English)—History and criticism
    I. Title
    823' .009'96

    ISBN 0-85255-552-0

Library of Congress Cataloging-in-Publication Data
Booker, M. Keith
    The African novel in English : an introduction / M. Keith Booker.
        p.   cm.— (Studies in African literature)
    Includes bibliographical references (p.   ) and index.
    ISBN 0-325-00030-1
    1. African fiction (English)—History and criticism. 2. Africa —In
    literature.   I. Title. II. Series.
    PR9344.B66   1998
    823.009'896—DC21   97-31166
                                                                 CIP

Editor: James Lance
Production: Elizabeth Valway
Cover design: Jenny Greenleaf
Manufacturing: Louise Richardson

Printed in the United States of America on acid-free paper

02   01   00   99   98   DA   1   2   3   4   5

Contents

▼▼▼▼▼▼▼▼▼

For Dubravka
And dedicated to the memory of
Patrice Lumumba, Amilcar Cabral,
Chris Hani, and all of those who have given
their lives in the struggle to set things right

Preface
▼▼▼▼▼▼▼

The rise to global prominence of African literature, and particularly of the African novel, is widely recognized as one of the most vital and dynamic events of world culture in the last quarter century. This textbook introduces American and British students to this exciting literary phenomenon. The book includes three basic components. Chapter 1 consists of introductions to a number of important issues that Western students must be aware of when approaching the African novel. Chapter 2 provides a brief historical survey of the development of the African novel within the context of broader developments such as colonialism, decolonization, and postcolonialism. The third, and longest, section of the book consists of a series of chapters that provide discussions of eight important African novels, ranging from founding texts such as Chinua Achebe's *Things Fall Apart* to recent contributions such as Tsitsi Dangarembga's *Nervous Conditions*. To help students place these discussions in context, each of the discussions of specific novels is followed by a survey of the text's historical background, as well as a survey of the author's life and career.

Because the African novel is such a large and diverse literary phenomenon, certain (sometimes very difficult) choices have had to be made in the formulation of this volume, particularly in the selection of individual texts for discussion in Chapters 3 through 10. A few prefatory comments regarding these choices are probably in order, especially as some of them are more complex than they may appear. For example, it is not at all a simple matter to define what constitutes an African novel to begin with. The novel is a rather vaguely defined genre in general, and this is especially the case in Africa, where the Western novelistic tradition often engages in productive dialogues with indigenous cultural practices. Even more importantly, the adjective "African" itself is not as easy to define as might first appear. Africa, unlike Europe (which is really a peninsula on the western side of Asia), is at least a well-defined geographic continent. But Africa has also been the object of a long Western tradition of imaginary constructions that have greatly distorted our perception of the continent, often in harmful and negative ways. Indeed, this tradition of imaginary misrepresentation is one of the greatest obstacles that must be overcome by American students who approach African culture for the first time. Africa is not just a dense jungle where Tarzan wrestles with cannibals, lions, and tigers. For one thing, most of the continent is not covered by jungle, and the continent has never contained any tigers nor many cannibals. Moreover, Africa is a large and diverse continent where many peoples and many cultures meet and interact. Ali A. Mazrui (1986), in an excellent introduction to some of the complexities of African culture and society, notes that the continent includes at least three different major cultural influences: the indigenous culture of traditional African societies, the Islamic culture brought to Africa by Arabs who eventually settled on the continent, and the European culture brought to Africa during the period of colonialism. Each of these three cultural forces is in itself quite complex and diverse, but in Africa various combinations of the three can create hybrid cultural phenomena that extend beyond any of the three original cultures.

The African novel is, in fact, one such hybrid phenomenon, which contributes to the complexity of its definition. For example, many novels by white European writers involve prominent African characters or are set largely or entirely in Africa. From founding texts such as Aphra Behn's 1688 work *Oroonoko* (arguably the first English novel) and the 1720 novel *Captain Singleton* by Daniel Defoe (regarded by many as the first English novelist), to nineteenth-century works of popular fiction such as H. Rider Haggard's *She* and *King Solomon's Mines*, to respected works of modern literature such as Joseph Conrad's *Heart of Darkness*, Joyce Cary's *Mister Johnson*, and Graham Greene's *The Heart of the Matter* and *A Burnt-Out Case*, the development of the English novel has been shaped by works about Africa. Some of the authors of these works spent extensive periods in Africa, and many European writers (Elspeth Huxley and Isak Dinesen are prominent examples) settled permanently in Africa during the period of colonial rule. British writers such as William Boyd and David Caute were in fact born in Africa during the colonial period, and Doris Lessing grew up there.

Unfortunately, many European novels about Africa show no real knowledge of Africa or Africans, presenting both in only the most ignorant and stereotypical ways. Even first-hand knowledge of Africa has not guaranteed that European writers could represent Africa and its people in fair and accurate ways. Indeed, settler writers such as Huxley and Dinesen have been among the worst offenders in promulgating condescending racist stereotypes of Africans, while writers such as Boyd and Caute have focused largely on European experience in an African setting. The works of all of these writers tend to be based upon fundamentally European aesthetic assumptions that show little influence of African cultural traditions. It has therefore been a relatively easy decision to exclude European works about Africa from this volume. It is, however, certainly valuable to compare novels of Africa by European novelists to the novels that I have considered as more properly African, especially because many African novelists react directly against the invidious portrayals of Africa and Africans conveyed by colonialist European novels.

By "African" writers I mean writers who were not only born and reared in Africa, but whose cultural roots are also in African societies, regardless of whether those writers later live and work outside of Africa. I thus include all writers who are native black Africans as African writers. I also include native white writers from South Africa in this category, because the white settler culture in South Africa has been established for enough generations that it now qualifies as "African." In this sense, I would also include the works of North African writers from areas such as Egypt, the Sudan, or the northwest African region known as the Maghreb (Morocco, Algeria, and Tunisia), and the works of such writers are briefly discussed in Chapter 2. However, the cultural traditions of North Africa differ substantially from those of sub-Saharan Africa, largely because Islam has supplanted earlier cultural traditions in North Africa so thoroughly that it now has essentially the status of an indigenous culture. On the other hand, pre-Islamic traditions are still strong in sub-Saharan regions such as Mali and Senegal that are now largely Muslim. The cultural climate of most of sub-Saharan Africa, especially the regions that were formerly British colonies, is largely a mixture of Christian and traditional African traditions. I have, therefore, chosen not to include North African writers in this volume, not because they are not African, but simply because I do not have enough space to deal with their work adequately. North African novels are probably even more culturally foreign to American readers than the works of writers from sub-Saharan Africa, especially those regions that (like the United States) are former British colonies.

As part of a general emphasis on accessibility to American and British undergraduate readers, I have decided to focus on novels by writers from former British colonies, most of whom write in English. These novels are thus linguistically available to American readers in an immediate way. In addition, former British colonies probably have more in common culturally with the United States than other regions of Africa do, so it is easier for American students to engage in productive readings of these novels rather than some other African novels. For one thing, Anglophone (English-language) African writers often engage in direct dialogues with works of British or American authors that American students may know. As a result, this book pays relatively little attention to African novels in French, Portuguese, Spanish, and African languages, though Chapter 2 does include a brief survey of novels in these languages. In addition, the emphasis on accessibility has led me to exclude important English-language novels such as Wole Soyinka's *The Interpreters* or Bessie Head's *A Question of Power*, largely because I find that these texts are extremely difficult for Western readers, especially those who are just beginning to study the African novel. I have, however, tried to include as many important works as possible, choosing novels that are widely read in Africa and have had a substantial influence on the works of other African writers. Within the basic focus on Anglophone novels, I have also tried to choose works that represent as many different aspects of modern African culture as possible that can also be read and studied together in productive ways.

The third section of the book begins with a treatment of Achebe's *Things Fall Apart*, one of the founding texts of the Anglophone African novel and probably the African novel that is best known in the West. Achebe's evocation of the precolonial Igbo culture of southeastern Nigeria—and of the impact of the colonial intrusion on that culture—makes a number of crucial points about the confrontation between Western culture and indigenous African cultures during the colonial period. Moreover, *Things Fall Apart* combines Western novelistic conventions with the conventions of African oral storytelling in ways that have been of central importance to the development of the African novel. The second text forms an interesting counterpart to Achebe's book. Buchi Emecheta's *The Joys of Motherhood* treats many of the same issues as *Things Fall Apart* but from a different perspective, partially because it takes place largely in an urban setting and in a slightly later period, but mostly because Emecheta addresses questions related to gender from a feminine perspective.

This pair of Nigerian texts is followed by a pair of texts by Ghanaian writers, again one by a man and one by a woman. These two texts, however, focus on the problems of the postcolonial period. Ayi Kwei Armah's *The Beautyful Ones Are Not Yet Born* is a biting critique of Ghana's social and economic problems in the 1960s, depicting an entire society overwhelmed by corruption brought about primarily by fascination with the "gleam" of Western commodity culture. Ama Ata Aidoo's *Our Sister Killjoy* also addresses the problem of cultural imperialism—the subtle ongoing domination of Africa by the West. By depicting the journey of an African protagonist to Europe, Aidoo's book also reverses the common scenario in which a European traveler goes to Africa, providing a fresh perspective on the relationship between the two cultures.

Among other things, my initial focus on these four West African novels indicates the historical importance of West African writers in the development of the African novel. The next two chapters grow out of a significantly different cultural, historical, and political context, discussing works by two South African writers and thus calling attention to the phenomenon of apartheid and its demise, two crucial events in African history. The first of these chapters treats *Burger's Daughter*, by Nadine Gordimer, a white South African writer whose status as a Nobel Prize winner indicates the respect her work has gained worldwide. Gordimer's book focuses on the evils of the apartheid regime in South Africa and on the opposition of white citizens, especially those affiliated with the South African Communist Party. The next chapter discusses Alex La Guma's *In the Fog of the Seasons' End*, which depicts the efforts of mostly black and "coloured" (persons of mixed race) South Africans to oppose apartheid not just through education and agitation, but also through violent revolution and guerrilla warfare.

The next chapter also focuses on a book that advocates violent revolution, the Kenyan Ngugi wa Thiong'o's *Devil on the Cross*. This chapter extends the coverage of this volume to East Africa. It also looks at Ngugi's important treatment of the phenomenon of neocolonialism in Kenya, where foreign interests continue to control much of the nation's economic and cultural resources decades after nominal independence from British colonial rule. *Devil on the Cross* (translated into English by the author) is also important because it was the first book Ngugi wrote in the Gikuyu language, though he had previously gained a substantial reputation as an English-language novelist. The book thus brings to the fore a number of issues surrounding the so-called language question in the African novel. Ngugi's novel focuses on the development and education of a female protagonist, as does Dangarembga's *Nervous Conditions*, the topic of the final chapter in this volume. However, because it was written by a woman, Dangarembga's book necessarily treats this topic in a somewhat different way. Dangarembga's book is set in colonial Rhodesia (later Zimbabwe), which expands this volume's coverage of southern Africa to include Zimbabwean history and culture. Together, these eight chapters should give students a good initial idea of the scope and variety of the African novel, of the issues it typically treats, and of the strategies it typically employs. Nevertheless, it should be emphasized that many other novels could have been chosen to achieve the same purpose.

I would like to express my appreciation to all of those who have provided encouragement and help during the evolution of this book. Perhaps foremost among these are the students at the University of Arkansas, both graduate and undergraduate, who provided me with an interactive forum for the initial development of the ideas expressed here. Special thanks are due to the scholars of African literature who have read all or part of this volume and provided me with their comments, including Katherine Fishburn, Abiola Irele, Dubravka Juraga, Christopher Miller, and Emmanuel Obiechina. I would also like to thank all of those who provided advice and encouragement in the early stages of the writing of this volume, including Chinua Achebe, Odun Balogun, Reed Way Dasenbrock, Ali A. Mazrui, V.Y. Mudimbe, and Wole Soyinka. Finally, I would like to thank Jean Hay and Jim Lance of Heinemann for believing in this project and for all of her help in bringing it to fruition.

Chapter 1

▼▼▼▼▼▼▼▼▼▼

Introduction:
Reading the African Novel

The Question of Relevance:
The African Novel and the Western Reader

Spurred partially by the newly energized civil rights and feminist movements of the 1960s, American literary scholarship in the past quarter of a
century has shown a greatly increased sensitivity to cultural perspectives
outside the mainstream of the Western literary heritage, a heritage dominated almost entirely by the "canonical" writers often now collectively referred
to as "dead white males." This new awareness of alternative perspectives has
led, within the context of American literature, to a dramatic increase in interest in works written by women, African Americans, Native Americans,
Hispanic Americans, and others. Published literary criticism now quite reg-
ularly deals with works by such writers, and the college literature curricu-
lum has been expanded in the past twenty years to include a number of
such works as well. Meanwhile, similar phenomena have occurred in Great
Britain, where the rapid decolonization of the early 1960s has contributed
to new respect for and attention to the works of writers from the former
empire. Indeed, because of the direct historical connection, the relevance of
literature from Africa and other former parts of the British Empire to Britain is especially obvious. But Africa looms large in American history as well.
Americans who tend to think of the European cultural tradition of Dante,
Shakespeare, and Milton as the background to American culture need to recall the central role played in the building of America by the tens of millions of Africans who were forcibly removed from their home continent
and brought to America on slave ships. The cultural roots of these slaves and
of their descendants, a large and important segment of the American population, are not in Europe but in Africa. Moreover, we are only just coming
to understand how profoundly even the mainstream "white" culture of
America has been influenced by the contributions of African-American art-

ists and how thoroughly even the works of white American writers have been conditioned by the particular nature of race relations in America.[1]

African literature has experienced a period of rich growth and development in the past forty years. There has been a dramatic increase in the number of novels produced by African writers during this period, and African novelists such as Chinua Achebe, Wole Soyinka, Nadine Gordimer, Naguib Mahfouz, Ngugi wa Thiong'o, Ousmane Sembène, Buchi Emecheta, Mariama Bâ, Bessie Head, Ayi Kwei Armah, Nuruddin Farah, and J. M. Coetzee have made important contributions to contemporary world literature and to the development of the novel as a genre. It might be noted, for example, that Gordimer, Coetzee, and Ben Okri have all been winners of Britain's prestigious Booker Prize in recent years and that Gordimer, Soyinka, and Mahfouz have been awarded the Nobel Prize for literature.

British and American students and scholars of literature have numerous reasons to be interested in the African novel. Not only is African literature a prominent component of contemporary world literature, but African culture is also a crucial part of the national cultural heritages of both Britain and America. We live in an increasingly global society, and scholars are beginning to realize the interconnectedness of the world's cultures and economies at the end of the twentieth century. For example, in much of his recent work, the American Marxist cultural critic Fredric Jameson has focused on this process of globalization, which he associates with the phenomenon he calls "late capitalism." Following the German thinker Ernest Mandel (1975), Jameson argues that late capitalism is the third historical stage of capitalist development, following the stage of classic capitalism delineated by Karl Marx and the stage of imperialism delineated by Vladimir Lenin. Late capitalism is fundamentally informed by the business operations of large multinational conglomerates whose resources (and loyalties) transcend the boundaries of any single nation. Jameson's suggestion that popular culture is a global, rather than national, phenomenon resonates with a number of recent theoretical discussions of the phenomenon of "cultural imperialism," that is, the continuing cultural domination by Europe and North America of the former colonial world. Indeed, the most striking characteristic of global culture at the end of the twentieth century is the almost totally dominant position occupied worldwide by "American" popular culture, which thereby becomes a sort of cultural successor to the British Empire. Indeed, many have described this phenomenon as "cultural imperialism"—that is, as a continuation of the earlier European colonization of much of the globe— but in subtle cultural forms rather than direct political ones. American film, television, and music enjoy an unprecedented prominence all over the world,

---

[1] See, for example, the recent study by Sundquist (1993).

though Jameson's remarks would suggest that, strictly speaking, the popular culture that emanates from America is more accurately regarded as the global culture of late capitalism. It is, after all, produced by large multinational entertainment corporations whose interests are not necessary the same as the national interests of the United States.

Cultural imperialism, in short, may be more complicated than the simple imposition of one nation's culture on others. Relevant here is John Tomlinson's argument that cultural imperialism needs to be seen not as an instance of some national cultures dominating others but as the simultaneous worldwide spread of capitalism and modernization. After reviewing a number of descriptions of cultural imperialism, Tomlinson concludes that all of them suggest a historical movement in which "imperialism" is replaced by "globalization" (Tomlinson 1991, 175). Tomlinson's concept of globalization derives from the work of a number of theorists of cultural imperialism, including Jameson's comments on late capitalism; for both Tomlinson and Jameson the distinctive characteristic of world culture at the end of the twentieth century is its participation in an interconnected global cultural system.

Indeed, by the end of the twentieth century, culture is such a global phenomenon that African and Western culture no longer exist as separate, pure phenomena, each independent of the other. As philosopher Kwame Anthony Appiah puts it, the circulation of cultures in our postmodern moment makes it inevitable that "we are all already contaminated by each other, that there is no longer a fully autochthonous echt-African culture awaiting salvage by our artists (just as there is, of course, no American culture without African roots)" (Appiah 1992, 155). Of course, to understand that Africa is now part of a global economic system and that African culture is a component of world culture is not to deny that it still retains distinctive characteristics. On the other hand, many observers—Jameson included—have worried that the global dominance of late-capitalist culture is gradually leading to a homogenization that robs the world of its former cultural diversity and richness. In his recent work, Jameson often figures the postcolonial world as one of the few remaining bastions of potentially productive cultural energy in the midst of a world that is otherwise caught entirely in the global net of late capitalism. Thus, he remarks that "the only authentic cultural production today has seemed to be that which can draw on the collective experience of marginal pockets of the social life in the world system," a category that for him includes such heterogeneous entities as Third World literature, black American literature, British working-class rock, women's literature, gay literature, and the *roman québécois* (Jameson 1992, 23). It may be problematic to group such diverse cultural forces or to describe a phenomenon as broad as Third World literature as a "marginal pocket," but Jameson's point is that these diverse cultural phenomena seem to share a common ability to resist the homogenizing tendencies of global capitalism and to tap into collective experience in ways that the more mainstream culture cannot.

African literature, in short, is relevant for Western students of literature not only because in a global society we need to know about African culture, but also because African literature provides new artistic perspectives that help us learn about the workings of art and literature in general. Westerners can thus profit from reading African literature both because Africa and the West are parts of the same global economic and cultural system and because African culture differs from Western culture in crucial ways that help us to gain insights into reality—insights that Western literature may not be able to provide. Moreover, at first glance, African literature is easily accessible to British and American readers. Much of it is written in English and in literary modes with which we are familiar. The novel, for example, has been a particularly popular genre among African writers. At the same time, however, African literature differs from American and European literature in certain crucial ways, and Western readers need to be aware of these important differences when they read African literature.

The Question of Cultural Difference: Orientalism vs. Universalism

Having acknowledged the relevance of the African novel to their lives, Western readers still need to be aware that African novels arise from a cultural and historical perspective that differs from their own in fundamental ways. African novels are first and foremost about *Africa,* however connected Africa may be to the rest of the world. Therefore, in reading African novels we need to know something about African history and African societies. Some of this knowledge, of course, can be gained from the novels themselves, though we need to resist the tendency (long common among Western readers of African literature) to see African literary texts as little more than odd and exotic curiosities that tell us something about the workings of an alien culture. As Henry Louis Gates, Jr., notes, Western readers have quite frequently used African literature merely as "evidence of African 'anthropology,' of traditional and modern African customs and beliefs" (Gates 1984, 5). Gates points out that for many years African novels were taught primarily in anthropology courses rather than in literature at American universities. He also notes that when Soyinka, a world-renowned literary figure, joined the faculty of Cambridge University in 1973, it was assumed there that he would be teaching not literature but anthropology!

We need to remember that African art is still art, though it is also true that the immediacy of the cultural and political problems addressed by post-colonial writing often gives that literature a relationship to reality that seems more direct and urgent than that found in Western literature. But we also need to understand that the criteria and conventions governing the production of art can vary dramatically from one society to another—or, for that matter, from one historical period to another within the same society. Not surprisingly, African novelists quite often make important use of formal strategies and techniques that are derived from African cultural traditions and that differ substantially from Western aesthetic conventions. For example, the rich tradition of African oral epics provides an important example of extended narratives in African culture that is at least as important as the European novel in constituting the background to the African novel. As readers, we therefore need some familiarity with those African traditions to appreciate certain technical aspects of many African novels and to resist the temptation to think of African aesthetics as a flawed version of European aesthetics—or as no aesthetics at all.

Having granted the African novel an aesthetic dimension, Western readers must avoid the temptation to judge African novels merely by our own aesthetic standards, thus giving the greatest value to the African novels that are most similar to the best European or American novels. Indeed (no doubt partially in response to anthropological readings that ignore the artistic component of African literature), influential early critics of African literature have often made this mistake. See, for example, the works of Charles Larson (1972) and Eustace Palmer (1972, 1983). Such critics have tended to argue for the aesthetic value of African literature merely through the use of universalist arguments that claim that African literature is worth reading because it is often quite similar to European literature. Such arguments obviously fail to respect the difference of African cultural traditions, but they are in fact quite typical of approaches to art and literature that have been prominent in the West for centuries. Indeed, such arguments participate in a tendency toward universalization that underlies virtually every aspect of European bourgeois ideology. Jameson notes the universalizing tendency of bourgeois aesthetics when he comments on the way the "restricted code" of bourgeois aesthetic values comes to be regarded as universal at the moment of the firm establishment of capitalism in Europe, when the bourgeoisie begins to feel that "its private experience is for a time that of the world itself" (Jameson 1992, 169).

Of course, such universalist approaches to literature can only be justified if one believes that literature somehow obeys its own laws in a way that is independent of historical context. This attitude is again typical of many Western visions of literature. Formalist critical approaches like the American New Criticism are the clearest example, and the slogan "Art for art's sake" is a central expression. The Nigerian critic Molara Ogundipe-Leslie, responding in particular to Larson, argues that such universalist treatments of African literature derive from Western cultural assumptions aligned with a privileging of capitalist economics and masculinist social structures (Ogundipe-Leslie 1973, 89). If nothing else, it is valuable for Western readers to study African literature because a sensitive reading of that literature makes it quite obvious that the different social and historical background of African literature leads to artistic criteria and conventions that differ from those of Europe or America. African literature thus provides an important demonstration that art cannot be separated from the social world, and that aesthetic criteria are not universal and timeless but arise in response to specific historical conditions and developments. As Achebe angrily suggested in a lecture on the relationship between art and society in the postcolonial world, the close connection between literature and politics in that world makes it clear that "art for art's sake is just another piece of deodorised dogshit" (Achebe 1975, 29).

Not surprisingly, African literary scholars have reacted against both anthropological and universalist readings of African literature. The prominent African critic Abiola Irele, for example, notes that African critics have felt pressure to conform to Western formalist approaches to literature in order to establish that African literature is worthy of serious critical attention at all. Thus, African critics of African literature have been hesitant to discuss the social and political implications of their literature because of Western tendencies to declare such discussions primitive by definition. For Irele, however, such readings of African literature are essential:

> The manifest concern of the writers to speak to the immediate issues of social life, to narrate the tensions that traverse their world—to relate their imaginative expression to their particular universe of experience in all its existential concreteness—this seems to me to leave the African critic with hardly any choice but to give precedence to the powerful referential thrust of our literature (Irele 1990, xiv).

Similarly, in his excellent introduction to the West African novel, Emmanuel Obiechina repeatedly emphasizes the social and political engagement of such novels, which are often overtly didactic in their attempt to convince their readers to support certain specific political ideas:

> Because the West African novel has risen at a time when large-scale social and economic changes are taking place, the writers show an almost obsessive preoccupation with the influence of these conditions. This is the condition of life; these are the ways in which people feel its pressure; these pressures demand expression (Obiechina 1975, 35).

Perhaps the most powerful response to Western criticism of African literature has come from the Nigerian critics Chinweizu, Onwuchekwa Jemie, and Ihechukwu Madubuike. In their controversial but important book *Toward the Decolonization of African Literature* (1983), these three critics review in detail the work of Western commentators such as Palmer and Larson in order to reveal the assumption of Western cultural superiority that lies behind their work, even when they are ostensibly attempting to serve as advocates for the value of African literature. Chinweizu, Jemie, and Madubuike have been especially influential for their impassioned insistence that critics of African literature should pay close and serious attention to the role played by African oral traditions in the development of modern African literature. To emphasize the dialogue between African and European literature at the expense of ignoring the specific Africanness of African literature is for these critics merely a subtle continuation of the European colonial domination of Africa. At the same time, Chinweizu et al. are perfectly aware that African writers have been influenced by Western models, so that the African novel is always a complex hybrid cultural phenomenon that combines Western and African cultural perspectives. They point out that "the African novel is a hybrid of the African oral tradition and the imported forms of Europe, and it is precisely this hybrid origin which needs most to be considered" when judging the effectiveness of African novels (Chinweizu et al. 1983, 8).

A proper appreciation of the hybridity of the African novel is perhaps the most important (and in some ways the most difficult) task facing the Western reader, especially because African writers are engaged in a concerted effort to contribute to the development of their own national cultures in ways that are independent of European domination. One might note here Biodun Jeyifo's argument that postcolonial writing in general falls into one of two basic categories. One kind of writing, which he calls "normative" or "proleptic" postcoloniality, seeks to speak "to, or for, or in the name of the post-independence nation-state." Postcolonial writers in this group are engaged in the "reassertion or reinvention of traditions which colonialism, not without considerable success, had sought to destroy or devalue." The other form of postcolonial writing is what Jeyifo calls "interstitial" or "liminal" postcoloniality. Writers in this category work within a complex combination of First World and Third World cultural paradigms, creating self-representations that are "diasporic, exilic, hybrid, in-between, cosmopolitan" (Jeyifo 1991, 53).[2]

It is one thing to acknowledge that the African novel incorporates both African and European literary traditions; it is quite another to resist the temptation to lean too far in one direction or another in appreciating this hybridity. It is crucial for Western readers to understand that the African novel differs from European and American ones both in its sociohistorical background and in its aesthetic conventions. At the same time, Western readers should resist the tendency to think of the African novel as an exotic alien artifact. As Jameson points out in an influential (and controversial) essay on Third World literature, Western critics who discuss such literature find them-

---

[2] These two kinds of postcolonial writing are not mutually exclusive. In this same article, for example, Jeyifo argues that Achebe combines the two modes in texts like *Things Fall Apart*.

selves torn between a tendency toward "orientalism"—in which the critics emphasize the radical difference of the Third World culture from their own First World culture—and a tendency toward "universalism"—in which difference is effaced and the cultural values of Western Europe and North America are assumed to apply worldwide (Jameson 1986, 77). Jameson further notes that any critical attempt to respect the otherness of Third World culture risks descending into a negative orientalism that converts that culture into an alien and exotic curiosity. Jameson himself opts to emphasize the difference between First and Third World literatures to call attention to the things we, as First World readers, might learn from Third World literature.

If Western critics of African literature must negotiate a path between undesirable alternatives, similar alternatives have long been central to the cultural climate in Africa. As the Caribbean-African intellectual Frantz Fanon has emphasized, the colonial situation is fundamentally informed by a stark, Manichean opposition between the colonizer and the colonized (Fanon 1968, 41). This opposition inherently leads to extremist attitudes. Drawing upon the ideas of both Jameson and Fanon, Abdul JanMohamed argues that a writer from a colonial society is caught in a double bind: if he rejects European culture and tries to draw upon indigenous cultural traditions in his work, he is seen as a primitive savage; if he attempts to emulate European culture he is seen as a "vacant imitator without a culture of his own" (JanMohamed 1983, 5). Thus, if African writers follow African examples in their work, that work seems to Europeans to be primitive and artless. If they follow European examples, then that only proves that African culture is unable to produce genuine art. One might note, for example, that the Nigerian writer Amos Tutuola—sometimes identified as the first English-language novelist in Africa—has been disparaged by many Western critics because his work (which draws extensively upon Yoruba oral traditions) does not conform to the conventions of the English novel.[3]

In the same vein, the important African thinker and revolutionary political leader Amilcar Cabral has noted that the cultures of colonized societies are in danger of annihilation through the attempts of their European colonizers to "create theories which, in fact, are only gross formulations of racism, and which, in practice, are translated into a permanent state of siege of the indigenous populations on the basis of racist dictatorship (or democracy)" (Cabral 1973, 40). Moreover, Cabral points out that these theories typically take one of two forms that seem distinctly different, but in the end they both amount to the destruction of indigenous cultures. On the one hand, there is the overt racism of "apartheid," in which Africans or other in-

---

[3] On Fagunwa's Yoruba-language narratives as predecessors of Tutuola's novels, see Irele (1990, 174–88) and Obiechina (1990, 16–17).

digenous peoples are viewed as radically different from and inferior to Europeans, while African culture is seen as primitive, debased, or even nonexistent. On the other hand, there is the theory of "assimilation" of indigenous populations into the culture of the colonizer, which seems more democratic, but which for Cabral "turns out to be only a more or less violent attempt to deny the culture of the people in question" (p. 40).

Western readers who would avoid a repetition of the cultural destruction cited by Cabral must resist the temptation to read African literature according to strictly Western criteria or to treat African literary texts as exotic specimens of cultural otherness. This project, however, is not an easy one. It requires constant vigilance and, in many cases, the radical reformulation of lifelong habits of reading. However, careful consideration of certain basic issues can do a great deal to help Western readers read African literature effectively. These include an understanding that postcolonial African literature reacts not only against the decades of European political rule in Africa, but also against a long legacy of negative representations of Africa and Africans in European and American writing. It is also important for Western readers to understand that many questions that seem to have simple answers in Western literature are not so simple in Africa. The very choice of a language in which to write can, for an African writer, be a highly political act. In addition, African writers have a problematic relationship to literary genres (like the novel) that are primarily European in their origin. Finally, the nature of African history requires that African writers have a fundamentally different relation to history than do European writers.

The Question of Background:
The Discourse of Colonialism

In his groundbreaking book *Orientalism* (1979), Edward Said convincingly demonstrates that European and American writers in a wide variety of disciplines have consistently tended since the eighteenth century to describe the Arabic culture and peoples of the Middle East in terms of a set of simplistic assumptions and negative stereotypes that together constitute what he calls the "discourse" of "Orientalism." Building on Said's description of orientalism, Christopher Miller has noted in his book *Blank Darkness* (1985) that Western descriptions of Africa tend to participate in a similar discourse of "Africanism." For Miller, however, Africanism differs from orientalism in certain crucial ways, most centrally in the far higher level of conscious uncertainty and far lower level of confidence that informs European attitudes about Africa, as opposed to European attitudes about the Middle East. Indeed, for centuries Europeans have regarded Africa as a mysterious and unknowable "dark continent." At the same time, European discourse about Africa does seem consistently certain of some things about Africa, most centrally that the continent and its inhabitants are fundamentally primitive. As early as 1888, the black thinker E. W. Blyden pointed out in his book *Christianity, Islam, and the Negro Race* that Europeans consistently tended to see Africans as undeveloped, even infantile, versions of themselves:

> The mistake which Europeans often make in considering questions of Negro improvement and the future of Africa, is in supposing that the Negro is the European in embryo—in the undeveloped stage—and that when, by and by, he shall enjoy the advantages of civilization and culture, he will become like the European; in other words, that the Negro is on the same line of progress, in the same groove, with the European, but infinitely in the rear (Blyden 1967, 276).

Blyden was accurate in his description of European scholarship, which thus managed to combine what Jameson refers to as universalist and orientalist perspectives on African culture and to do so in ways that were disadvantageous to Africans on both counts. Because of their presumed primitivity and savagery, Africans were seen as radically different from Europeans, yet the African road to civilization was assumed to be the same as the European road, so Africans could become civilized only by discarding their own primitive ways and seeking to become like Europeans. Modern Europe was seen as the only possible model for civilization, thus discounting any possibility that African culture might present viable alternatives.

In a similar vein, R. H. Lyons notes the consistency with which nineteenth-century European commentators regarded blacks as inferior to whites, quite often comparing the two along the lines of children versus adults:

> Though they did disagree among themselves about which European "races" were inferior to others, Western racial commentators generally agreed that Blacks were inferior to whites in moral fiber, cultural attainment, and mental ability; the African was, to many eyes, the child in the family of man, modern man in embryo (Lyons 1975, 86–87).

Indeed, as the African philosopher V. Y. Mudimbe notes, an entire array of nineteenth-century European discourses on Africa quite consistently envisioned Africa as radically separated from Europe in terms of temporal development. European writers in fields like botany, anthropology, and phrenology "attempted to prove that in Africa the physical environment, the flora and fauna, as well as the people, represent relics of a remote age of antiquity" (Mudimbe 1988, 107). Powerful currents in nineteenth-century European thought, including a fascination with evolution, history, and social progress, all envisioned the course of both nature and society as an ongoing forward movement in time. Moreover, such models tended to be global in scope, treating Africa and Europe as part of the same process, with Europe simply farther along on the temporal scale. Africa, in fact, came to be treated as the locus of primitivity in virtually all subject areas, thus serving as a sort of anchor point against which the progressive development of Europe could be measured.

Central to this vision of world history was the philosophy of the German thinker G. W. F. Hegel, who saw history as the inexorable movement toward the realization of an ultimate goal that is identified with God's plan for humanity. This vision of history led Hegel to the ethnocentric conclusion that his contemporary European culture was the culmination of that plan and to the nationalistic belief that his own Germany was supreme among the nations of the earth. In short, his model of history provided a justification for European imperial conquest of Africa and other "undeveloped" regions, because it envisioned Europe as closer to the fulfillment of God's plan for all of humanity. Africa, meanwhile, is for Hegel a primitive land outside the flow of history. It is

> the land of childhood, which lying beyond the day of self-conscious history, is enveloped in the dark mantle of Night.... For it is no historical part of the World; it has no movement or development to exhibit....What we properly understand by Africa, is the Unhistorical, Undeveloped Spirit, still involved in the conditions of mere nature (Hegel 1956, 91, 99).

European historians, ethnographers, anthropologists, and philosophers consistently espoused such views of Africa in the nineteenth century. Many of these stereotypes still persist today. European literature about Africa has contributed to this Africanist discourse in important ways as well. American readers are probably all aware of the depiction of Africans as savage cannibals in Edgar Rice Burroughs's Tarzan novels, even if they know those novels only through their numerous film adaptations. Such simplistic stereotypes about Africa are not limited to Western popular culture. *Heart of Darkness,* perhaps the best known European novel about Africa, virtually ignores Africans as individual human beings and consistently depicts the entire continent as backward and primitive. Conrad's protagonist, Charlie Marlow, describes the African jungle as the "primeval forest" (Conrad 1988, 29); traveling up the Congo is for him like going "back to the earliest beginnings of the world" (p. 35); and the Africans in Marlow's crew "still belonged to the beginnings of time" (p. 42). The atrocities that the European Kurtz apparently committed while he was in Africa in search of wealth are clearly attributed to his reversion to primeval ways, to "the awakening of forgotten and brutal instincts" (p. 65). The comments of Blyden and Lyons also shed new light on Marlow's acknowledgment of a "remote kinship" with black Africans (p. 38). After all, to Marlow the remoteness of this kinship resides precisely in the fact that Africans are remote from Europeans in time and development. Marlow sees black Africans as embodying a primeval, natural truth of the human condition, a truth "stripped of the cloak of time" that still lies at the heart of the existence of the contemporary white European, but that is now buried beneath the many layers of civilization that Europe has accumulated over two thousand years (p. 38).

Marlow's point, however, is not that the Africans are equally capable of developing an advanced civilization. Rather, he shows a typical turn-of-the-century European anxiety (exemplified by texts such as Robert Louis Stevenson's *Dr. Jekyll and Mr. Hyde*) over the possibility that civilized Europeans might under certain conditions revert to primitive savagery; he suggests that civilization is all that prevents Europeans from reverting to the condition of savages.[4] Marlow's view of Africans as primitive versions of Europeans reveals an ideological bias in which the European perspective is always maintained as primary. Further, Marlow gives the primitivity of Africans a consistently negative slant, as when he appears to assume that all the Africans he encounters are cannibals. Marlow (and, presumably, Conrad) participates here in a quite common aspect of Africanist discourse, in which the cannibalism of most Africans seems to have been taken for granted. In reality, however, European accounts of the savagery and cannibalism of Africans in the late nineteenth century appear to have been greatly exaggerated, if not fabricated outright. Patrick Parrinder (1992) argues that European reports of African cannibalism were highly unreliable and seldom (if ever) based on confirmed evidence. Indeed, he notes that there were very few actual reports of cannibalism in central Africa during the first four centuries of European contact. In the late nineteenth century, however, a belief in African cannibalism suddenly became extremely convenient as European missionaries fanned out across the continent in search of converts and European powers scrambled to gain control of their share of what only then came to be known as the "dark" continent. The characterization of Africans as cannibals (and thus as primitives in need of salvation) helped to make the European loss of life in "civilizing" the continent seem worthwhile, while at the same time justifying European rule.

Heart of Darkness clearly participates in this phenomenon. Moreover, despite Marlow's occasional expressions of sympathy with the Africans he sees being beaten and starved by their European masters, his sympathy is extremely condescending, and the Africans themselves are consistently described as "cannibals," "niggers," and "savages." It is thus not surprising that Achebe (in a controversial lecture first published in 1977) concludes that "Joseph Conrad was a thoroughgoing racist" (Achebe 1988b, 257) and that *Heart of Darkness* is an "offensive and deplorable book": "I am talking about a book which parades in the most vulgar fashion prejudices and insults from which a section of mankind has suffered untold agonies and atrocities in the past and continues to do so in many ways and many places today" (p. 259).

---

[4] For a discussion of the prominence of this fear of "degeneration" in European and American writing around the beginning of the twentieth century, see Kershner (1986).

Achebe thus argues that *Heart of Darkness,* perhaps more than any other work, is informed by a conventional European tendency to "set Africa up as a foil to Europe, as a place of negations at once remote and vaguely familiar, in comparison with which Europe's own state of spiritual grace will be manifest" (pp. 251–52).

At first glance, Joyce Cary's *Mister Johnson* (1989, first published in 1939), another book Achebe has openly criticized, differs greatly from *Heart of Darkness.* After all, the central (title) character of Cary's book is an African, whereas Conrad presents no vivid African characters at all. Moreover, Cary's treatment of Mr. Johnson is ostensibly sympathetic, even to the point of suggesting that the British colonial intrusion into Nigeria is ultimately responsible for Johnson's tragic fate. Cary, in fact, was widely praised for his success in portraying (perhaps for the first time in European literature) an African character in a convincing and sympathetic manner. But a close look at *Mister Johnson* makes it clear why Achebe might object to Cary's book as well. Despite being presented as a character with whom readers are obviously intended to sympathize, the clerk Johnson is consistently described via conventional Africanist stereotypes. He is nothing if not childish, and his relationship to Harry Rudbeck, the British colonial administrator for whom he works, is very much one of child to parent.

Johnson is presented as a naive, childlike figure who would prefer to spend his time singing and dancing and who is very much out of place in the adult world he sees during his employment by the British. He is emotional and irrational, and he consistently responds to difficult situations with confusion and panic. Little wonder, then, that he eventually runs up large debts or that his troubles eventually lead him to the accidental killing of the British storekeeper Gollup, a deed for which Johnson is finally executed. Moreover, stereotypical African though he may be, Johnson is a great admirer of British culture, and his attitude toward Britain is one of almost abject reverence. His central goal in life is to be thought British, as can be seen by the refrain of loyalty that he loves to sing:

> England is my country
> Oh, England, my home all on de big water.
> Dat King of England is my King,
> De bes' man in de worl', his heart is too big.
> Oh, England, my home all on de big water (Cary 1989, 36).

At the same time, Johnson's attitude toward traditional African culture is one of dismissive contempt. He feels far superior to non-Westernized Africans, whom he refers to as "savages" (p. 27), as superstitious (p. 39), and even as "bush apes" (p. 103). Understandably, this attitude sometimes leads to self-contempt as well: Johnson knows deep down that he is an African and that, because of his race, he will never be fully accepted by the British as one of their own.

Cary's book demonstrates the cruelty of a colonial system that encourages Africans to be loyal to Britain but refuses to offer them a fully British status. In particular, the poignancy of Johnson's dilemma highlights the psychic damage inflicted upon Africans by their own internalization of the British racialist stereotypes. But Cary seems unable to imagine or present alternatives to these stereotypes, and at no point does he suggest that the Africanist vision of Africans (as inherently less rational, responsible, and practical than Europeans) may itself need to be revised. Many Western works about Africa are overtly contemptuous in their racist depictions of Africans or simply ignore the reality of Africans altogether, treating the continent as an uninhabited wilderness where courageous European characters can have exciting adventures of a kind no longer available in Europe. It may be, however, that works like *Heart of Darkness* (which is often highly critical of European colonialism in Africa) and *Mister Johnson* (which at least attempts to be sensitive to the humanity of individual Africans) indicate the true extent to which negative Africanist stereotypes underlie the entire tradition of Western representations of Africa.

Confronting this tradition is clearly one of the major tasks facing African novelists. Not only must African writers attempt to demonstrate that Western ideas about Africans are largely erroneous, but (as the internalization of Africanist stereotypes by Cary's Mr. Johnson indicates) such writers must also counter the feelings of cultural inferiority that the Western tradition has inculcated in Africans themselves. Indeed, one of the most important things for Western readers of the African novel to remember is that the primary audience for most African novelists is not Western readers, but Africans. This central fact underlies a number of the other issues that should be considered in our reading of African literature, including the choice of the language in which African texts are written.

The Question of Language: Words and Worlds

JanMohamed appropriately observes that "the African writer's very decision to use English as his medium is engulfed by ironies, paradoxes, and contradictions" (JanMohamed 1984, 20). Indeed, African writers who continue to work in the languages of their former colonial rulers risk the perpetuation of colonialist ideas, especially ideas involving the cultural and linguistic superiority of Europe. But the factors involved in the use of European languages by African writers are actually far more complicated. Fewer Africans are literate in any given African language than are literate in English or French. African writers can thus reach a larger African audience by writing in European languages, and they can reach a Western audience as well. The economics of the publishing industry thus creates great pressures for the use of European languages. At the same time, *most* Africans are *not* literate in European languages. Thus, the primary African audience for novelists who write in European languages is the educated elite—precisely those people who have been most thoroughly inculcated with the Western cultural traditions that these novelists want to challenge or overcome.[5]

Further, JanMohamed notes that European and African languages quite often operate on fundamentally different premises. In particular, European culture from the Renaissance forward is primarily a written culture, and European languages reflect this fact. Most traditional African culture, however, is oral in nature, and most African languages did not have written forms before the arrival of colonialism. The very act of writing is to a certain extent a European activity, though there certainly are traditions of written culture in Africa. We are all aware, for example, that Egyptian hieroglyphics existed long before the development of written cultures in Europe. Nevertheless a clash between written and oral cultural forms is one of the defining characteristics of African postcolonial literature, which is itself written, but which often draws upon the traditions of oral culture. And it is important to recognize that the differences between oral and written culture go far beyond superficial questions of medium. Following the work of theorists of oral culture like Walter J. Ong (1982) and Jack Goody (1977, 1987), JanMohamed notes that oral and written cultures tend to conceptualize the world in fundamentally different ways.

African writers have attempted to deal with the conflict between oral and written cultural forms in a number of ways, most obviously through the incorporation of materials from African oral culture into their written texts.[6] Tutuola is a good case in point; his texts are marked first and foremost by the "ability to assimilate elements peculiar to the oral tradition with elements peculiar to the literary tradition: in other words, to impose a literary organization upon essentially oral narrative material" (Obiechina 1990, 50). Obiechina goes on to argue that Tutuola's close relation to oral culture may arise from his lack of formal education (p. 60). Achebe, on the other hand, draws upon a great deal of education in Western culture to produce a similar combination of oral and written forms. JanMohamed, for example, argues that in novels such as *Things Fall Apart* and *Arrow of God* Achebe manages a "syncretic" combination of written and oral cultural energies (JanMohamed 1984, 36).[7]

---

[5] Moreover, due to the material realities of the publishing industry and to the relatively low rate of literacy in most African countries, many African novels actually sell more copies in Europe and America than in Africa.

[6] Much study has been done on the relationship between the African novel and African oral culture. See, for example, the recent book by Eileen Julien (1992).

[7] To a certain extent, the confrontation between oral and written culture that is often enacted in the African novel is a confrontation between indigenous culture and the culture of Africa's European colonizers. However, it is also important to recognize that in postcolonial Africa this confrontation is a matter of class as well. Most upper-class Africans can now read and write; most lower-class Africans cannot. Thus, as Miller notes, "the border between literate and illiterate is the most accurate indicator of class in Africa" (Miller 1990, 255).

Achebe, like Tutuola, writes his novels in English. Moreover, as he explains in the essay "The African Writer and the English Language," he feels that English is now part of his African cultural heritage: "I have been given the English language," he writes, "and I intend to use it" (Achebe 1975, 102). At the same time, Achebe sees the necessity of developing a new kind of English that goes beyond the limitations of the imperial past:

> I feel that the English language will be able to carry the weight of my African experience. But it will have to be a new English, still in full communion with its ancestral home but altered to suit new African surroundings (p. 103).

The "new English" cited by Achebe often involves an attempt to express the "feel" of oral culture in written texts. In this sense, Achebe's attitude resembles that expressed by the Indian postcolonial novelist Salman Rushdie in his influential article "The Empire Writes Back." Rushdie is very clearly a great lover of the English language, noting in this article that "I don't think there's another language large or flexible enough to include so many different realities." However, in this same article he also shows a profound appreciation for the historicity and political embeddedness of language, arguing that the vestiges of empire are still to be found in the "cadences" of the English language itself. On the other hand, he sees the political charge that inheres in language to be potentially energizing. Citing the great Irish writers Joyce, Beckett, and O'Brien as predecessors, Rushdie argues that much "vitality and excitement" can be derived from attempts to "decolonize" the English language. In this vein, Rushdie acknowledges the work of such African writers as Achebe and Ngugi, who are resisting the history of imperialism within the English language not only by "busily forging English into new shapes" but also by placing politics at the very centre of their art" (Rushdie 1982, 8).

Many African writers have been less confident than Achebe or Rushdie that English can adequately express the realities of African life. Both Soyinka and Armah, who themselves write in English, have suggested that African writers should begin to work toward the eventual development of a pan-African literary language, perhaps Swahili. Sembène, meanwhile, writes his novels in French, but he has devoted much of his energy in the last two decades to making films rather than novels, thus extending the accessibility of his work to a wider African audience, especially because many of his films use the Wolof language. Similarly, Ngugi, having made a worldwide reputation as an English-language novelist, has written a number of plays in Gikuyu, thus making his work available to Gikuyu peasants and workers who do not know English or cannot read. Indeed, though identified by Rushdie as a leading "decolonizer" of English, Ngugi has since eschewed the use of English in his writing, preferring to write his later original texts in

Gikuyu. Ngugi is quite adamant in texts like *Decolonising the Mind* about the responsibility of African writers to reject the languages inherited from their former imperial oppressors. Language, he argues, is central to one's cultural identity, and Africans will never be able to establish a strong sense of self as long as they continue to express their deepest thoughts in European languages (Ngugi 1992, 4).[8]

Far from being an auxiliary matter, the language question lies at the very heart of African literature. Among other things, this situation is indicative of numerous other complexities amid which postcolonial African nations attempt to wrest stable cultural identities from the chaos wrought by colonialism. Thus, Irele notes that the seeming incongruence of African literature written in European languages is representative of the postcolonial condition:

> The peculiar position of the new literature of Africa written in the European languages involving, at least at first sight, a divorce between the substance of this literature and its linguistic medium, is in itself a reflection of what I would call the state of incoherence within our societies (Irele 1990, 27).

American readers are, by and large, limited to reading African novels in English. Even novels like Ngugi's *Devil on the Cross* (1988) and *Matigari* (1989)are generally accessible to us only in English translation. We should, however, ask ourselves whether such translations do not, in fact, have a very different status than African novels written originally in English. In any case, we should strive not to take language for granted and to recognize the important social and political issues that are at stake in the use of European language by African writers.

The Question of Genre: The Novel and African Culture

Many readers think of literary genre as a purely formal consideration, regarding an author's choice of the genre in which he or she works as roughly analogous to the choice of food items from a cafeteria menu. On the other hand, it is clear that different genres become popular in different societies and at different points in history. Thus, numerous writers in late-sixteenth-century England began to write sequences of sonnets at roughly the same time. Such phenomena are partially a matter of conscious fashion: writers naturally tend to work in forms that they themselves have enjoyed reading, and there is also a natural tendency to choose forms that are likely to be well received by readers. For example, we now know that a writer such as Shakespeare who is often regarded as a sort of universal genius and whose work transcends such

---

[8] Thus far, Ngugi has had relatively few followers in the production of literature in African languages. An exception, however, is recent Tanzanian literature, which (spurred by direct government support) has been largely produced in Swahili. There is, nevertheless, a substantial body of literature in various African languages. See Gérard (1981) for a survey of many of these works.

matters, made many of his artistic decisions in a conscious effort to produce plays that would draw a large and congenial audience in Elizabethan London. It has long been noticed that Shakespeare's career moved through various phases, concentrating on romantic comedies in his early work, on dark tragedies in the middle of his career, and on seemingly whimsical fantasies as his career drew to a close. Critics have often attempted to relate these changes to developments in Shakespeare's personal life, but a broader perspective shows that many of Shakespeare's contemporaries went through similar phases and that the evolution of Shakespeare's writing to a large extent simply followed changing fashions on the Elizabethan stage.[9]

One cannot, however, attribute changes in dominant literary modes simply to fashion. There must be reasons why certain things are fashionable at certain times. Many recent critics and theorists of literature have noted that this is especially the case with fundamental factors like choice of genre. Jameson notes the social function of genre, pointing out that "genres are essentially literary *institutions,* or social contracts between a writer and a specific public, whose function is to specify the proper use of a particular cultural artifact" (Jameson 1981, 106). In other words, when a writer chooses to work in a particular genre, he or she announces an intention to address certain specific expectations on the part of a specific audience of readers. Moreover, Jameson argues that generic expectations and conventions reflect social and political forces at work in the world at large. In short, genre is ultimately a political and historical phenomenon, and changing fashion in genre can be taken as an indication of more fundamental changes in the social world. "Genre," writes Jameson, "is essentially a socio-symbolic message" (p. 141).

Because societies are complex and multiple phenomena, the question of genre is complex as well. In particular, Jameson notes that genre theory must always do more than merely account for the dominance of certain genres at certain times: it must account for the simultaneous availability of other generic forms as well. There may be specific historical reasons why the sonnet sequence was popular in Elizabethan England, but Elizabethan writers worked in numerous other forms as well. In this sense, the novel for Jameson becomes a special genre because its "eclecticism" simultaneously shows the impact of a variety of different available social messages (Jameson 1981, 143). Here Jameson's work recalls that of the Russian thinker Mikhail Bakhtin, perhaps the most influential of all modern theorists of the novel. For Bakhtin, one of the most important characteristics of the novel is its generic multiplicity, its ability to incorporate and make use of the conventions normally associated with any number of other genres, even those not usually consid-

---

[9] The most influential work on Shakespeare's close relationship to his contemporary historical context has been done by the American critic Stephen Greenblatt (1988).

ered literary. Thus, a novel can incorporate poems, songs, letters, sermons, diary entries, newspaper articles, and so on, and still be regarded as a novel.

Bakhtin's vision of the novel is quite broad and includes forms in the tradition of the novel dating back to ancient Greece. Most historians of the novel, however, regard it as a relatively modern form. For example, the Marxist critic Walter Benjamin has pointed out in his influential essay "The Storyteller" that the rise of the novel as the dominant narrative genre in Europe can be directly associated with a turn toward written culture in Europe at the expense of the loss of oral forms of culture (such as storytelling) that had formerly been prominent (Benjamin, 1955). For Benjamin, the rise of the novel is associated with specific material developments, such as improvements in printing technologies and a concomitant spread in literacy, but these developments themselves are closely associated with social and political changes in Europe. In the same vein, critics such as Arnold Kettle (1951) and Ian Watt (1957) have pointed out that the novel rose to prominence as a European genre as part of the great historical process through which feudal society was transformed into modern capitalist society and through which the bourgeoisie supplanted the aristocracy as Europe's ruling class.

Indeed, it is by now quite conventional to regard the novel as the quintessential bourgeois genre, the genre in which the European bourgeoisie most effectively express their particular class consciousness or view of the world. However, this description probably holds true only for the great realistic novels of the nineteenth century; many modern European novels actually challenge the premises upon which such novels are based. The novel has also been one of the most important genres in which postcolonial writers from Africa and elsewhere have attempted to assert their independence from European cultural domination. The very choice of the novel as a genre, like the choice to write in European languages such as English, is a complex and highly political one for African writers. For example, if African cultural traditions are primarily oral, it follows that African writers must to a certain extent draw upon European literary traditions in their own work, especially since most African writers themselves have had Western educations, either in colonial schools in Africa or in European and American schools and universities. As Appiah notes,

> Postcoloniality is the condition of what we might ungenerously call a comprador intelligentsia: of a relatively small, Western-style, Western-trained, group of writers and thinkers who mediate the trade in cultural commodities of world capitalism at the periphery. In the West they are known through the Africa they offer; their compatriots know them both through the West they present to Africa and through an Africa they have invented for the world, for each other, and for Africa (Appiah 1992, 149).

This phenomenon is closely involved in the question of genre. Timothy Brennan thus warns that, in the Third World, the novel has typically been the genre of a Western-educated elite:

> Almost inevitably it has been the form through which a thin, foreign-edu-
> cated stratum (however sensitive or committed to domestic political inter-
> ests) has communicated to metropolitan reading publics, often in
> translation (Brennan 1990, 56).

No matter how important it may be to understand and appreciate that
African novels are *African,* it is also important to recognize that they are still
novels, which means that they have certain relationships to the Western novelistic tradition, even if African novels draw upon a number of African cultural traditions outside the Western tradition. But if the novel is the generic
embodiment of the process through which written culture replaced oral culture as the dominant form in Europe, then the use of the novel is obviously
problematic for African writers who seek to preserve, rather than supplant,
African oral cultural traditions. Not only is the novel as a genre generally
considered European in origin, but this origin is also closely associated with
the rise of capitalism in Europe, a historical process that also led eventually
to the European colonization of Africa, making the novel in many ways the
central literary expression not only of European bourgeois ideology, but of
European colonialist ideology as well.

The novel as a genre provides a particularly rich site for the enactment
of many of the issues that are crucial to postcolonial culture. For example,
Said, in his recent *Culture and Imperialism,* focuses on the importance of imperialism as a motif in the British novel, where he suggests that allusions to
empire probably appear "with more regularity and frequency" than in any
other cultural text of the nineteenth century (Said 1993, 62). Moreover, Said
not only insists on the relatively obvious fact that European literature and
culture consistently reflect the fact of empire, but he also argues that these
disciplines work in complicity with imperialism and are to a certain extent
constitutive of it. Little wonder, then, that novelists like Conrad and Cary
often convey colonialist ideas in their work.

Postcolonial African novelists are thus to some extent working in a
genre that is foreign—and even hostile—to their cultural context. On the
other hand, one should also consider here Bakhtin's influential vision of the
novel as a genre that has an almost infinite flexibility, a genre that can change
shape and adapt to almost any conditions because it can establish a close and
direct contact with the contemporary world around it. According to Bakhtin, rather than functioning according to rigidly defined principles, the novel
by its very nature challenges its own principles and thereby remains ever
new, ever in touch with contemporary reality. To maintain this dynamic
adaptive ability, the novel must continually challenge predefined notions of
what it should be. It is therefore an inherently antiauthoritarian genre, "a
genre that is ever questing, ever examining itself and subjecting its established forms to review. Such, indeed, is the only possibility open to a genre

that structures itself in a zone of direct contact with developing reality" (Bakhtin 1981, 39). The novel as a genre is "both critical and self-critical, one fated to revise the fundamental concepts of literariness and poeticalness dominant at the time" (p. 10).

In short, the novel for Bakhtin is an ever-evolving genre because the best novels, drawing energies derived from their historical context, always challenge and go beyond the conventions established by previous novels. From this point of view, the novel is the ideal genre for postcolonial literature, which, in its engagement with the European literary tradition, represents not the smooth continuation of European conventions, but instead entails a direct challenge to a tradition that often worked in direct complicity with the European colonial domination. Moreover, drawing upon the work of Bakhtin, Brennan (1990) has argued that the novel is especially important as a postcolonial genre not only because of its inherently "composite" nature, but also because of the close historical involvement of the novel in the rise of nationalism in Europe. The nationalist orientation of the novel thus potentially makes it the ideal genre for postcolonial writers who are seeking to contribute to the development of new national cultural identities.

Sometimes African novels mount quite direct and explicit challenges not only to the Western novelistic tradition, but also to specific novels. For example, Achebe's first two novels—*Things Fall Apart* (1994b, first published in 1958), and *No Longer at Ease* (1994a, first published in 1960)—were both written at least partially as responses to British novels about Africa (especially *Mister Johnson*) that were often ostensibly sympathetic to Africans but nevertheless continued colonialist stereotypes of Africans as lazy, irresponsible, irrational, and excessively emotional. More generally, African novels as a whole are faced with the task of overcoming a general complex of negative stereotypes about the social and cultural inferiority of Africa and Africans that were promulgated through a variety of European texts (both literary and scientific) during the colonial period.

In any case, if theorists such as Jameson and Bakhtin argue that the European novel is an inherently complex, hybrid genre, then it is clear that an African novel is even more so. Moreover, the hybridity of the African novel is a complex phenomenon that involves more than a simple additive combination of cultural perspectives. This hybridity often involves complex dialogues—and sometimes violent confrontations—between African and European cultures. To understand these dialogues, we need to understand certain aspects of the historical relationship between Africa and the West that have important consequences for the relationship between African novelists and their Western predecessors (and contemporaries). At the same time, studies of the African novel can potentially add a great deal to our understanding of African history, especially the relationship between Africa and Europe.

The Question of History: The African Novel and the African Past

Jameson (to a great extent following his great Marxist predecessor Georg Lukács) has recently emphasized that the entire history of the world from the Renaissance forward should be understood within the context of the "bourgeois cultural revolution," the long, slow historical process through which the bourgeoisie gradually supplanted the aristocracy and the Catholic Church as the most powerful ruling force in Europe. For Jameson, this revolution begins with the early challenge by the rising European bourgeoisie to the feudal-aristocratic power of church and monarch and concludes with the era of late capitalism, when the dominance of capital (and of bourgeois ideology) has spread over the globe. In particular, Jameson argues that written histories from the nineteenth century onward, in one way or another, always tell the story of the rise of bourgeois power, which makes the bourgeois cultural revolution "the only true Event of History" (Jameson 1992, 226–27). In short, history in the modern sense is an invention of the European bourgeoisie, designed to narrate (and legitimate) the centuries-long process through which they became the dominant class in Europe.

This is not, of course, to say that history (in the sense of the events that occur in the world) was literally an invention of the bourgeoisie. Nor is Jameson unaware that numerous writers had recorded historical events before the rise of bourgeois historiography in the eighteenth and nineteenth centuries. But "historians" before the bourgeois era were largely engaged in a mere chronicling of events without any attempt either to verify the detailed accuracy of their descriptions or to explain the events in terms of any particular theory of history. Bourgeois history (sometimes referred to as "scientific" history) attempts to perform both of these tasks. Bourgeois historians try to support their narratives with detailed documentation. They also structure these narratives within the context of a specific theoretical model of history—in particular the Hegelian notion of history as progress, where progress is defined in terms of various improvements in material and intellectual life that are basically synonymous with the rise of the bourgeoisie as the ruling class in Europe.

If history as we know it is thus, like the novel, largely an invention of the bourgeoisie to explain their rise to power in Europe, then it makes sense that there would be a close connection between the novel and history. Indeed, history has long been regarded as a crucial issue for the novel as a genre. For example, Bakhtin's description of the close contact between the novel and contemporary reality is simply another way of saying that the novel as a genre is especially closely related to history. In addition, the narrative form of the novel, especially the realistic novel, closely resembles the narrative form of bourgeois historical models such as that proposed by Hegel. In both cases, one event leads logically to another in sequential fashion as the plot marches inexorably toward some predetermined goal. Both bourgeois history and the bourgeois realistic novel seek to portray the world as a place where events make sense and, in particular, where it makes sense for the bourgeoisie to be the ruling class.

Probably the most influential description of the close connection between the realistic novel and bourgeois history is that provided by Lukács in his book *The Historical Novel* (1983). Lukács argues that, if the realistic novel is in some ways the central literary expression of the point of view of the European bourgeoisie, then the historical novel is especially so. This is especially clear in the early nineteenth century when the bourgeoisie had risen to power very recently and recognized that this rise represented a radical historical change. A powerful sense of history thus informs the work of many early-nineteenth-century novelists, and this sense of history (like Jameson's vision of the bourgeois cultural revolution) centers on the revolutionary process through which the feudal world was shattered and replaced by modern capitalism. Lukács identifies the British novelist Sir Walter Scott as a paradigm of this phenomenon and describes at great length the way Scott's novels narrate the collapse of feudalism and the beginnings of the rise of capitalism.

The development of the novel is thus closely associated with notions of history that are specific to the European bourgeoisie, which introduces another complication into the relationship between European and African versions of the novel. After all, African history differs from European history in obvious and important ways. For thousands of years, European and African culture developed almost independently of one another, though there were certainly some points of contact.[10] And even when, in recent centuries, European and African culture have come more and more into contact, it has been in asymmetrical ways that affected the two continents differently.[11] If the major event in recent European history is the bourgeois cultural revolution, then the major event of African history in the past century is surely the phenomenon of colonialism and its postcolonial aftermath.[12] In this regard, readers of African literature need to be aware of the impact of colonialism on this literature and of the relatively recent end of European colonial dom-

---

[10] See, for example, Martin Bernal (1987) and Cheikh Anta Diop (1974) for arguments that Greek civilization, so often regarded as the cradle of European culture, derived in direct and important ways from African cultures such as that of Egypt.

[11] For a discussions of the European exploration of Africa, see McLynn (1992). For discussions of the formal European colonization of Africa, see Pakenham (1991) and Wesseling (1996).

[12] On the other hand, as Mazrui emphasizes, the colonial experience was a relatively brief episode in African history, which stretches for millennia (Mazrui 1986, 14). Mazrui's book is a good introduction to the history of Africa, as is the collection of essays edited by Olaniyan (1982). Also very accessible (especially to Western readers) are the numerous works of African history by Basil Davidson (see Works cited). Coquery-Vidrovitch's recent (1988) book is good as well, though a bit more advanced.

ination. Lewis Nkosi thus insists that "modern African writing has its origins in the politics of anti-colonial struggle and still bears the marks of that struggle" (Nkosi 1981, 1). And it is certainly no coincidence that decolonization corresponds roughly to the beginnings of the rise of the African novel to prominence on the world literary scene. African novelists thus centrally participate in the effort to develop viable postcolonial cultural identities within African societies whose histories and traditions have been radically disrupted by the intrusion of foreign political, economic, and cultural forces. As Irele puts it, "our writers are groping implicitly, through the imagination, towards the creation of a new order of Africa" (Irele 1990, 28).

To some extent the European bourgeois cultural revolution and the colonization of Africa are related phenomena, and it was no coincidence that the European bourgeoisie turned to the colonization of most of the rest of the globe only after they had solidified their power in Europe itself. In addition, the phenomenon of decolonization in Africa appears in some ways to be analogous to the European bourgeois revolution. Colonialism had numerous feudal characteristics, and the African nations that emerged from decolonization were largely ruled by the African bourgeoisie.[13] But, as thinkers such as Fanon have emphasized, the postcolonial African bourgeoisie are far different from their European predecessors. They have not risen to power through the historical process of cultural revolution but have merely been placed in power by their former colonial rulers. As a result, according to Fanon, the African bourgeoisie lack the historical energy and vitality of their European predecessors, of whom they are merely a weak and prematurely decadent echo (Fanon 1968).

The question of history in the African novel is complicated especially by the way history itself was employed as a crucial tool of European domination during the colonial era. Colonialist historians contributed to the consistent description of Africa as primitive by envisioning Africa as a timeless place without history, mired in the primeval past and unable to move forward until the European colonizers brought new energies and new knowledge to the continent. Catherine Coquery-Vidrovitch thus notes that

> colonialist histories have long perpetuated the myth of a sub-Saharan Africa conquered fairly easily and profiting from pacification. . . . The local populations, according to these histories, were finally delivered by the "colonial peace" from the internal struggles of little local rulers forever raiding their neighbors' territories in search of slaves or livestock (Coquery-Vidrovitch 1988, 66).

Mudimbe notes that such colonialist histories "speak neither about Africa nor Africans, but rather justify the process of inventing and conquering a continent and naming its 'primitiveness' or 'disorder,' as well as the subse-

---

[13] On the feudal aspects of colonialism, see Benedict Anderson (1991).

quent means of its exploitation and methods for its 'regeneration'" (Mu-dimbe 1988, 20). Such discourse claims that African civilization came into existence only through the creation of colonies by European powers, who came to Africa on a civilizing mission. Indeed, as Raymond Williams notes, the very word "civilization" came to be regarded in Europe from the eighteenth century forward as synonymous with the "achieved condition of refinement and order" of the emergent bourgeoisie (R. Williams 1977, 13). As a result, Eurocentric versions of history define African history and culture as essentially nonexistent, with serious consequences for Africans. As Albert Memmi points out, "the most serious blow suffered by the colonized is being removed from history" (Memmi 1965, 91). This removal, which produces the stereotype of Africans as "people without history," to use Eric Wolf's well-known phrase, denies Africans access to a useable past upon which they can build a viable future (Wolf 1982). Without a useable past, Africans are unable to counter the ongoing neocolonial definition of the cultural and personal identities of Africans by foreign forces.

African thinkers and writers have employed a number of strategies to restore a sense of history to African societies and thereby recover a past that can support viable cultural identities in the present. One version of this effort involves what Appiah calls "nativist" discourses of African history—discourses that espouse a return to the precolonial past and a rejection of the entire colonial period as an aberration, a break in the flow of history. Such discourses typically seek to emphasize the positive aspects of precolonial African culture and attempt to draw upon this culture as a model for the present. For Appiah, these discourses are best represented by the work of Chinweizu, Jemie, and Madubuike, particularly in their "now-classic manifesto of African cultural nationalism, "*Toward the Decolonization of African Literature*" (Appiah 1992). On the other hand, Chinweizu and his fellow *bolekaja* critics do not simply romanticize the African past.[14] Indeed, they warn against a tendency toward such romanticization in the writers of the Négritude movement in French African literature, noting that such romanticization might "imprison the contemporary imagination in a bygone era" (Chinweizu et al. 1983, 258).[15] Nevertheless, such critics do emphasize the supposed cultural superiority of the precolonial past, which is presented as a positive alternative to a present degraded by the colonial encounter. Supporters of this attitude recommend that African writers should return for their inspiration to precolonial cultures and traditions if they are to overcome the problems that colonialism imposed.

---

[14] *Bolekaja*—meaning "come down, let's fight"—is a term used to describe the aggressive behavior of callers attempting to attract customers to the "mammy wagons" that serve as buses in western Nigeria. It refers to the intense political commitment of these critics.

[15] For good discussions of the Négritude movement, see Jahn (1968, 239–69) and Irele (1990, 67–124).

The attempt to restore a sense of a useable past to present-day Africans is complicated, however, by the fact that modern versions of history are so thoroughly European (and bourgeois) in their origin. In other words, the restoration of African history requires more than the simple narration of precolonial events via the typical techniques of scientific history, though parts of Africa do, in fact, have glorious and eventful precolonial histories. For one thing, the primarily oral nature of most precolonial African culture means that the kind of detailed documentation usually demanded by European versions of scientific historiography is simply not available. For another, researchers argue that oral and written cultures tend to conceive of history in fundamentally different ways, largely due to this difference in available documentation.[16] Ong emphasizes that, without the ability to record knowledge in written form, oral cultures must emphasize the repetition of important ideas and insights so that they will not be forgotten. This need thus tends to establish in oral cultures "a highly traditionalist or conservative set of mind that with good reason inhibits intellectual experimentation" (Ong 1982, 41). At the same time, Ong argues that, because of the preciousness of memory in oral cultures, these cultures cannot afford to retain memories that are not of direct use in the present. Such cultures tend to "live very much in a present which keeps itself in equilibrium or homeostasis by sloughing off memories which no longer have present relevance" (p. 46).

Writing, as Ong points out, can be conservative in its own ways, but written cultures generally tend to encourage more innovation: "By storing knowledge outside the mind, writing and, even more, print downgrade the figures of the wise old man and the wise old woman, repeaters of the past, in favor of younger discoverers of something new" (p. 41). This difference clearly means that concepts such as "progress" are likely to be valued more in written than in oral cultures. Further, the kinds of linear narrative forms that support the particular European bourgeois notion of progress are more characteristic of written than of oral cultures, which are likely to place more emphasis on narrative as a form than written cultures do, but which tend to employ more episodic and nonlinear narrative structures (pp. 141–51). As a result, African versions of history that draw upon the precolonial past will differ from European histories not only in content but in fundamental matters of structure and form. Thus we might expect that African novels would employ different narrative strategies than European novels and that African historical novels might differ from European ones in particularly radical ways.

Yet, ironically, African writers have quite often employed the historical novel—the form so favored by European bourgeois writers—as part of a

---

[16] For a good summary of much of this research, especially as it applies to the African postcolonial situation, see JanMohamed (1984).

program to generate new postcolonial cultural identities that transcend this inherited tradition of bourgeois historiography and that escape definition by the colonial past. Given the material impact of colonialism on African history and the symbolic impact of colonialist historiography on the African imagination, it is obvious that history is a crucial area of contestation for African writers who seek to wrest control of their cultural identities. Any number of African novelists have thus produced works that challenge the tradition of colonialist historiography. For example, each of Ngugi's novels focuses on a particular moment in Kenyan history, and, together, his novels— ranging *from The River Between* (1965) to *Matigari* (1989)—constitute a sweeping historical narrative that tells the story of Kenya from the early days of British colonialism to the contemporary postcolonial period. While identifying colonialism and neocolonialism as crucial determining events in the history of Kenya, Ngugi places his emphasis on the strong Kenyan tradition of resistance to oppression, seeking thereby to contribute to the recovery of a useable past that can help Kenyans to move forward to a better future. In a similar (if less politically specific) manner, Achebe's novels, from *Things Fall Apart* (1994b) to *Anthills of the Savannah* (1988a), collectively trace the colonial and neocolonial history of Nigeria. Other representative examples of African historical novels include Sembène's dramatization of a 1947–1948 railway strike in French colonial Africa in *God's Bits of Wood,* (Sembène 1960), M. G. Vassanji's imaginative retelling of the history of Tanzania in *The Gunny Sack* (Vassanji 1989), Farah's elaboration in his trilogy *Variations on the Theme of an African Dictatorship* (Farah 1979, 1981, 1983) on the Siyad Barre period in Somalia, Ben Okri's attempt to capture the spirit of modern Nigerian history through an Africanized magical realism in *The Famished Road* (Okri 1991), Yambo Ouologuem's somewhat notorious depiction of African history as a never ending cycle of abject violence in *Bound to Violence* (Ouologuem 1968), and Ayi Kwei Armah's *Two Thousand Seasons* (1979b), a more positive and mythic version of African history (written partially in response to Ouologuem).[17]

Together such novels constitute a major component in the process of historical recovery now under way throughout postcolonial Africa. Indeed, the contributions of the African historical novel to the restoration of African history constitute one of the more visible ways in which African literature as a whole is attempting to make a positive contribution to the construction of viable cultural identities throughout Africa. This process gives African literature a relevance and a vitality that students of literature

---

[17] For a useful and interesting survey of a selected range of postcolonial historical literature, see Dasenbrock (1985–86). For excellent account of Ouologuem's controversial text, see Miller (1985, 216–45). See also Lang (1987) for a comparative reading of *Bound to Violence* and *Two Thousand Seasons*.

should find quite exciting. At the same time, the obvious importance of literature to the social and political world of Africa can teach us valuable lessons about the social and political relevance of literature in general. And if the African novel raises a number of formal and ideological issues that are different from those we typically encounter in the European novel, this very difference can help us understand Western literature better. Western readers thus have every reason to study the African novel, both so that we can become familiar with one of the most powerful and exciting cultural forces in the world today and so that we can learn to see our own culture in new and different ways.[18]

---

[18] See Katherine Fishburn's recent (1995) study of the work of Buchi Emecheta for some extremely useful discussions of this topic and for an effective attempt to remind American readers of the pitfalls of approaching African literature from a Western perspective.

Chapter 2

▼▼▼▼▼▼▼▼▼▼

A Brief Historical Survey
of the African Novel

The following brief survey of the African novel provides a general overview of some of the major works in the genre. Some attempt has been made to place these works within a historical framework, but the history of the African novel is far too complex to be comprehended adequately by such a brief survey. Of course, history itself is a complex phenomenon, and historians must always make a number of fundamental decisions in telling coherent stories of the human past. They must choose beginning and ending points to the stories they tell, and they must select events and phenomena to convey what they believe are the salient features of the movement of history between these two points. The history of the African novel is no different. That history—like all histories—is complex and multiple. There is no precise beginning and no single line along which this history proceeds. The history of the African novel is complicated by the fact that African novels draw upon literary traditions that are not African (particularly the Western novel) and African cultural productions that would not generally be considered to be novels (particularly oral narratives). Moreover, if (as Bakhtin and others have emphasized) the novel is the most complex and multiple of all genres, "Africa" is also a complex and multiple entity that involves not just geography but a long and complicated history of symbolic representations. In addition, while it is often assumed that the development of written literature in Africa was a direct consequence of European colonization, there were indigenous African written languages prior to the European intrusion, and written Arabic had also made a significant impact on some parts of Africa.[1] The Af-

---

[1] See, for example, Obiechina for an account of the growth of written literature in West Africa that begins by acknowledging that "the Arabic script had already been in existence several centuries before the arrival of the Roman script in West Africa" (Obiechina 1990, 1).

rican novel is thus an especially complex historical phenomenon, and this complexity is only increased by the fact that history itself is such a major issue of concern to African novelists. The following survey is presented with the recognition that it is necessarily partial and involves a number of assumptions that might have been made differently. The organization of this chapter into subheadings is purely a matter of practical convenience and should not be taken as either absolute or complete. In particular, because this is a book about African novels in English, the chapter emphasizes Anglophone novels, though it indicates the broad outlines of the development of the African novel in other languages as well. It presents an introduction to the historical development of important issues and trends in the African novel; it also provides a historical framework that will allow the novels discussed in the remainder of this text to be understood better in terms of their place in African literary history.

For more detailed surveys of various movements within the African novel, students are referred to the numerous book-length studies that have been published on the subject. Some of the most useful of these include general works such as those by Schipper (1989), Dathorne (1974), and Gérard (1990), works by Obiechina (1975, 1990), Nkosi (1981), and Gikandi (1987) on the Anglophone novel; Irele (1990), Ngaté (1988), Mortimer (1990), and D'Almeida (1994) on the Francophone novel; Harrow (1991) on the influence of Islam; Kaye (1992) on North African literature; and Jad (1983) on the Egyptian novel. Also useful are the collections edited by Gurnah (1994, 1995), Ngara (1995), and Riemenschneider and Schulze-Engler (1993), which discuss more recent African fiction, at least through the 1980s. Also of great usefulness are reference works such as Owomoyela's recent compilation of the histories of various aspects of African literature (1993) and the extensive encyclopedia of postcolonial literature in English compiled by Benson and Conolly (1994).

The West African Anglophone Novel

West African novels occupy a special place of importance in the development of the African novel in English. Writers from countries such as Nigeria and Ghana have been especially important in the development of the African novel, partially because Nigeria is the most populous country in Africa, and Ghana was the first African colony to achieve independence from British rule. The areas now occupied by Nigeria and Ghana also had particularly rich histories in the precolonial era, and they maintained a certain connection to their traditional cultural heritage through the years of colonization. For example, Nigerian novelists can draw upon an especially strong tradition of oral storytelling: certain traditional African narratives had already been published in the area even before the advent of what might properly be considered the beginnings of the Nigerian novel in English. Thus Amos Tutuola, often considered the first African novelist in English, is preceded not only by the rich tradition of Yoruba oral folk tales but also by the work of D. O. Fagunwa, whose Yoruba narratives were published as early as 1938.[2]

If one must select a starting point for a history of the West African Anglophone novel, however, Tutuola's *The Palm-Wine Drinkard*, (Tutuola 1952) first published by the well-known British publisher Faber and Faber in 1952, might be a good choice. This book relates the fantastic adventures of its narrator, an inveterate drinker of palm wine, who travels to the Land of the Dead in an attempt to retrieve his recently deceased palm-wine tapster, the only person capable of tapping palm wine to the drinkard's satisfaction. The premise of Tutuola's book has precedents in Western literature that include the trips to the underworld (such as Homer's *Odyssey* and Virgil's *Aeneid*), and the fantastic elements of *The Palm Wine Drinkard* have numerous analogs in the works of Western writers such as Franz Kafka and James Joyce. But Tutuola's story of his protagonist's various adventures and meetings with fantastic otherworldly creatures remains firmly rooted in the Yoruba folk tradition. Tutuola's book was a major success upon its publication, and if Tutuola is not the first West African writer of fiction, he was certainly the first to achieve international recognition. However, there is some disagreement over whether his works can properly be considered novels. His writing has often been regarded by Western critics as "primitive" because of his extensive reliance on traditional oral narratives for his subject matter and because of the strong influence of local Nigerian rhythms and inflections on his language and style. Tutuola has sometimes been rejected by Nigerian critics as well, both because his work lacks originality (by simply retelling traditional folk tales) and because his focus on certain sensational aspects of the folk tradition (witches and wizards, the violence of jungle life, and so on) merely feed a Western taste for the exotic.

On the other hand, one could argue that this concept of originality itself was imported from post-Romantic Europe. Tutuola's reputation has been somewhat rehabilitated in recent years, and his place as an important early figure in the history of the African novel now seems secure. In particular, he can be seen as a sort of bridge between traditional African oral narratives and the more conventionally literary African novels that began to be published soon after his work first appeared. Obiechina notes that Tutuola seems to have a unique ability to "assimilate elements peculiar to the oral tradition with elements peculiar to the literary tradition: in other words, to impose a literary organization upon essentially oral narrative material" (Obiechina 1990, 50).

---

[2] For a detailed study of Fagunwa's novels, see Bamgbose (1974).

It is perhaps this sense of Tutuola as a transitional writer, rather than a full-blown novelist, that leads so many critics to consider not Tutuola, but Chinua Achebe to be the founding figure of the modern African novel and even of modern African literature as a whole. Simon Gikandi discusses at some length the reasons why Achebe has been seen as such a seminal figure in the growth of African literature, even though he in fact had a number of important predecessors. Gikandi concludes that Achebe's importance lies in the fact that his work was a genuine breakthrough in its direct confrontation with the cultural traditions of colonialism, in its ability

> to evolve narrative procedures through which the colonial language, which was previously intended to designate and reproduce the colonial ideology, now evokes new forms of expression, proffers new oppositional discourse (Gikandi 1987, 4).

In particular, Gikandi argues, Achebe is able to use the colonial language of English and the Western genre of the novel to mount a powerful challenge to the myth of European cultural superiority, thereby recovering elements of African experience that have been effaced by colonialism and producing a viable sense of an alternative African cultural identity. "I want to insist," writes Gikandi, "that Achebe was possibly the first African writer to be self-con-scious about his role as an African writer, to confront the linguistic and his-torical problems of African writing in a colonial situation, and to situate writing within a larger body of regional and global knowledge about Africa" (pp. 5–6).

Whatever the reasons, Achebe has been an inspirational figure for the generation of African writers who followed him, not only in West Africa, but in the entire continent. His *Things Fall Apart* (1994b), first published in 1958, remains the best-known and most widely read African novel nearly forty years later, and all of Achebe's novels have received considerable attention from readers and critics. Achebe's status as a role model for other African writers thus arises both because the impressive quality of his novels provides important aesthetic models for an African writing practice and because his commercial and critical success have encouraged Africans to write for pub-lication and publishers to publish the works of African writers. In addition, his numerous critical and theoretical statements on his own writing and on African literature as a whole have done a great deal to establish the standards and conventions within which African novelists work.

Achebe's individual importance and influence may, in fact, be one of the reasons why West African novels (especially Nigerian ones) have been so prominent in the development of the genre in Africa. On the other hand, as Obiechina points out in his influential study of a number of early West Af-rican novels, there are also important social and historical reasons why the novel would develop in a particularly rich way in this area. Obiechina emphasizes that the "peculiarities" of the West African novel are "clearly determined by the West African cultural tradition and environment" (Obiechina 1975, 3). He illustrates this point with readings of a number of specific novels, focusing especially on the works of Achebe. He also provides significant discussions of other Nigerian novels, including Timothy Mofolorunso Aluko's *One Man, One Wife* (1959), Cyprian Ekwensi's *Jagua Nana* (1975), Nkem Nwankwo's *Danda* (1964), Gabriel Okara's *The Voice* (1964), Wole Soyinka's *The Interpreters* (1965), and Elechi Amadi's *The Concubine* (1966). The Ghanaian Ayi Kwei Armah's *The Beautiful Ones Are Not Yet Born* (1969) is also an important text in Obiechina's study. All of these novels can now rightfully be regarded as classics of African literature, and together they illustrate many of the important trends in the early development of the West African novel.

Aluko's *One Man, One Wife*, though set in the relatively late 1940s and 1950s, details life in traditional Yoruba society in a mode reminiscent of Achebe's description of traditional Igbo life. It is largely a satire of Christian converts who turn their backs on their traditional culture, though the religious aspect of traditional life comes in for considerable satire as well. Aluko's satire is relatively lighthearted, employing a variety of exaggerations and caricatures to produce a humorous vision of Yoruba society in a time of transition, that for Obiechina displays "a Dickensian sense of the comically grotesque" (Obiechina 1975, 88). Aluko's writing draws extensively on Yoruba oral traditions in this and his six subsequent novels, a fact that has combined with his simple, straightforward style to make his works extremely popular in Nigeria.

Ekwensi's *Jagua Nana* focuses on the experiences of its title character, an aging prostitute who prowls the bars and nightclubs of modern Nigeria in search of customers, but also longs to be a wife and mother and to live the kind of life her pastor father would have wished for her. The book focuses on the private experiences of its protagonist, but it does so in a way that allows Ekwensi to address a number of important public social and political issues affecting modern Nigeria. In the course of the book, Jagua travels back to her own village of Ogabu and to Bagana, the traditional home of the family of Freddie Namme, the young man she hopes to marry. Ekwensi is thus able to set up a direct contrast between life in these villages, still powerfully influenced by traditional cultural practices, and life in Lagos, dominated by modern customs imported from Europe. Jagua thus finds life in the villages "totally different from the Lagos atmosphere. That driving, voluptuous and lustful element which existed in the very air of Lagos, that something which awakened the sleeping sexual instincts in all men and women and turned them into animals always on heat, it was not present here" (p. 180). She thus characteristically interprets the cultural difference between village and city in sexual terms, but the book presents this difference in other ways as well.

For example, it describes the contrast between the violence and corruption of politics in Lagos and the rather utopian functioning of politics in the villages, where Chief Ofubara of Krinameh's dedicated leadership brings a certain amount of modernization to his village while maintaining most of the communal values of traditional society.

As Obiechina points out, such contrasts between urban and rural societies constitute a major motif in the West Africa novel (Obiechina 1975). Indeed, Ekwensi himself continues to explore this theme in later novels such as *Beautiful Feathers* (1963), though his work is noted primarily for its depictions of urban life. Nwankwo's *Danda* involves a similar confrontation between traditional and modern cultures, though in the Nigeria of Nwankwo's book the modern forces are more clearly on the ascendant. Indeed, *Danda*, like Nwankwo's later *My Mercedes Is Bigger Than Yours* (1975), is a satirical account of the erosion of traditional values amid the corruption and grasping materialism of modern Nigeria. Danda himself is a sort of trickster figure who clearly derives from the prominent presence of such figures in African oral narratives. Traditional dance and music play important roles in the novel as well. In its criticism of conditions in the waning days of colonialism and even in the days after independence, Nwankwo's work resembles that of many other African writers, though his novels are unusual in the extent to which he employs comedy to achieve his effects.

Okara's *The Voice* represents another important early trend in the West African novel. Known primarily as a poet, Okara constructs his novel in a highly poetic and symbolic vein, conveying his ideas through powerful central images rather than realistic detail. Like Achebe, Ekwensi, and Nwankwo, Okara comments extensively in his novel on political corruption and social decay, but he does so largely through linguistic effects and through the poetic evocation of a dark and brooding atmosphere rather than specific events or characters. As Obiechina points out, "The most striking feature of Okara's art is the repetition of single words, phrases, sentences, images or symbols, a feature highly developed in traditional narrative, especially in the folk-tale with its scope for dramatic pauses" (Obiechina 1975, 173). Okara is thus no "wild man of the African novel." His highly inventive language may deviate substantially from the conventions of Western realism, but it does so primarily because of its close relationship to African oral traditions. Okara's work may not represent Nigerian society in a conventionally realistic manner, but what it does convey is the "linguistic reality of West Africa" (Obiechina 1975, 171). In this sense, *The Voice* recalls Bakhtin's argument: "Language in the novel not only represents, but itself serves as the object of representation" (Bakhtin 1981, 49). But Okara's book also serves as a vivid reminder of the inadequacy of purely Western concepts for the appreciation of African novels.

A similar point might be made about the Ghanaian Kofi Awoonor's poetic novel *This Earth, My Brother* (1972), but the leading work in this vein might be Soyinka's *The Interpreters*. Soyinka's work employs an array of literary devices usually associated with Western modernism (or even postmodernism), but it also draws in important ways on African sources. The complex, fragmented narrative structure of *The Interpreters* also serves an important mimetic function, reinforcing the book's content to create a vivid picture of the chaotic and confusing conditions that inform life in postcolonial Nigeria. The book focuses on the educated elite of Soyinka's generation, who attempt to use their Western education to provide links between Nigeria and the West, often only to find themselves caught in the middle and alienated from both cultures. Soyinka employs a similarly complex narrative form in his later novel *Season of Anomy* (1973), a dystopian fiction informed by graphic violence and abject imagery that grow directly out of the experience of the Nigerian civil war (1967–1970). Both books draw upon African oral traditions in important ways, but it is probably fair to say that Soyinka, more than most African writers, has absorbed the lessons of modern Western literature and put them to good use in his work. This is especially the case in his drama, which shows an intimate connection with traditional African oral performances, but which also conducts extensive intertextual dialogues with Western dramatists such as Bertolt Brecht and Samuel Beckett. Soyinka's drama is, in fact, his best-known work, and it is most responsible for his winning of the Nobel Prize in 1986. He was the first black African to win that honor, which announced the growing world recognition of the importance of African literature.

The West African writer whose satirical vision most closely resembles that of Soyinka may be Armah, whose first three novels—beginning with the now-classic *The Beautyful Ones Are Not Yet Born* (1969)—constitute one of the most scathing critiques of postcolonial African society ever produced. Writing from a distinctive political perspective strongly influenced by the work of Frantz Fanon, Armah indicts postcolonial Ghanaian society for its failure to live up to the independence movement's utopian dreams and its descent into corruption and moral decay under the impact of the dazzling lure of Western capital and commodities. Armah's sophisticated novels, which combine substantial influences from African oral culture with impressive technical mastery of Western novelistic forms and devices, represent one of the most important contributions to the development of the West African novel as a hybrid of African and Western cultural forces. Moreover, if *The Beautyful Ones Are Not Yet Born* can be taken as a paradigm of the satirical treatment of postcolonial society in African fiction, later Armah novels such as and *The Healers* (1979) and *Two Thousand Seasons* (1979) represent important contributions to the development of the African historical novel and to the African attempt to generate, through literature, a positive vision of the African past that escapes the stereotypes of colonialist histories of Africa.

Elechi Amadi has also written both plays and novels, though (unlike Soyinka) his reputation rests primarily on his novels. *The Concubine* is still his best-known work and one that, in its presentation of traditional rural society in Nigeria, provides a useful supplement to the satire and largely urban focus of writers such as Ekwensi, Nwankwo, and Soyinka. In some ways reminiscent of Achebe's depiction of traditional Igbo society in *Things Fall Apart*, *The Concubine* portrays the traditional society of the village of Omokachi in rather idealized terms. Amadi's villagers live a serene existence, comfortable in their place in the communal society of the village and free of the alienation and existential angst that beset the characters of modern Western fiction or African urban fiction. The people get along well and understand and accept the roles they are expected to play in their society. Amadi maintains a similar focus through most of his work. Even the recent *Estrangement* (1986), whose title suggests the breakup of traditional idyllic life, continues to concentrate on rural life, during and after the Nigerian civil war.

Amadi has sometimes been praised for the sensitive treatment of strong and dynamic female characters, as has his Nigerian compatriot John Munonye (in works such as the 1966 *The Only Son*). However, perhaps not surprisingly, it has been left to West African women writers to provide the most vivid depictions of the role of women in West African life.[3] Obiechina discusses no women writers in his survey of the West African novel through the 1960s, though there were in fact several important novels written by West African women by that time. This omission is indicative of the lack of serious and sensitive critical attention that African women writers suffered in the early years of independence. Most important among these early women novelists are the Nigerians Flora Nwapa and Buchi Emecheta and the Ghanaian Ama Ata Aidoo, all of whom have produced works that are worthy of standing with those of Achebe, Ekwensi, Nwankwo, Soyinka, and Amadi as early classics of the West African novel.

Nwapa's *Efuru* (1966) was the first English-language novel published by a West African woman. The book constituted a breakthrough in the access of women writers to publication. It was, for example, the first work by a woman to be published in Heinemann's African Writers Series, the major market for African novelists from the late 1950s to the late 1980s. *Efuru* is set in the late 1940s and early 1950s and tells the story of a strong, independent woman who is modeled on the women of Nwapa's own Oguta, an impor-

---

[3] Indeed, some feminist critics have seen Amadi's depiction of women as stereotypical and even downright misogynistic (Stratton 1994, 85–86). Stratton also points out that Munonye's book focuses on a rather traditional African woman who is self-sacrificing in her nurturing devotion to her son (Stratton 1994, 134).

tant trading town in eastern Nigeria. Efuru triumphs over marital difficulties to establish a meaningful life of community service. Nwapa herself also
triumphed over difficulties, overcoming the early rejection of her work by
male critics to attain a reputation as the "mother" of West African women's
fiction. While her second novel, *Idu* (1970), resembles *Efuru* in its focus on
traditional Igbo life, Nwapa's later novels, *Never Again* (1975), *One is Enough*
(1981), and *Women Are Different* (1986), concentrate on the experiences of
women in modern Nigeria. Nwapa's work thus has a scope that rivals that
of any African male writer, and her writing well deserves the increased critical attention it has received in recent years.

Aidoo's *Our Sister Killjoy* (1994b) was copyrighted in 1966—before the
publication of *Efuru*—but was not published until 1977. In the intervening
years, Aidoo established a significant reputation as a dramatist, poet, and
short-story writer. *Our Sister Killjoy*, with its poetic treatment of neocolonialism from a feminine perspective, is an important addition to the African
postcolonial tradition of satirical writing. Moreover, the novel—set primarily in Germany and England—marks an expansion in the scope of the West
African novel, which had previously tended to be set in West Africa itself.
Aidoo's treatment of feminist concerns from a decidedly African perspective
also indicates the substantial ways in which the problems and concerns of
African women sometimes differ from those of Western women and thus
serves as a warning against the uncritical application of Western feminist criteria to African literature and society.

The internationalism of *Our Sister Killjoy* is also a hallmark of the writing of Emecheta, perhaps the most successful of all West African women
writers. Emecheta's first two novels, *In the Ditch* (1994c, first published in
1972) and *Second-Class Citizen* (1983c, first published in 1974), are set in
London and derive from the author's own experiences as a member of the
African immigrant community there. Later Emecheta novels such as *The
Bride Price* (1976) and *The Slave Girl* (1977) focus on the lives of women in
traditional Igbo society, while Emecheta's best-known novel, *The Joys of
Motherhood* (1988b, first published in 1979), features a female protagonist
who is caught between the traditional values of her native village and the
modern values of urban Lagos, where most of the novel's action takes place.
More recently, Emecheta has written novels on the Nigerian civil war, on
the special problems of the educated elite in postcolonial Nigeria, and on the
plight of a poor Caribbean woman living in the immigrant community of
London. Emecheta's concern with the travails of postcolonial Nigeria and
with the conflict between the traditional values of urban Nigeria and the
modern values inherited from the colonial intrusion parallels that of male
writers such as Achebe and Ekwensi, but her distinctively feminine focus
provides insights unavailable in the works of the male writers.

While there is a certain continuity in all of these early works by West African writers, Jonathan Peters suggests that Tutuola, Achebe, Ekwensi, and Okara join writers such as William Conton, Onuora Nzekwu, Timothy Aluko, and Obi Egbuna in what might be considered the "first wave" of West African fiction writing, a group of texts in which "a limited number of themes emphasized either colonialism and its clash with autochthonous cultures or village life" (Peters 1993, 23). For Peters, the second wave of West African fiction deals with the problems of postcolonial corruption and disillusionment. This wave was ushered in by Soyinka's *The Interpreters* and includes texts such as Achebe's *A Man of the People* (1989b); Amadi's *The Concubine*, Armah's *The Beautyful Ones Are Not Yet Born, Fragments* (1970), and *Why Are We So Blest?* (1974); and Kole Omotoso's *The Combat* (1972); as well as the works of women writers such as Nwapa, Aidoo, and Emecheta.

More recent West African fiction, in Peters's scheme, can be considered a third wave of texts. These texts deal with a wide variety of social, political, and historical issues, but they are tied together by a number of common themes, including a turn toward writing clearly for an African, rather than a Western, audience. As with any contemporary literary movement, the most important texts of this wave have yet to be clearly established, especially as recent African writing is marked by a dramatic increase in the sheer number of texts that are being produced. Of course, many of the major figures of the earlier decades of West African writing continue to work in the third wave as well, and texts such as Achebe's *The Anthills of the Savannah* (1988a), Amadi's *Estrangement*, Nwapa's *Women Are Different*, Emecheta's *The Family* (1990), and Aidoo's *Changes* (1993) are clearly among the most important novels written by West African writers in the past decade. But a number of important new voices emerged in that decade as well. Among these are numerous writers of popular fiction such as fantasies and detective thrillers, a development that indicates the rising readership for fiction in West Africa. Moreover, an awareness of this readership has led writers such as the Ghanaian Amu Djoleto to pursue the themes of West African literature in a more accessible style reminiscent of popular literature. Also more accessible for a newly literate African audience are a number of new political novels by writers such as Kole Omotoso and Festus Iyayi, who write from an avowedly socialist perspective. (These novels also tend to reject the criteria of complexity and ambiguity often invoked by Western literary critics.) Works such as *The Man Who Came in from the Back of Beyond* and *The Sympathetic Undertaker and Other Dreams* (both 1991) by the Ghanaian Biyi Bandele-Thomas tend toward fantasy and absurdism. Probably the leading figure in this vein is the Nigerian Ben Okri, whose extremely complex and difficult novels have received considerable praise among Western critics.

Djoleto began his career in 1967 with the novel *The Strange Man* (1967), essentially a critique of the abuses of the colonial educational system in Ghana. He continued his writing in the 1975 *Money Galore* (1975), which focuses on the activities of the businessman and politician, Kafu, in a satire of postcolonial corruption reminiscent of *The Beautyful Ones Are Not Yet Born*, but written in a lighter and simpler style that has been compared to that of Aluko. Djoleto's latest novel, *Hurricane of Dust* (1987), continues in this vein, focusing on the activities of Doe Hevi, a construction worker. Doe espouses strong support for a recent revolutionary coup in Ghana, but he uses the ensuing confusion as an opportunity to expand his operations as a small-time criminal. Djoleto ironically undercuts Doe's revolutionary rhetoric in ways that radically challenge the notion that any military coup could ever bring social justice. Doe himself runs afoul of the new regime and is arrested and tortured for his involvement in a petty theft. Indeed, the book is filled—despite its generally light tone—with instances of torture, brutalization, and murder perpetrated by soldiers of the new socialist regime. The most positive character in the book is John Wudah, a government bureaucrat of the kind typically satirized in African fiction, but who in this case turns out to be a decent, honest, hard-working civil servant. Djoleto's book, in its critique of socialism and its positive presentation of the bourgeois Wudah, thus runs against the grain of most African political fiction and helps to indicate the complexity of the African political climate.

Iyayi, on the other hand, is a committed socialist whose novels have much in common with the Soviet movement of socialist realism and the leftist "proletarian fiction" that arose during the depression years of the 1930s in Britain and the United States. Iyayi's first novel, *Violence* (1979), relates the travails of a young Nigerian couple, Idemudia and Adisa, as they attempt to make a life for themselves in a modern Lagos dominated by the corrupt manipulations of politicians and businesspeople. Narrated in a straightforward, down-to-earth style that should make its message accessible to large numbers of Nigerian readers, *Violence* addresses a number of crucial issues, including the exploitation of workers by dishonest bosses and the ill functioning of public services such as hospitals because of corruption and incompetence among administrators and managers. The book's description of the relationship between Idemudia and Adisa also provides a sensitive exploration of relations between the genders in modern Nigeria. In its vivid contrast between the dire poverty of the honest, hard-working couple and the decadent luxury of a rich couple, Obufun and Queen, *Violence* presents a striking indictment of the inequities in postcolonial Nigerian society. In particular, as its title indicates, the book shows the violence (both physical and psychological) that is perpetrated by the rich against the poor. On the other hand, in the final solidarity between Idemudia and Adisa and in certain hints of the potential for successful collective action among workers against their unscrupulous bosses, the book includes a strong utopian dimension that suggests the possibility of a better future. Iyayi continues to combine a critique of postcolonial corruption with the suggestion of possible alternatives in his subsequent novels, *The Contract* (1982) and *Heroes* (1986). *Heroes* joins a large body of Nigerian fiction that deals with the cataclysmic Nigerian civil war, but it is distinctive for its suggestion that soldiers on both sides of the war would have been better-off to band together in a class war against their bosses.

Okri's fiction also frequently deals with the civil war. Okri has recently become one of the brightest new stars of African literature, especially after his magnum opus, *The Famished Road* (1991), was awarded the prestigious Booker Prize in 1991. (The Booker Price is an award annually given for the best novel written by a writer from the British Commonwealth.) Okri began his career with the novel *Flowers and Shadows*, published in 1980 and written when he was nineteen years old. In addition to *Flowers and Shadows*, Okri's early works include the novel *The Landscapes Within* (1981) and two books of short stories, *Incidents at the Shrine* (1986) and *Stars of the New Curfew* (1988). These works to a certain extent continue the motif of disillusioned critique of postcolonial society begun by writers such as Achebe and Armah, though Okri's work is marked by a distinctive poetic style and by a departure from the realistic mode that has been dominant in much of postcolonial African literature. Okri's fiction in some ways harkens back to the work of Tutuola, especially in its effacement of the line between the worlds of the living and the dead. It also employs a number of experimental strategies reminiscent of Western modernism and the avant-garde. Okri's work reaches its full power in *The Famished Road*, a brilliant tour de force that combines indigenous traditions of oral narrative with a use of fantastic images for purposes of social and political critique. This use of fantastic images has much in common with the mode of "magical realism" pioneered by Latin American writers such as Gabriel García Márquez, a mode increasingly used by Third World writers who find straightforward realism inadequate to the sometimes bizarre nature of life in the postcolonial world. Centering on the experience of Azaro, a young boy who moves back and forth between the material world and the world of the spirits, *The Famished Road* becomes a sort of summation of modern Nigerian culture and society. Azaro himself becomes very much what Fredric Jameson would call a national allegory because his childhood adventures closely parallel the tribulations encountered during the growth of the young Nigerian nation. The book is uncompromising in its critique of the violence and corruption of modern Nigerian society, but (like the work of Iyayi) it ends with a vision of a better future and a call to "redream" the world. Magical realism is also central to Syl Cheney-Coker's *The Last Harmattan of Alusine Dunbar* (1990), while Okri himself continues in this vein in *Songs Of Enchantment*, a 1993 sequel to *The Famished Road* that further traces the adventures of the boy Azaro—and of postcolonial Nigerian society. In his highly sophisticated literary style and his rich intertextual relationship with the literature and culture of societies around the globe, Okri's work indicates a new internationalism in West African fiction, even as his work draws heavily upon distinctively Nigerian narrative traditions and maintains a vivid contact with Nigerian reality.

The Anglophone Novel in East Africa and Southern Africa

Despite the dominance of West African writers in the development of the Anglophone African novel, some of the most important examples of the modern African novel have emerged from East Africa and southern Africa, especially in the works of the Kenyan novelist Ngugi wa Thiong'o. Ngugi stands with figures such as Achebe, Soyinka, and the Senegalese writer and filmmaker Ousmane Sembène as the true giants of modern African literature. Indeed, Ngugi's career in many ways is the paradigm of the development of East African literature as a whole. Ngugi first began to consider writing seriously while he was a student at Makerere University in Kampala, Uganda, in the early 1960s, which points to the crucial role that university played as an intellectual center in the early years of modern East African literature. Ngugi wrote his first novel, *The River Between* (1965), in 1961, but he became particularly determined to write after attending the African Writers' Conference in Kampala in 1962. This conference inspired him and other East African writers (particularly Kenya's Grace Ogot) because there were so few East African writers present. Finally, Ngugi's intense engagement with social and political issues in Kenya and in Africa as a whole stands as a model of the social responsibility that is the hallmark of modern African literature.

The River Between, a meditation on the conflict between traditional and modern values in the Gikuyu society of colonial Kenya, was not published until 1965. Ngugi's first published novel (and the first modern novel to be published by an East African writer) was *Weep Not, Child*, written in 1962 but published in 1964. Both of these novels detail the sometimes devastating impact of colonial domination on Kenya's traditional societies. *Weep Not, Child* focuses particularly on the so-called Mau Mau rebellion against British rule, the first of a number of novels that focus on that crucial conflict, including Ngugi's own *A Grain of Wheat* (1967). Indeed, the Mau Mau period is a major concern of East African fiction, especially Kenyan fiction, though the treatment of the Mau Mau movement varies considerably in the works of different writers. For example, Charles Mangua's *A Tail in the Mouth* (1972), while it is highly critical of the "home guards" (the Kenyan troops who sided with the British to suppress the rebellion) can by and large be read as a satirical treatment of the Mau Mau freedom fighters. The book might thus be seen as a parodic response to Ngugi's positive vision of those fighters as paradigms of anticolonial resistance, though it can also be argued that Ngugi's understanding of the Mau Mau in this way did not fully congeal until his turn toward a more radical vision in the later novels *Petals of Blood* (1977), *Caitaani Mutharaba-ini* (first published in 1980; trans. *Devil on the Cross*, 1982), and *Matigari ma Njiruugi* (first published in 1986; trans. *Matigari*, 1989). Meja Mwangi's novels *Carcase for Hounds* (1974) and *Taste of Death* (1975) are more ambivalent, depicting the suffering of both the freedom fighters and their opponents. Mwangi's Mau Mau novels show a basic sympathy with the goals of the Mau Mau movement, but they sometimes veer dangerously close to a repetition of colonialist myths of the Mau Mau as primitive savages driven by blood lust. The same might also be said for Godwin Wachira's *Ordeal in the Forest* (1968), which combines a biting critique of colonialism (especially through its depiction of the racist British officer Major Cook) with a seeming acceptance of a number of colonialist stereotypes about Africans. The story collection *Potent Ash* (1968), by Leonard Kibera and Sam Kahiga, and Kibera's novel *Voices in the Dark* (1970) are also sympathetic to the Mau Mau cause, but they focus on the nightmarish conditions that the rebellion created and on the deplorable social and political conditions of postcolonial Kenya that the rebellion indirectly fostered. Charity Waciuma's *Daughter of Mumbi* (1969), on the other hand, is far more consistent in its support for the Mau Mau cause through a depiction of the justice of their opposition to conditions in colonial Kenya.

Ngugi's first two novels were soon followed by Ogot's *The Promised Land* (1966), the first East African novel by a woman writer and the first novel to be published by Nairobi's East Africa Publishing House, which would become a major force in the development of East African literature. *The Promised Land*, like *The River Between*, focuses on the impact on traditional village society of modern values derived from the colonial presence in Kenya. Ogot would go on to develop a reputation as a short-story writer, particularly for the stories published in the collections *Land Without Thunder* (1968), *The Other Woman* (1976), and *The Island of Tears* (1980a). Ogot's stories combine traditional Luo storytelling techniques with nationalistic sentiments to express a passionate concern for the plight of women in East African society.

Another important early contribution to the East African novel in English was the long poem *Song of Lawino* (1966), which can be described as a sort of novel in verse and which was written by the Ugandan poet, Okot p'Bitek. p'Bitek had already published an Acoli-language novel, *Lak Tar*, in 1953, which shows that the "birth" of the East African novel in the early 1960s was not a sudden event but grew out of a number of indigenous cultural forces in addition to the impact of colonialism and colonial education. *Song of Lawino* would soon be joined by *Song of Ocol* (1970a) and *Two Songs: Song of Prisoner and Song of Malaya* in (1971) to form a sort of trilogy that established p'Bitek as a major poet who is sometimes compared to Nigeria's Christopher Okigbo.[4] *Song of Lawino*, p'Bitek's masterpiece, is the comic lament of Lawino, a traditional woman who has been abandoned by her Westernized husband, Ocol. It thus again deals with the conflict between traditional and modern cultures, though in a mode unique not only for its comic irony, but also for its impressive use of the techniques of traditional Acoli oral culture. Indeed, p'Bitek is the son of accomplished Acoli oral artists, and all of his work is marked by the strong influence of African oral culture. One of the major motivations of his work is to challenge the colonialist vision of this culture as primitive and undeveloped. In 1974, for example, he demonstrated the richness of Acoli oral culture in *The Horn of My Love* (1974), a compilation of English translations of traditional Acoli songs. p'Bitek has also published scholarly studies of African culture, religion, and philosophy, including *African Religions in Western Scholarship* (1970b) and *Artist, the Ruler* (1986).

By the time Idi Amin seized power in Uganda in a 1971 coup, initiating a dark period for Ugandan literature, p'Bitek had gone into exile in Kenya where he joined Ngugi and the Ugandan writer Taban lo Liyong on the faculty of the University of Nairobi, which at that time supplanted Makerere as the leading center of intellectual activity in East Africa. Ngugi, meanwhile, continued his work as the most important figure in East African fiction. *Petals of Blood* is his longest novel and the one that makes the most extensive and sophisticated use of narrative techniques learned from Western models. *Caitaani Mutharaba-ini*, on the other hand, marked a major change in direction for Ngugi, not only because it was written in Gikuyu rather than English, but also because it draws extensively upon the traditions of Gikuyu oral narrative in its style and structure. *Matigari* continues in this vein, using folk traditions and supernatural imagery to make Ngugi's most radical statement in favor of revolutionary change in postcolonial Kenya.

Ngugi's major political concern is international capitalism's neocolonial exploitation of Kenya and the complicity of the postcolonial Kenyan regime in this exploitation. But Ngugi's work is also particularly marked by an intense concern with the special difficulties faced by women in Kenyan society. In this sense, his work resonates with that of Ogot and numerous other important women writers from East Africa. Ogot is a popular writer in Kenya, though her work has received relatively little critical attention in the West.[5] In 1980, she published a second novel in English, *The Graduate*

---

[4] Okigbo, killed while fighting for the Biafran side in the Nigerian civil war, is himself the central figure in an extremely interesting East African novel, *The Trial of Christopher Okigbo* , by the Ugandan intellectual Ali A. Mazrui (1971).

[5] See Stratton's chapter on Ogot for an attempt to rectify this situation (Stratton 1994).

(1980b),which focuses on the political disempowerment of women in postcolonial Kenya. Perhaps more significantly, Ogot produced a number of works in the Luo language in the 1980s, perhaps following the lead of Ngugi. These works, including *Ber Wat* (1981a), *Aloo Kod Apul-Apul* (1981b), *Miaha* (1983a; trans. *The Strange Bride*, 1989), and *Simbi Nyaima*, (1983b) have found a substantial readership in Kenya and have done a great deal to advance the notion of writing in African, as opposed to European, languages.

Like her male compatriot Ngugi, Ogot criticizes the neocolonial domination of Kenya, but her principal focus is on the masculine bias of postcolonial Kenyan culture itself. In this sense, she has remained a leader among East African women writers. Another important women writer is Charity Waciuma, who (in addition to writing *Daughter of Mumbi*) has been a leader in the production of children's literature in Kenya. Also noteworthy is the Kenyan Rebeka Njau's *Ripples in the Pool* (1975), which contrasts the nature-oriented wisdom of a traditional medicine man with the coldly scientific approach to medicine (and the world) imported from the West. Njau employs poetic language and supernatural imagery to evoke the traumatic effect on the Kenyan peasantry of the dispossession of their land in the colonial period, an effect that continues to have ramifications well into the postcolonial era. Njau has also written short stories and a play, showing an ability to work in multiple genres that is typical among African women writers.

If Njau's approach in *Ripples in the Pool* anticipates the turn toward fantastic imagery in Ngugi's *Matigari* (or even the rise of magical realism in the works of writers such as Ben Okri), other writers have moved toward more and more direct descriptions of reality. Neil Lazarus identifies the naturalistic style developed by Mwangi, his fellow Kenyan Thomas Akare, and the Zimbabwean Dambudzo Marechera as one of the most important developments in politically engaged African literature since 1970 (Lazarus 1990, 209). In addition to his two Mau Mau novels in the mid-1970s, Mwangi has published a number of novels that focus on the plight of the urban poor in postcolonial Nairobi, including *Kill Me Quick!* (1973), *Going Down River Road* (1976), and *The Cockroach Dance* (1979). Mwangi's work is particularly distinctive for its description of the poor in their own idiom. His latest novel, *Weapon of Hunger* (1989) continues his social concern in its vivid treatment of civil war as an emblem of the moral and political chaos that have marked much of postcolonial African history.

Mwangi's novels, partially because of their use of vernacular language, have been extremely popular in Kenya, which has developed a lively tradition of commercially successful popular literature in the past two decades. Mangua's *Son of Woman* (1971) is generally acknowledged as the founding text of this trend, in which crime stories and spy thrillers—both heavily influenced by Western models—have been particularly popular. But it is David

Maillu who is the undisputed king of Kenyan popular literature, both because of his own writings and because of his founding of Comb Books (and later of Maillu Publishing House), one of the major publishers of popular novels in East Africa. Maillu's numerous works have often been judged inferior in quality by critics, either because of his overt didacticism or because of his lack of mastery of literary technique. On the other hand, Emmanuel Ngara has argued that Maillu's work deserves more serious critical attention and that the social vision embodied in his works constitutes a profound literary expression of the social problems facing postcolonial Africa (Ngara 1985, 55). Focusing on *My Dear Bottle* (1973) and *After 4:30* (1974), Ngara demonstrates Maillu's intense concern with the plight of women and of the working class in Kenya, though Ngara acknowledges Maillu's stylistic limitations and grants that Maillu's success as a political writer is compromised by his lack of a fully articulated socialist vision. Ngara concludes that Maillu "may with some justification be condemned as a 'pornographic jester,' but his style should not obscure the fact that he raises questions capable of pricking the consciences of those in positions of power and authority" (p. 58).

Maillu's work continues to be popular in the 1990s, though in recent years he has turned more and more to the production of children's books. Of course, the turn to crime thrillers and other forms of "entertainment" literature in the 1970s can also be attributed to the fact that increasingly oppressive political conditions in Kenya made it unsafe for writers to treat contemporary reality in more profound ways. There has been a notable decline in the political engagement of Kenyan fiction in the last two decades. Ngugi himself, because of the uncompromising political engagement of his writing, was detained in prison for nearly a year in the late 1970s and then forced into exile in the late 1980s. The trend toward popular fiction has also been followed by writers such as Marjorie Oludhe Macgoye. Her 1986 *Coming to Birth* (1986) is a serious social novel, but she moved to a more popular mode in the 1987 *Street Life* (1987). Similarly, Ugandan fiction has never quite recovered from the traumatic effect of the political turmoil both before and after Amin's 1971 coup, though several important works have been produced, mostly by writers working in exile. These include Peter Nazareth's *In A Brown Mantle* (1972), which critiques the regime of Amin's predecessor Milton Obote; Eneriko Seruma's *The Experience* (1970); and Alumidi Osinya's *The Amazing Saga of Field Marshall Abdulla Salim Fasi, or How the Hyena Got His!* (1977), a hilarious satirical send-up of the Amin regime.

The work of the Somali writer Nuruddin Farah is also worthy of note in any account of East African Anglophone literature, even though Farah's Somali culture draws upon a number of traditions (especially Islamic ones) that are outside those that are central to most Anglophone African writers. Farah's complex and sophisticated novels combine important influences from the strong tradition of Somali oral poetry with an impressive mastery of the literary techniques of Western modernism to produce some of the most noteworthy works of modern East African literature. Farah's consistent focus on gender issues has gained him a reputation as one of the most "feminist" of all African male writers. His first novel, *From a Crooked Rib* (1970) is set in the colonial Somalia of the 1950s and focuses on the tribulations of its protagonist Ebla, an illiterate Somali woman who attempts to escape her treatment as the property of men. By and large, however, Farah's work concentrates on the postcolonial period. *A Naked Needle* (1976) focuses in an impressionistic fashion on the experiences of the young man Koschin, a scholar of the work of James Joyce and an inhabitant of Mogadishu in the confusing years following the 1969 coup that placed Somalia under the rule of General Mohammed Siyad Barre.

Farah's most substantial work to date is the trilogy *Variations on the Theme of an African Dictatorship*, which consists of the volumes *Sweet and Sour Milk* (1979), *Sardines* (1981), and *Close Sesame* (1983). These volumes are extremely literary, including allusions to a wide range of other texts from a variety of disciplines and employing an extensive array of experimental narration techniques reminiscent of Western modernism. But the political engagement of Farah's fiction is unquestionable. All three volumes are set in a fictional dystopian Somalia of the 1970s ruled by a fictional "General" who is quite obviously based on Siyad Barre. Farah's critical commentary on oppressive conditions in Somalia is thus quite direct. (Farah was forced into exile and his works banned.) All in all, *Variations on the Theme of an African Dictatorship* is one of the most sophisticated literary works in the global dystopian tradition.

One of the themes of Farah's trilogy is the impact of Soviet support for Siyad Barre in the 1970s. In *Maps* (1986), however, Farah demonstrates that Siyad Barre's later switch to the American side in the Cold War did little to alleviate the oppressive conditions in Somalia. *Maps* also employs an even more inventive narrative style than its predecessors, moving from the realm of modernism into that of postmodernism. Its protagonist Askar is another example of "national allegory" in African fiction, and it is clear that his experiences are representative of postcolonial Somalia as a whole. Farah's literary production continued unabated in exile, through the tumultuous conditions in Somalia in the 1990s. In 1992 he published *Gifts*, (1992) which explores the subtle ramifications of international efforts to provide aid to war-torn and drought-ridden Somalia.

Other Anglophone novels from East Africa and southern Africa include those produced by Zambia's Dominic Mulaisho (e.g., *The Tongue of the Dumb*, 1971) and Tanzania's M. G. Vassanji (e.g., *The Gunny Sack*, 1989). In addition, a number of important novels have been produced by writers from the southern African republic of Zimbabwe. Zimbabwe (then the British colony of Southern Rhodesia) was the childhood home of the British novelist Doris Lessing, many of whose later novels are set in colonial Zimbabwe. In novels such as *Martha Quest* (1952), *A Proper Marriage* (1954), *A Ripple from the Storm* (1958), and *Landlocked* (1965), Lessing presents powerful critiques of the ideology of colonialism from a Marxist-feminist perspective. A similar critique of colonialism informs much of the early fiction of black Zimbabwean writers. Recently, a new generation of exciting young writers has turned its attention to the particularly tumultuous conditions of Zimbabwe's movement toward independence from European (and later, local white) domination in the 1960s and 1970s and to social conditions in postcolonial Zimbabwe. Perhaps most prominent among these is Dambudzo Marechera, whose violent, fantastic novel *The House of Hunger* (1978) was awarded the Guardian Prize for Fiction in 1979. While this novel focuses on poverty in the slums of colonial Salisbury, Marechera's second novel, *Black Sunlight* (1980), focuses on similar conditions in London. Marechera also published a volume of short stories and one of plays, prose, and poetry, but his career was cut short by his death in 1987 at the age of thirty-five. Other important Zimbabwean novels include Shimmer Chinodya's 1989 *Harvest of Thorns*, which details the impact on its protagonist of the long and difficult war of liberation from white rule, and Tsitsi Dangarembga's female bildungsroman *Nervous Conditions* (1989a), no doubt one of the most important fictional explorations of the social conditions of African women's lives to be published in the last decade. The poet Chenjerai Hove has recently turned to the writing of novels as well. His 1988 novel *Bones* is a powerful evocation of the impact of Zimbabwe's fight for liberation on the experiences of rural women, while his 1991 *Shadows* presents the story of innocent lovers who struggle against poverty, oppression, and generational conflicts in their desire to be together.

The South African Anglophone Novel

The literature of the Republic of South Africa is a special case in the history of African culture, because the history of South Africa—the postcolonial African nation with the largest population descended from European settlers, differs from that of most African nations in important ways. In particular, South African history has been blighted by the phenomenon of apartheid, through which the white minority population sought to maintain economic and political control through brutal repression of the black majority. Apartheid, based on a strict separation of races and on an assumption of the absolute superiority of whites over nonwhites, was part of a long legacy of racism in South Africa. It was the official government policy from 1948 to 1990. The election of Nelson Mandela in 1994 as the first president of post-apartheid South Africa was the first genuinely free election in the country's history.

The fact of apartheid dominates post–World War II South African literature, which, to its credit, consists almost entirely of works that are critical of apartheid and of the ruthless manner in which it was generally carried out. However, the history of South African printed literature goes back to the early years of the twentieth century, when a surprising number of works were published in indigenous languages, especially Sotho and Zulu. Most of these early works were produced by presses controlled by missionaries working in the area and are little more than religious tracts. However, at least one, Thomas Mofolo's Sotho-language novel *Chaka* (submitted for publication as early as 1910, but first published in 1925) has claim to considerable literary merit and continues to receive extensive critical attention even today. Indeed, since the publication of Daniel Kunene's new English translation in 1981, *Chaka* has achieved a new prominence in critical discussions of South African literature. Mofolo's book, based on the story of an early nineteenth-century Zulu king, can be taken as an early attempt to recover elements of the African past that were suppressed in colonialist histories, thus initiating what would become one of the major projects of later African literature. South African literature has shown a special intensity in its engagement with history, perhaps out of a sense of the urgency of speaking out against apartheid.

One of the important founding figures of black South African literature in English was Peter Abrahams, who became politically aware in the 1930s and then went into exile in 1939 better to pursue his ambition to be a writer. After two years at sea, Abrahams settled in London, where he married an English woman and became an editor of the Communist Party organ *Daily Worker*. Abrahams's first two novels, *Song of the City* (1943) and *Mine* (1946), show the influence of this work with their overtly Marxist themes of opposition to class-based oppression under industrial capitalism (which, in South Africa as in the United States, is inseparable from racial oppression). Abrahams's third novel, *The Path of Thunder* (1948) is optimistic in its treatment of the possibility of love across racial barriers. Taken together his first three novels are informed by a powerful hope that conditions in South Africa can be greatly improved if only white South Africans can be taught to see beyond their traditional habit of racial hatred. With the publication of *Wild Conquest* (1950), Abrahams turned his attention to more historical themes in an attempt to locate the roots of apartheid in the early history of encounters between the indigenous Matabele people and Afrikaner settlers during their "Great Trek" into the interior of South Africa in the 1830s and 1840s. One of Abrahams's most important works is *Tell Freedom* (1954), the first published autobiography by a black South African. The 1956 novel *A Wreath for Udomo* (1956) is also especially important because its indictment of colonialism and its understanding of the dangers of neocolonialism anticipate the works of later writers such as Achebe, Armah, and Ngugi. Abrahams extends this theme in *This Island Now* (1966), a critique of neocolonialism in an island nation modeled on Haiti and Jamaica. Other important works by Abrahams include *A Night of Their Own* (1965) and *The View from Coyaba* (1985), which employ South African and Jamaican settings, respectively, to explore the role of the writer in the liberation of the black race.

Abrahams has been an important inspiration for a number of other black South African writers, though many of these writers draw upon indigenous oral traditions to go beyond Abrahams's relatively conventional adherence to a Western aesthetic. Es'kia Mphahlele is another important early figure in the development of a black South African literature. Perhaps his most important single work is his autobiography, *Down Second Avenue* (1959), which joins Abrahams's *Tell Freedom* as the two most important South African works in that genre. Mphahlele is also the author of two novels, *The Wanderers* (which was published in 1971 and which helped Mphahlele earn his doctorate at the University of Denver) and *Chirundu* (1971, 1979). But Mphahlele's most important contributions to South African fiction may be in the genre of the short story, especially his work with the important literary magazine *Drum*, which became one of the major forces in the development of South African literature. Mphalele's short story collections include *The Living and the Dead* (1961), *In Corner B* (1967), *The Unbroken Song* (1981), and *Renewal Time* (1988). Mphalele is also an important critic, known for volumes of commentary such as *The African Image* (1962) and *Voices in the Whirlwind* (1972) and for his sometimes controversial stands. He has vigorously opposed the ideology of the Négritude movement, and like Ngugi, he is skeptical of the ultimate ability of literature in English to contribute to the development of a genuinely African cultural identity.

The short story has been a particularly important genre in modern South African literature, partially because of the influence of magazines such as *Drum* and *Classic*. In addition to Mphahele, important short-story writers have included Richard Rive, James Matthews, Njabulo Ndebele, Mbulelo Mzamane, and Alex La Guma. Rive's 1964 novel, *Emergency* (1964), though banned in South Africa, was also an important contribution to the development of that genre in South African literature. *Emergency* describes events surrounding the 1960 police massacre of dozens of peaceful demonstrators at Sharpeville. Rive's engagement with political developments in South Africa continued in his other novels, including *"Buckingham Palace," District Six* (1986) and *Emergency Continued* (1990). La Guma's politically engaged novels have made him perhaps the most important of all nonwhite South African novelists. As Abdul JanMohamed puts it, "The life and fiction of Alex La Guma perfectly illustrate the predicament of nonwhites in South Africa and the effects of apartheid on their lives" (JanMohamed 1983, 225).

Born and raised in the notorious District Six, the "coloured" ghetto of Cape Town, La Guma experienced the tribulations of South Africa's poor and oppressed firsthand.[6] His communist parents exposed him to leftist politics at an early age, and by 1948 (at the age of twenty-three) he had joined the South African Communist Party. When it was outlawed two years later, La Guma was forced into a particularly marginal position in South African society. In the 1950s his active involvement in trade union politics led to his harassment and detention by the authorities on several occasions, eventually forcing him to leave the country for England in 1966. By this time he had established a considerable international reputation as a writer, both for his short stories and for the novels *A Walk in the Night* (1967b, first published in 1962) and *And a Threefold Cord* (1964). *The Stone Country* (1967a) was also written while he was still in South Africa. These novels combine an uncompromising description of the squalor of life in South Africa's urban slums with a strong commitment to the possibility of radical political change. La Guma's novels written in exile, *In the Fog of the Seasons' End* (1972) and *Time of the Butcherbird* (1979), continue this passionate political commitment and concern for the plight of those whom Fanon called "the wretched of the earth."

La Guma's novels are all informed by a sophisticated Marxist understanding of the problems of South African society and the steps necessary for their ultimate solution. The novels are also distinctive in their journalistic style, which is reminiscent of the works of American naturalist writers such as Frank Norris and Theodore Dreiser, but the closest American analog is probably the proletarian fiction produced by 1930s writers such as Mike Gold, Jack Conroy, and James T. Farrell. La Guma himself characterized his work as socialist realism, thus indicating the crucial influence of Soviet writers such as Maxim Gorky, Fyodor Gladkov, and Mikhail Sholokhov. La Guma's dialogic relationship with a number of international literary movements parallels his extensive international reputation, though his works were banned in South Africa and were virtually unknown there until the 1980s.

While La Guma's journalistic realism is typical of the dominant mode of black South African fiction, poets such as Sipho Sepamla and Mongane Serote have written novels that show the clear influence of their poetic backgrounds. Serote was perhaps the best-known poet in South Africa in the early 1970s. He writes in a street-smart mode influenced by Amiri Baraka and other African-American activist writers of the 1960s. This poetry is marked by the same intense political commitment that distinguishes his only novel, the 1981 *To Every Birth Its Blood* (1981). The first part of this novel presents a vivid evocation of township life as background to the personal

---

[6] The racist regime of apartheid South Africa categorized citizens according to strict racial designations. "Coloured" South Africans are those of mixed race, generally part white and part black, though potentially part Asian.

angst of its protagonist, Tsi. But the second part of the novel expands its scope into the public sphere by suggesting the possibility for change through collective resistance to the madness of apartheid. Sepamla's novel *A Ride on the Whirlwind* (1981) focuses on the experiences of its protagonist, Mzi, who returns to South Africa to work for the violent overthrow of the government after training abroad in revolutionary techniques. Its focus on both interracial violence and violence among blacks (especially as perpetrated by blacks who collude with the South African regime) anticipates the specific incidents that marked life in South Africa in the 1980s. This novel thus echoes the earlier *The Root Is One* (1979) in its concern with the possibility of change through violent political action. But, like Iyayi, Sepamla's real subject is the everyday violence, both psychic and physical, that apartheid wrought on the lives of ordinary black people in South Africa. His later novels, *Third Generation* (1986) and *A Scattered Survival* (1989) focus particularly on the breakdown of personal relationships under the squalid conditions of life in South Africa's black townships.

Also of note among recent South African novels is Lewis Nkosi's *Mating Birds* (1983), a blistering indictment of the crippling effects of apartheid on personal relationships in South Africa. This novel focuses on an aspiring writer who is in a South African prison awaiting execution; it participates in a tradition of prison novels that has, not surprisingly, been a prominent aspect of South African literature. Important earlier examples of the prison genre include D. M. Zwelonke's *Robben Island* (1973) and Moses Dlamini's *Hell Hole, Robben Island* (1984); prison and jail experiences also figure prominently in many of La Guma's works. Nkosi's novel shows a large degree of sophistication, which might be expected because Nkosi has taught African literature in universities around the world and is the author of numerous works of literary criticism, including the important *Tasks and Masks: Themes and Styles of African Literature* (1981).

Black South African women writers have been more active in the short story than in the novel. However, one nonwhite woman, Bessie Head, became one of Africa's leading women novelists, though her career was cut short by her premature death in 1986. It is indicative of conditions in South Africa that all of Head's novels were written in exile—in Botswana, where most of her fiction is also set. Like so many African novels, her first novel, *When Rain Clouds Gather* (1969) is a story of conflict between modern and traditional societies. The book takes on special political force, however, because modern ideas are brought to the rural Botswanan village of Golema Mmidi not by white colonizers, but by political exiles fleeing from the apartheid regime in South Africa. Indeed, the book's major English character, Gilbert Balfour, is a positive figure, an agricultural expert who tries to help the poor villagers modernize their farming methods and thus decrease their poverty.

In *Maru* (1971), Head continues her focus on Botswanan village life, but she considerably increases the complexity of her fictional technique. The novel presents a basic love story about the competition of two men, Maru and Moleka, for the affections of the same woman, Margaret. But it is also a complex, multilayered narrative that explores the psychic consequences of tribalism, racism among different groups of blacks, and the oppression of women. The major characters all have a rather allegorical quality, standing as representatives of social, racial, and gender positions in the book's exploration of traditional African prejudices. In its final affirmation of the individual will as opposed to the demands of social conventions, Head's vision would appear to be more in line with European individualism than with African socialistic traditions, but the book nevertheless makes some important points about Botswanan village society.

Head's best-known novel is unquestionably the 1974 *A Question of Power*, a frighteningly intense and at least partially autobiographical exploration of psychological instability in the context of Botswanan village. The protagonist, Elizabeth (who seems directly modeled on Head herself) is a coloured South African woman in exile in Botswana who must battle to find a stable sense of identity in the midst of a mental breakdown. Her search is complicated by her social position as an exile and by her situation as a woman in a strongly male–dominated society. Head's style powerfully evokes Elizabeth's simultaneous experience of mental illness and social marginalization, and it is clear that Elizabeth's nightmarish psychic pain and fragmentation represent both Head's own personal experiences and the larger social damage wrought in South Africa by the insane policy of apartheid. The book ends, however, on a positive (if somewhat unconvincing) note, with a suggestion of the healing power of individual love and the positive potential of communal activities such as cooperative gardening.

In *Serowe: Village of the Rain Wind* (1981) Head turns to a more historical focus, telling the story of the development of Botswana from 1880 to 1970 through a compilation of oral accounts based on interviews with the real inhabitants of Serowe. The book is thus one of the more interesting African experiments in the blending of written and oral narrative. Head's last novel, *A Bewitched Crossroad: An African Saga* (1984), also focuses on themes in Botswanan history, mingling fact and fiction in an ambitious attempt to tell the story of Botswana from a human perspective. Head's short stories, many of which are collected in the volumes *The Collector of Treasures and Other Botswana Tales* (1977) and *Tales of Tenderness and Power* (1989), are also important.

South Africa's best known novelist on an international scale is the white woman Nadine Gordimer, who won the Nobel Prize for literature in 1991. Indeed, the tradition of novels by white South African women goes back to the late nineteenth century in the work of Olive Schreiner, whose *Story of an African Farm* (1883), first published in 1883, is still widely read today. Indeed, though Schreiner's work can be criticized for its focus on white settlers almost to the exclusion of South Africa's indigenous black population, this work has inspired a number of later women novelists. For example, Lessing credits Schreiner with having taught her that it was possible to write seriously about Africa. Gordimer is unquestionably the most important white South African woman novelist working today, and her combination of deft literary technique with an uncompromising sense of social responsibility stands as a model for novelists worldwide.

Gordimer's first few novels, including *The Lying Days* (1953), *A World of Strangers* (1958), and *Occasion for Loving* (1960b), treat conditions in South Africa in a mode of relatively light satire and have been described by Adbul JanMohamed as works of Gordimer's "bourgeois phase" (JanMohamed 1983, 88). For JanMohamed, however, novels such as *The Late Bourgeois World* (1982b, first published in 1966), *A Guest of Honour* (1970), and *The Conservationist* (1975) can be taken as examples of a "postbourgeois" phase in which Gordimer's growing outrage brings her to a more and more urgent criticism of the social and political conditions in South Africa. *The Conservationist*, which was the first novel by an African writer to win the Booker Prize, marks the beginning of Gordimer's recognition as a major novelist on the world scene, but it can also be regarded as the culmination of Gordimer's early career, with its tendency toward a lyrical style and a focus on the subjective experiences of individual characters within the context of South African racism and oppression.

In *Burger's Daughter* (1980a) and *July's People* (1982a), Gordimer's work takes on a substantially more public and political dimension. These works, which JanMohamed considers the beginning of the "revolutionary" phase in Gordimer's writing, suggest that the intolerable conditions in South Africa are leading inevitably to an explosion and that individuals have an obligation to take political action amid the growing crisis. This same sense of a need for political commitment can also be found in *A Sport of Nature* (1988) and *My Son's Story* (1991b). Gordimer's first post-apartheid novel, *None to Accompany Me* (1994) focuses on the chaotic attempts to establish a new South Africa in the wake of apartheid. She has also published numerous influential volumes of short stories and essays.

The tradition of white men's writing in South Africa goes back for some time as well, though the early years after the official establishment of apartheid in 1948 were a particularly rich period. Works in English such as Alan Paton's *Cry, the Beloved Country* (1948), Dan Jacobson's *Evidence of Love* (1960), and Jack Cope's *The Dawn Came Twice* (1969) typically mix a commitment to liberal values with a critique of apartheid, though there is generally a growing sense of pessimism in such works. By far the most important white male English-language novelist in South Africa today is J. M. Coetzee, who has combined a self-consciously postmodern and experimental literary style with an intense concern with the evils of apartheid. His novels are marked both by technical sophistication (perhaps showing the influence of his doctorate in literature from the University of Texas and his long-time role as professor of literature at the University of Cape Town) and powerful and disturbing content (showing the impact of South African political and social reality). Coetzee's novels begin with the 1974 *Dusklands*, a parody of colonialist discourse reminiscent of the work of postmodern European writers such as Samuel Beckett and Vladimir Nabokov, and *In the Heart of the Country* (1977), a stream-of-consciousness exploration of the master-slave mentality of South African society.

Coetzee's best-known novel is probably the 1980 *Waiting for the Barbarians* (1980). It combines starkly realistic descriptions of violence with almost surrealistic scenes of symbolic imagery to comment upon the phenomenon of imperialism in general and apartheid in particular. Coetzee was the second African writer to win the Booker Prize with the 1983 novel *The Life and Times of Michael K* (1983), which marks an increasing turn toward metafictional explorations of the nature of fiction and its role in the world. The Kafkaesque *Michael K* employs typically European experimental modes of writing to explore themes of official oppression versus individual freedom but with distinctly South African (anticolonial, antiapartheid) resonances. *Foe* (1986) is even more self-consciously literary, drawing upon the plots of Daniel Defoe's eighteenth-century novels *Robinson Crusoe* and *Roxana* to construct a profound philosophical fiction that explores both the nature of artistic creation and the impact of political oppression on such creation. *Age of Iron* (1990) similarly explores the impact of social marginalization on the writer, while *The Master of Petersburg* (1994), Coetzee's first postapartheid novel, continues his engagement with the European literary tradition with a fictional re-creation of the life of the nineteenth-century Russian novelist Fyodor Dostoevsky.

Coetzee is also the editor, with André Brink, of the anthology *A Land Apart (1986),* which includes fiction, poetry, and autobiography from a number of South African writers in both English and Afrikaans. Brink, like Coetzee, is a professor of English at the University of Cape Town. He is the only South African writer working in Afrikaans who has any significant critical reputation. Brink, however, translates his own work into English and thus might be considered an English-language novelist. It is certainly in English that his work is best known and widely read. Novels such as *Looking on Darkness* (1974), *A Dry White Season* (1979), and *A Chain of Voices* (1982) draw directly upon South African history to produce powerful antiapartheid statements that make Brink, along with Gordimer and Coetzee, one of the leading figures in South African literature today.

The Francophone African Novel

By the end of the colonial period, France and Great Britain were the two major colonial powers in Africa, and French and English are the two most widely used European languages in Africa. As with English, there is an extensive African literature written in French, and no survey of the African novel can claim to be complete without at least a brief mention of the Francophone African novel. Not only have there been a number of extremely important novels produced by African writers working in French, but the development of the Francophone novel in many ways runs slightly ahead of the development of the Anglophone novel, so that one might argue that Francophone writers have often led the way for Anglophone writers. In any case, there has been a great deal of mutual influence among Francophone and Anglophone African novelists, and the two traditions cannot be considered as entirely independent.

René Maran's *Batouala* (1921) is sometimes considered the first Francophone novel. Though Maran was originally from the island of Martinique, a French colony in the Caribbean, he spent some of his childhood in Africa and worked for over twenty years in the French colonial administration in Africa. Maran's novel won the Prix Goncourt (a French equivalent to the Booker Prize), and this recognition certainly encouraged subsequent African writers. The important thinker (and leader of the Négritude movement) Léopold Senghor declared Maran the father of the African novel, and Abiola Irele has designated Maran "the creator of the modern African novel" (Irele 1990, 132). Maran's distinctive combination of literary techniques derived from the European tradition (such as French symbolism) with elements of African oral storytelling traditions produced a vivid depiction of conditions in French colonial Africa that would set the tone for many African novels to come, in both French and English.

Several other African novels in French (by Maran and others) were published in the 1920s, 1930s, and 1940s, but many critics consider Camara Laye's *L'enfant noir* (1953; trans. *The Dark Child*, 1954) as the beginning of the modern African novel in French. By this time, however, the most important phenomenon in Francophone African literature was the Négritude movement. Writers such as Senghor and Aimé Césaire drew upon techniques similar to those used by the French surrealists to try to develop a distinctively African mode of literary expression that would contribute to the development of a positive cultural identity for black Africans—and all black people. Controversial and often criticized, the Négritude movement nevertheless made major contributions to the development of African (especially French African) literature, though these contributions were more important in poetry than in fiction.

Laye's work owes relatively little to Négritude in a stylistic sense, but its idealized portrayal of conditions in a traditional Malinke society untouched by colonial contamination clearly owes something to the influence of the movement. Indeed, Senghor defended Laye against charges of excessive idealization and sentimentality. Subsequent Francophone writers continued Laye's elaboration of an African cultural identity but in more explicitly anticolonial and politically engaged ways. Laye himself would move in this direction with works such as *Dramouss* (1966; trans. *A Dream of Africa*, 1968), the sequel to *L'enfant noir.* A similar project was pursued by such writers as Bernard Dadié, from the Ivory Coast, and the Cameroonian Mongo Beti. Dadié's 1956 novel *Climbié* (1956) is a semiautobiographical exploration of the author's own identity, while several books describing Dadié's travels in the West detail his search for identity through an explicit engagement with Western culture. Beti, meanwhile, employs humor and satire to excoriate colonialism (especially as purveyed through Catholic missions) and to contribute to the development of a sense of African identity. In novels such as *Le pauvre Christ de Bomba* (1956; trans. *The Poor Christ of Bomba*, 1971) and *Mission terminée* (1957; trans. *Mission to Kala* 1964), Beti provides important early examples of the Francophone satirical novel. Beti fell silent in the tumultuous 1960s, but reemerged in the 1970s as a writer exploring the political situation in postcolonial Africa in works such as *Perpétue* (1974; trans. *Perpetua and the Habit of Unhappiness,* 1978), *Remember Ruben* (first published in 1974, English translation, 1980).

Another important early satirist was the Cameroonian Ferdinand Oyono, whose *Le vieux nègre et la médaille* (1956a; trans. *The Old Man and the Medal,* 1967) satirizes colonialism through the eyes of an old Cameroonian man who has long been loyal to his French masters but comes to question his earlier attitudes. Oyono's *Une vie de boy* (1956b; trans. *Houseboy* 1966) is another excellent example of satire. It is striking for its depiction of the reaction of colonized Africans to the behavior of their French colonizers as bizarre, nonsensical, and even obscene, thus effectively reversing a number of European stereotypes about Africa. A strong element of humor continues to inform the Francophone novel throughout its history, as in more recent works such as the Congolese Henri Lopes's *Le pleurer-rire* (1982; trans. *The Laughing Cry,* 1987), a comic dystopian satire of conditions in a fictional postcolonial African dictatorship.

Cheikh Hamidou Kane's *L'aventure ambiguë* (1961; trans. *Ambiguous Adventure,* 1963) set the stage for another important trend, the Francophone philosophical novel. Largely a meditation on the spiritual impoverishment of a European culture devoted to material wealth, the book tells the story of Sambo Diallo, a young man from Senegal who moves from an early devotion to Islam to education in French colonial schools in an attempt to discover the secrets of European power. He eventually moves to Paris to study philosophy, but he is disappointed to find that Europe's ultimate secrets remain hidden. Meanwhile, he finds himself in an ambiguous cultural position, trapped between the spiritual values of his early upbringing and the material values of capitalist Europe, but now unable to participate fully in either culture.

Perhaps the most important African philosophical novelist is V. Y. Mudimbe, himself a scholar and philosopher of considerable prominence in African letters. In works such as *Entre les* (1973; trans. *Between Tides*, 1991), *Le bel immonde* (1976; trans. *Before the Birth of the Moon*, 1989), and *L'écart* (1979; trans. *The Rift*, 1993), Mudimbe effects a sophisticated dialogue between African and European intellectual traditions to explore their impact on the consciousnesses of individual Africans trapped in the confluence of these traditions. Mudimbe's works have, in fact, been criticized as too sophisticated for the average African (or European) reader, both in terms of their philosophical content and in terms of their sometimes difficult, multilingual style.

One of the most important—and controversial—early Francophone novels was Yambo Ouologuem's *Le devoir de violence* (1968; trans. *Bound to Violence*, 1971). Indeed, while reviewer Matthieu Galey's characterization of Ouologuem's book as "the first African novel worthy of the name" is surely an exaggeration, it is certainly the case that *Le devoir de violence*, awarded the prestigious Prix Renaudot in 1968, became one of the first African novels to receive substantive critical acceptance in the West (Galey 1968, 219). Employing a narrative voice reminiscent of the traditional African griot (combined with a liberal dash of modern irony), the book tells the story of the fictional Nakem Empire from its early conquest by Arab invaders, through the later years of French colonial rule, into the postcolonial era of the nation of Nakem-Ziuko. This scope allows Ouologuem to remind readers that the era of French colonialism was preceded by an earlier era of Arab conquest and domination. Moreover, Ouologuem suggests the Saïf dynasty (which rules this empire through murder and terror from the early thirteenth century onward) remains firmly in control of Nakem even during the French colonial period. The Saïfs and the local "notables" who support them manipulate the naive French colonizers to their own advantage and even assassinate any French officials who fail to play along. Meanwhile, the common people of Nakem consist primarily of an abject underclass of *négraille*, or "nigger-trash," that suffers the same kinds of oppression regardless of the nominal identities of their rulers.

Ouologuem's text was extremely important for its inventive adaptation of the French language and for its sweeping historical scope. On the other hand, the book soon became an object of considerable controversy. For one thing, its subject matter is informed principally by abject violence and transgressive sexuality. It thus threatens to confirm and reinforce negative Western stereotypes—especially because Ouologuem attributes most of the violence and abjection to indigenous cultural forces rather than to the impact of colonialism. In addition, Ouologuem's textual appropriation of works by European writers like André Schwarz-Bart, Graham Greene, and Guy de Maupassant seemed to many critics an outright case of plagiarism. Greene went so far as to file suit for plagiarism, and the English translation of Ouologuem's book was reissued in a "corrected" edition with certain passages corresponding too closely to passages in Greene's *It's a Battlefield* (1934) expurgated.[7] The French original was essentially suppressed and is now out of print. It is, however, the close similarity between *Le devoir de violence* and Schwarz-Bart's *Le dernier des justes* (1959) that has triggered the most controversy.[8] On the other hand, Ouologuem has had numerous defenders as well, with critics like Christopher Miller identifying the cut-and-paste construction of *Le devoir de violence* as an effective literary strategy that challenges the dominant position of Western discourse.[9] In addition, Miller has argued that Ouologuem's book represents an effective response to the stereotyping so prevalent in Western discourse on Africa, despite coming perilously close to simply repeating those stereotypes (Miller 1985, 216–45).

Also marked by a particularly inventive use the French language is Ahmadou Kourouma's *Les soleils des indépendances* (1968; trans. *The Suns of Independence*, 1981), which adapts French to the rhythms and syntax of Malinke to produce a distinctively African style of French prose. Indeed, this kind of adaptation of the French language is a central element in the Francophone African literature, with writers such as Lopes, Labou Tansi, and Tierno Monénembo also exploring distinctively African modes of literary expression in French. Kourouma's book also joins *Le devoir de violence* in its focus on political subjects that go beyond the confrontation of the colonizer and the colonized, though it could be argued that *Les soleils des indépendances* offers a more positive exploration of African cultural identities. Meanwhile, Kourouma's later *Monnè, outrages et défis* (1990; trans. *Monnew*, 1993) resembles *Le devoir de violence* in its engagement with West African history, though

---

[7] On the other hand, see Wolitz (1973) for a close comparison of the texts of Ouologuem and Greene which concludes that Ouologuem's is actually more inventive.

[8] The opening lines of both books are almost identical, and they bear considerable structural similarities. Eric Sellin has been particularly vocal in his criticism of Ouologuem's "plagiarism," identifying *Le dernier des justes* as the "blueprint" for *Bound to Violence*. For a summary of the plagiarism controversy and Sellin's role in it, see Sellin (1976).

[9] Moreover, numerous twentieth-century Western authors have employed similar methods of composition, ranging from the collage-like constructions of modernist writers such as James Joyce and T. S. Eliot, to the large-scale textual borrowing (which has also sometimes led to charges of plagiarism) by writers such as D. M. Thomas in *The White Hotel* or Danilo Kiš in *A Tomb for Boris Davidovich*. The *White Hotel* controversy triggered a *Times Literary Supplement* symposium on plagiarism published on April 3, 1982. On the controversy over Kiš's text, see Juraga and Booker (1993).

Monnè limits itself to the French colonial period, from the initial French conquest in the late nineteenth century to the eve of independence in the late 1950s. In *Monnè* Kourouma modifies French less radically than in *Les soleils des indépendances*, but he nevertheless employs the language in distinctive ways that allow him to supplement his exploration of the relationship between colonizer and colonized with a dialogue between European and African linguistic and narrative traditions. Kourouma thus produces not only an intense meditation on African history, but also an exploration of "the literate form of the novel as both the medium of an engagement with history and as a creative transformation of orality within writing in its formal realization" (Irele 1993, 167).

Beginning with the Senegalese Nafissatou Diallo's *De Tilène au plateau: Une enfance dakaroise* (1975; trans. *A Dakar Childhood*, 1982), works by women have been extremely important in the development of the African Francophone novel. In addition to Diallo, prominent Francophone women writers of fiction include Ken Bugul of Senegal and Werewere Liking of Cameroon. Liking exemplifies a movement from the mid-1970s onward to sophisticated feminist explorations of topics such as the social construction of gender. In works such as *Elle sera de jaspe et de corail* (1983), Liking combines comic satire and song-like language to produce innovative cross-generic works that demonstrate the broad flexibility of the novelistic tradition. More conventionally realistic, but particularly important, is the work of the Senegalese Aminata Sow Fall, whose intensely engaged political novels combine a feminine perspective with a class-based call for the liberation of Africa's poor and oppressed from economic and political tyranny. Sow Fall's work is relatively little known in the United States, where the Cold War encouraged a political climate inhospitable to leftist writers. Indeed, at this writing only one of her novels has been translated into English. Nevertheless, she has been extremely influential in Africa. Sow Fall's first novel, *Le revenant* (1976) details the experiences of a young man who has just been released from prison, only to find that social conditions in postcolonial African constitute a larger kind of prison. Sow Fall's best-known novel (and the only one in English translation) is *La grève des bàttu* (first published in 1979; trans. *The Beggars' Strike*, 1981). Like much Western proletarian literature, it focuses on the motif of a strike to comment upon social inequities and the exploitation of workers by unscrupulous bosses. In *L'appel des arène* (1984), *Ex-père de la nation* (1987), and *Le jujubier du patriarche* (1993) Sow Fall continues this mode of intense political commitment and detailed, realistic representation of the social conditions that inform the lives of Africa's poor and downtrodden.

Perhaps the best known Francophone African novel by a woman (especially among readers of English translations) is Mariama Bâ's *Une si longue lettre* (1980; trans. *So Long a Letter*, 1981), a brief epistolary novel that explores the special problems that women face in the social and political context of postcolonial Africa. The novel particularly focuses on the practice of polygamy and the difficulties faced by its protagonist, Ramatoulaye, after her husband decides to take a second wife. Polygamy joins interracial marriage to provide the central issues in *Un chant écarlate* (1984; trans. *Scarlet Song*, 1985), which was published shortly after Bâ's untimely death.

Finally, no survey of the Francophone African novel, however brief and incomplete, can fail to mention the towering contribution of the Senegalese Ousmane Sembène, almost certainly the single most important novelist in the African Francophone tradition. Sembène's long and productive career began during the colonial 1950s, when he was an important contributor to the early development of the African Francophone novel. Stylistically, Sembène's fiction derives directly from the Western tradition of realism, and it is particularly related to the politically committed motif of socialist realism that was dominant in the Soviet Union through much of the twentieth century. Nevertheless, Sembène has declared a close relationship between his work and traditional African oral narratives, linking the role of the modern writer to that of the traditional griot in a preface to his novel *Referendum* (1965a).

Sembène's working-class background clearly informs all of his novels. He began writing not after a university education, but after a stint as a dock worker in Marseilles in the 1950s, beginning with the 1956 *Le docker noir* (trans. *The Black Docker*, 1987), which details the travails of a young Senegalese man working on the docks in Marseilles while struggling to become a writer. Sembène's second novel, *O pays, mon beau peuple!* (1957) moves from France to a small fishing village in Senegal and treats the theme of prejudice by juxtaposing white racism against blacks with black prejudice against a European woman who marries an African man. Sembène moved to the front rank of Francophone novelists with the publication in 1960 of *Les bouts de bois de Dieu* (trans. *God's Bits of Wood*, 1962), still regarded as one of the masterworks of African literature. The book dramatizes a 1947–1948 strike against the Dakar-Niger railway, paying particular attention to the crucial role played by African women in support of the striking men. While the strikers are black and their bosses are white, Sembène makes clear his socialist orientation by presenting the strike in terms of class struggle rather than racial oppositions. The 1965a *Referendum* evokes the spirit of independence that was blowing, irresistible as the Harmattan wind, across colonial Africa in the late 1950s. Like Fanon, however, the book suggests that independence alone cannot bring genuine freedom, which can only be achieved through socialism.

Many of Sembène's early short stories were published in the volume *Voltaïque* in 1962 (trans. *Tribal Scars and Other Stories*, 1975), while two brief novels, *Vehi-Ciosane* and *Le mandat* were published together (1965b; trans. *The*

Money Order, with White Genesis, 1972). These novellas explore the break-down in Senegalese society under the impact of colonialism, but they are careful to suggest that the alternative to the bourgeoisification of Africa is not a return to the traditional past but a forward movement to a socialist fu-ture. In 1973, Sembène turned his attention from the colonialism to neoco-lonialism with the short novel *Xala* (trans. *Xala* 1976). Employing a mode of comic satire, Sembène explores the ongoing neocolonial exploitation of Senegal by depicting a member of the rich, decadent indigenous bourgeoi-sie who continues to do the bidding of his French masters in order to main-tain his wealth and status. However, vestigial remnants of precolonial social practices (such as polygamy) are satirized as well, and Sembène again makes clear his belief that liberation in Africa must be achieved through socialism rather than through a return to precolonial tradition. Sembène's latest full-length novel, *Le dernier de l'empire* (1981; trans. *The Last of the Empire*, 1983), is a dystopian satire that focuses on a fictional political confrontation be-tween a party of neocolonialists and a party of staunch nationalists to sug-gest that neither of these attitudes can bring liberty and justice to Senegal. Also published in the 1980s were the novellas *Niiwam* and *Taaw* (published together in 1987; trans. *Niiwam and Taaw*, 1991).

Sembène's later fiction is characterized by a particularly cinematic use of visual imagery, cutting from one scene to another—which is not surprising because by this time he had also become one of Africa's premier filmmakers. Sembène's work is marked by a strong socialist political perspective and a spe-cial concern for the plight of women in African society. His work has pro-vided a major source of inspiration for an entire generation of African writers, Francophone and otherwise. Contrary to the linguistic experimen-tation that distinguishes so many African Francophone novels, Sembène em-ploys a relatively straightforward prose style that attempts to make his work accessible to a wider African audience. However, aware that most inhabitants of the former French Africa are not able to read French, Sembène has devot-ed much of his career to the production of films, frequently based on his own fiction. Importantly, his later films have been produced mostly in the Wolof language, which is widely spoken in Senegal. Sembène has had such success as a filmmaker that he is widely considered the father of African cinema.

Other Traditions, Other Voices

Africa is a large and culturally diverse continent, and English and French are not the only former colonial languages that continue to have a major pres-ence in Africa. There is, for example, an important Lusophone African liter-ature, that is, African literature in the Portuguese language. There is also a substantial literature in African languages, especially Swahili. Finally, it is necessary to remember when employing sweeping designations like "African literature" that in most of northern Africa Islam has long been a far more powerful cultural force than either indigenous African traditions or traditions inherited from European colonialism. This area has a rich literature as well, most of it written in Arabic. And, despite the cultural differences between this area and most of sub-Saharan Africa, it is nevertheless worth remembering that Algerians and Moroccans and Egyptians are Africans too.

Portuguese-language literature has received considerably less attention than African literature written in English and French, no doubt partially because far fewer people can read Portuguese and because Portuguese literature generally is far less known than French or British literature. There are also practical reasons: few Lusophone African novels have been published in French or English translation. However, Lusophone African literature has a long tradition. Gerald Moser (1967) notes that this literature began as early as the middle of the nineteenth century and argues that it can thus be considered the first African literature. Portuguese remains the official language of the nations of Angola and Mozambique, both of which have produced important contributions to African fiction. In 1969 Luís Bernardo Honwana's short-story collection *We Killed Mangy-Dog* (originally *Nós matamos o Cão-Tinhoso*, 1964) was the first Lusophone African fiction to be published in English translation in the Heinemann African Writers Series. Honwana, who combines a Portuguese linguistic matrix with the rhythms of the Ronga language, remains the most influential fiction writer from Mozambique. Angola has also produced numerous important works of fiction, many of which grow out the tumultuous climate of political instability and civil war that reigned there in most of the 1960s, 1970s, and 1980s. Of particular note are the works of José Luandino Vieira, a linguistically innovative writer of short political fables; Uanhenga Xitu, who combines the Portuguese and Kimbundu languages in works such as the novel *Manana* (1978, first published 1974); Manuel Rui, who focuses on urban Luanda in the story collection *Sim camarada!* (1977; trans. *Yes, Comrade!* 1993); and Pepetela, whose work includes the important 1980 leftist political novel *Mayombe*.

In addition to early figures such as Mofolo and Fagunwa and more recent figures such as Ngugi, numerous writers have produced important works of African fiction in African languages. For example, Henry Masila Ndawo published a novel in Xhosa (*uHambo lukaGqoboka*) as early as 1909. Another important early Xhosa novel was A. C. Jordan's *Ingqumbo yeminyanya*, (1940) published in 1940. Perhaps the most important African-language literature has been produced in Swahili: written manuscripts date back to at least the seventeenth century. The novelist, poet, and essayist Shaaban Robert did much to promote the status of Swahili as a literary language in the 1940s and 1950s, and the Swahili literary tradition remains particularly strong today in Tanzania. Government support for literature in Swahili has helped writers such as Euphrase Kezilahabi to produce important novels, many of which unfortunately are yet to be translated into English, partially because of their leftist political perspective. The thriving Tanzanian Swahili tradition, combined with the recent endorsement of Swahili as a pan-African literary language by important writers such as Wole Soyinka and Ayi Kwei Armah, suggests a bright future for literature in Swahili—and in other African languages as well.[10]

Much of northern Africa, especially the northwestern region known collectively as the Maghreb, was formerly under French colonial domination, and it is important to remember that Francophone African literature also includes the contributions of writers from this region. For example, Jean Déjeux (1992) points out that the first novel in French by an Algerian was published in 1920 and that more than four hundred novels and short story collections by writers from the Maghreb were published from 1945 to 1989. Writers such as Mohammed Dib, Kateb Yacine, Rachid Boudjedra, Tahar Ben Jelloun, and Driss Chraïbi have produced novels that have made important contributions to ongoing attempts to create a viable North African cultural identity that combines a basic Islamic orientation with lessons learned from the European colonial experience. Ben Jelloun's novel *La nuit sacrée* (1987; trans. *The Sacred Night*, 1989) was awarded the 1987 Prix Goncourt. Probably the most important North African literature, however, has been written in Arabic, and the trend in recent years has been toward a progressively greater emphasis on writing in Arabic. Indeed, though writings in Arabic have been widely produced in the Maghreb for more than a thousand years, there has been a particularly rich growth in Arabic literature in the decades following independence. For example, Abdelhamid Benhedouga's *Rih al-janub*, published in 1971 can be considered the first Algerian novel in Arabic (Bois 1992, 105). Other important participants in the burgeoning phenomenon of Maghrebian Arabic novels include Tahar Ouettar, Ismaïl Ghamouqat, Merzak Bagtache, and Ezeddine Madani, and the Francophone novelist Boudjedra has now written several novels in Arabic.[11]

Finally, important fiction has also been produced by writers from northeast Africa. A notable recent example is Hama Tuma's English-language story collection *The Case of the Socialist Witchdoctor and Other Stories* (1993), a searing satirical indictment of conditions in Ethiopia under the Soviet-backed Mengistu regime of the late 1970s and 1980s that serves as a com-

---

[10] For a useful survey of Swahili literature published between 1975 and 1984, see Bertoncini (1987). For more details on literature in African languages, see Gérard (1971, 1981) and Cancel (1993).

[11] For a number of excellent recent discussions of North African literature, especially from the Maghreb, see the recent special issue of *Research in African Literatures*, edited by Patricia Geesey (1992).

panion piece to Farah's *African Dictatorship* trilogy. But most of the important northeast African fiction is written in Arabic. Particularly well known, at least in the West, is the work of the Sudanese novelist Tayeb Salih, especially *Mawsim al-hijrah il'a al-shamal* (1966; trans. *Season of Migration to the North*, 1969). There is an especially rich tradition of Arabic literature in Egypt, which was the center of attempts to create a modern Arabic literature during the nineteenth-century Arabic Literary Renaissance. Particularly important in recent years are women writers such as Alifa Rifaat and Nawal el-Saadawi, who have produced feminist explorations of Islamic culture and society. On an international scale, however, undoubtedly the most prominent Arabic-language novelist is the Egyptian Naguib Mahfouz, winner of the 1988 Nobel Prize for literature. The only Arabic writer to be so honored, Mahfouz is the author of a large and impressive body of work, including some forty novels and story collections, many of which are now available in English translation. He is also the author of several stage plays and more than thirty screenplays. His novels include both historical fictions about the Egyptian past and social novels about colonial and contemporary Egypt. Mahfouz's work, marked by influences from a number of European writers, is written largely in a realistic mode, though many of his later novels are more experimental in form and technique. He is best known for the *Cairo Trilogy*, consisting of *Bayn al-qasrayn* (1956; trans. *Palace Walk*, 1990), *Qasr al-shawq* (first published in 1957; trans. *Palace of Desire*, 1991), and *Al-sukkariyah* (1958; trans. *Sugar Street*, 1992). In these novels Mahfouz traces three generations of a Cairo family from World War I until the days following the overthrow of King Farouk I in 1952. In so doing he presents a panoramic view of Egyptian culture and society during these four crucial decades of rapid and profound historical transformation.

Chapter 3

Chinua Achebe:
Things Fall Apart

Things Fall Apart (1994b) is almost certainly the African novel that is most often read by Westerners and most often taught in British and American classrooms. Not only is it a staple of college courses in African literature, but it is also widely taught in courses in world literature. It is also frequently taught in courses on African culture, society, and history as an introduction to the workings of a precolonial African community. As a result, Achebe's book is frequently the first African novel encountered by its Western readers, and rightfully so. Not only is it one of the earliest African novels (it was first published in 1958), but it also exemplifies many of the fundamental issues that face Western readers of African novels. For most readers, the most memorable part of the book is its vivid evocation of Igbo society in the early twentieth century, at the time of the first major incursions of British colonialism. Achebe has made it clear that his principal purpose in the book was to give African readers a realistic depiction of their precolonial past, free of the distortions and stereotypes imposed in European accounts. The Africans of Achebe's book live not in primitive savagery, but in a sophisticated society

> in which life is rounded and intricate and sensitively in correspondence with a range of human impulses. It admits both the aristocratic and the democratic principles. It is a life lived by a dignified clan of equals who meet together in an Athenian way (Walsh 1970, 49).

Achebe's reminders that precolonial African societies functioned in such sophisticated ways are, of course, valuable to both African and Western readers. On the other hand, the detailed depiction of the workings of Igbo society in *Things Fall Apart* makes the book particularly vulnerable to the kind of anthropological readings that have sometimes prevented African novels from receiving serious critical attention as literature rather than simply as documentation of cultural practices. Ato Quayson (1994) argues that much of the published criticism on the book is typical of criticism of African literature as a whole: it treats the text as a transparent and direct representation of reality without paying sufficient attention to the book's aesthetic dimensions, especially those related to African oral traditions.

However, *Things Fall Apart* is such an intricately crafted work of fiction that many critics have acknowledged its aesthetic merits, while noting the importance of its reminders that precolonial African societies were complex and sophisticated structures bearing little relationship to European myths of African savagery and primitivism. Thus, even the "anthropological" material in the book has a strong aesthetic dimension. As Obiechina points out, "the integrative technique in which background and atmosphere are interlaced with the action of the narrative must be regarded as Achebe's greatest achievement" in works such as *Things Fall Apart* and *Arrow of God* (Obiechina 1975, 142).

Noting the critical acclaim for Achebe's depiction of traditional Igbo society, Solomon Iyasere argues that it fails to do justice to the novel's complexity. "On closer examination, we see that it is provocatively complex, interweaving significant themes: love, compassion, colonialism, achievement, honor, and individualism" (Iyasere 1978, 93). Donald Weinstock and Cathy Ramadan, noting this same structural complexity, argue that Achebe blends realistic and symbolic modes of writing in a manner akin to that employed by novelists such as Joseph Conrad, James Joyce, and D. H. Lawrence (Weinstock and Ramadan 1978, 126–27). Indeed, the formal strategies employed by *Things Fall Apart* are so complex and sophisticated that they do recall the works of Western modernism. As a result, however, Western critics are in danger of falling into old habits of formalist reading and thereby of failing to do justice to the important social and political content of Achebe's book.[1] By circumscribing Achebe's book within European aesthetic traditions, such readings are in danger of perpetuating precisely the colonialist gestures that the book is designed to surmount. *Things Fall Apart* thus illustrates particularly well Achebe's warning that the Western critic of African literature "must cultivate the habit of humility appropriate to his limited experience of the African world and be purged of the superiority and arrogance which history so insidiously makes him heir to" (Achebe 1975, 8).

Readers and critics of Achebe's novel must pay close and careful attention not only to the style and the content of the book, but also to the intricate relationships between them. The content of the first part of the book is striking for its depiction of traditional Igbo society; the style and structure of the entire book are striking for the way in which they incorporate ele-

---

[1] See Irele for a discussion of the inadequacy of Western formalist criticism for the African novel (Irele 1990, xiii).

ments of Igbo oral traditions. Many critics have remarked on the sophistication with which Achebe wove traditional oral forms into his written text. According to Obiechina (1993), for example, the way embedded forms—such as proverbs and folk tales—contribute directly to the impact of Achebe's main narrative is similar to the way they are used in African oral epics. Indeed, Iyasere (1978) notes that much of the complexity of Achebe's narrative technique arises from his effective use of strategies derived from Igbo oral culture. Similarly, JanMohamed, while emphasizing the fundamental differences between oral and written—or chirographic—cultures, concludes that *Things Fall Apart* manages to achieve an impressive combination of the two modes and to remain "delicately poised at the transition from the epic (oral) to the novel (chirographic)" (JanMohamed 1984, 34).

The very existence of Achebe's text as a written, bound book places it in dialogue with the Western novelistic tradition, even as it draws heavily upon Igbo oral traditions for its style and content. Moreover, it is important to note that Achebe wrote the book in direct reaction to the demeaning and objectionable depictions of Africans in novels such as Joseph Conrad's *Heart of Darkness* and Joyce Cary's *Mister Johnson*. Innes discusses the way in which Achebe not only responds to Cary's stereotypical vision of Africans, but also shows that Cary's "African" figure Mr. Johnson is a purely European creation many of whose characteristics (such as his individual isolation and lack of contact with family or relatives) are almost unimaginable from an African point of view (Innes 1990, 21–41). In keeping with its integration of style with content, of atmosphere with narrative, and of written with oral forms, *Things Fall Apart* is itself a complex cultural hybrid that is a product not only of the Igbo cultural traditions it so vividly portrays, but also of the encounter between those traditions and the culture of the West.

On the other hand, Achebe's book is a striking demonstration of Fanon's observation that "the colonial world is a Manichean world" (Fanon 1968, 41). In the book, European and African societies come together in a mode of radical difference. The resulting encounter between the two cultures (in an atmosphere of mutual misunderstanding) leads to cataclysmic results for the African society, which is no match for the Europeans in terms of military and economic power. Of course, depictions of Africans and African society as strange and incomprehensible to Westerners can be found in many examples of Africanist discourse, including literary works like *Heart of Darkness*. One of the most valuable aspects of *Things Fall Apart*, for Western readers at least, is its presentation of the estrangement between European and African cultural traditions from an African perspective: it reminds us that there are two sides to this story of encounter between alien cultures. Achebe presents Igbo society in a way that makes its workings perfectly comprehensible, carefully weaving Igbo customs and Igbo words into his narrative in a way that makes them accessible to Western readers. Meanwhile, the Europeans of Achebe's book are depicted as peculiar, incomprehensible, and even vaguely ridiculous—as when a white missionary has his translator speak to the people of Mbanta in Igbo, not realizing that the translator speaks a different dialect from the audience. The translator's words seem strange (and sometimes comical): he continually says "my buttocks" whenever he means to say "myself" (p. 144).[2] Such reversals from the norm of British literature (in which Africans or Indians struggle, often comically, with the English language or English customs) make a powerful statement about the importance of point of view in confrontations between foreign cultures and thoroughly undermine the Western tendency to think of our values as absolute and universal.

On the other hand, *Things Fall Apart* establishes numerous points of contact between European and African cultures, and Achebe is careful to avoid depicting African society as totally foreign to Western sensibilities. For example, many critics have observed the parallels between Achebe's precolonial Umuofia and ancient Greece. Achebe himself has acknowledged these parallels in an interview with Charles Rowell, arguing (in a mode reminiscent of the work of Martin Bernal (1987) and Cheikh Anta Diop (1974)) that the similarities may arise because Greek culture was itself heavily influenced by African culture (Achebe 1990). *Things Fall Apart* as a whole has often been compared to Greek tragedy.[3] Michael Valdez Moses notes the "strikingly Homeric quality" of the book and compares its protagonist Okonkwo to Homer's Achilles (Moses 1995, 110). Okonkwo also resembles Oedipus: he is banished from Umuofia for the accidental killing of a fellow clansman, thus recalling Oedipus's punishment for the inadvertent murder of his father. In this vein, Rhonda Cobham argues that Achebe has chosen to present "those aspects of Igbo traditional society that best coincide with Western-Christian social values," thereby establishing a worldview that is not limited to the precolonial past but can speak to the postcolonial present as well (Cobham 1991, 98). As Achebe himself has put it, a point that is "fundamental and essential to the appreciation of African issues by Americans" is that "Africans are people in the same way that Americans, Europeans, Asians, and others are people" (Achebe 1991, 21).

Achebe does an excellent job of presenting characters whose humanity Western readers can recognize. However, as Florence Stratton points out, the

---

[2] A similar motif occurs in Ferdinand Oyono's *Houseboy* (1990), in which the missionary Father Vandermayer attempts to deliver his sermons in the Ndjem language, but with such poor pronunciation that virtually all of his words "had obscene meanings," resulting in sermons "full of obscenities" (pp. 9, 35).

[3] For a good introduction to the tragic aspects of Achebe's work, see Irele (1978). On more specific parallels between *Things Fall Apart* and the Greek concept of tragic drama, see Killam (1977, 13–34) and Landrum (1970).

complex characters of the book tend to be male, while the female characters are depicted in vague and superficial ways (Stratton 1994, 29). Okonkwo's wives have virtually no identities outside their domestic roles. His daughter Ezinma is the strongest female character, yet her strength is repeatedly attributed to her more masculine characteristics. Moreover, she essentially disappears late in the narrative, determined to pursue a conventional role as wife and mother. The patriarch Okonkwo dominates the text. If *Things Fall Apart* is first a story of the disintegration of a traditional African society, it is also the personal tragedy of a single individual, whose life falls apart in the midst of that same process. Indeed, Okonkwo unites these communal and individual elements. Obiechina, for example, emphasizes Achebe's achievement in presenting Okonkwo both as embodiment of certain traditional Igbo cultural values and as a distinct "individual with obvious personal weaknesses" (Obiechina 1975, 204).

A careful consideration of Achebe's presentation of Okonkwo as both an individual and as an allegorical representative of his entire society provides a fruitful framework within which to read Achebe's novel. For example, the initial section of the book is devoted principally to a description of everyday life at the end of the nineteenth century in Umuofia, a group of nine villages in the Igbo area of what is now southeastern Nigeria. This section also introduces the protagonist Okonkwo, one of the leaders of the village of Iguedo in Umuofia. We learn a great deal about Okonkwo's background, including his struggle to overcome what he regards as the legacy of weakness and lack of achievement left him by his father Unoka. This section describes the hard work and dedication that have made it possible for Okonkwo to rise from humble beginnings to a position of prominence in his village. We also learn of Okonkwo's physical prowess and of the way he became famous as the greatest wrestler in Umuofia by defeating the champion Amalinze the Cat in what has become a near-legendary match. This section also provides details about Okonkwo's family life. We learn, for example, that he has three wives and eight children. We also learn something of the texture of the everyday life in Okonkwo's household, which consists of a compound that includes Okonkwo's private hut and separate huts for each wife and her children.

Okonkwo rules this household "with a heavy hand," and the first part of *Things Fall Apart* presents not only extensive descriptions of his sometimes harsh treatment of his wives and children, but also detailed background on the causes behind his rather authoritarian personality (p. 13). Okonkwo's major motivation (and the principal reason for his domineering behavior) is his determination to succeed where his musician father (whom he regards as cowardly and effeminate) failed. Okonkwo thus goes out of his way to behave in what he considers to be a staunchly masculine manner and to demonstrate his strength in every way possible. This strength, however, arises from a kind of weakness. "His whole life," the narrator tells us, "was dominated by fear, the fear of failure and weakness. . . . It was the fear of himself, lest he should be found to resemble his father" (p. 13).

Achebe, a master storyteller, dramatizes this aspect of Okonkwo's personality in a number of ways, especially in the story of Ikemefuna, a boy from the neighboring village of Mbaino. Ikemefuna and a young girl are sent to Umuofia to compensate for the killing of an Umuofian woman in Mbaino. The girl is given as a replacement wife to the dead woman's husband, while Ikemefuna goes to live in the household of Okonkwo until the boy's final fate can be determined. Ikemefuna lives with Okonkwo for three years and becomes like a member of the family, growing especially close to Okonkwo's eldest son, Nwoye. Then, however, the Oracle of the Hills and Caves decrees that Ikemefuna must be killed as a sacrifice. Okonkwo, as a leader of Umuofia, knows that he must abide by this decision. However, he does more than simply accept the fact that Ikemefuna must die. Although warned by the elder Ogbuefi Ezeudu not to participate in the killing, Okonkwo himself strikes the fatal blow, cutting the boy down with his machete because "he was afraid of being thought weak" (p. 61). Okonkwo, in seeking to meet his society's standards of admirable conduct, performs a deed that is considered reprehensible by many in that society, including his good friend Obierika, who is horrified by Okonkwo's participation in Ikemefuna's killing, even though he himself regards that killing to be justified. "If the Oracle said that my son should be killed," Obierika tells Okonkwo, "I would neither dispute it nor be the one to do it" (p. 67).

The episode of the killing of Ikemefuna is pivotal for a number of reasons. This sacrifice dramatizes aspects of Igbo society that seem harsh, cruel, or even savage by modern Western standards and thus illustrates Achebe's determination to provide a realistic description of traditional Igbo society and his refusal to romanticize that society to impress a Western audience. As Oladele Taiwo puts it, "Besides the strengths in tribal society he gives the weaknesses. We therefore have a true and complete picture in which the whole background is fully realised" (Taiwo 1976, 112). It is important to recognize, though, that the killing of Ikemefuna, however startling by Western standards, does not necessarily demonstrate a weakness in Igbo society. This act has a genuine justification from the Igbo point of view. Moses thus notes that the ritual killing of Ikemefuna (who had nothing to do with the original crime) "is cruel and violates liberal norms of justice," but the sacrifice "does serve to prevent a war between the two clans and therefore helps to ensure the long-term security of both villages." This action, for Moses, "suggests not the absence of ethical standards among the Igbo people, but the existence of a strict premodern morality that values the welfare of the clan and tribe above that of the individual" (Moses 1995, 115). In this way, the episode serves not only to provide a striking illustration of Okonkwo's personality, but also to make an important point about the differences between Igbo social values (which place the good of the community above that of any single person) and Western liberal standards of individualism.

One of the most important aspects of *Things Fall Apart* is its delineation of a society that operates on principles quite different from the individualistic notions that shape most Western ideas of social justice. The book thus asks us to challenge our assumption that individualism is an absolute and universal good. Achebe achieves this goal in a number of ways. Much of the description of Igbo society focuses on presenting the crucial role played by communal activities such as the Week of Peace and the Feast of the New Yam. And many of the book's more dramatic scenes (such as the killing of Ikemefuna or Okonkwo's exile from Umuofia after he accidentally kills Ezeudu's son during Ezeudu's funeral) are built around confrontations between the good of the community and what Westerners would regard as the "rights" of individuals. But this aspect of Achebe's book is built into the text in more profound ways as well. For example, Innes notes that the narrative voice of the text is itself a sort of amalgam of traditional Igbo voices, in contrast to modern Western expectations that the narrator of a story will be a distinct individual (Innes 1990, 32).

By problematizing Okonkwo's relationship to the values of his society, the killing of Ikemefuna calls attention to the book's central focus on the relationship between the individual and the community in Igbo society. It is clear that Okonkwo can, to a certain extent, function as an allegorical stand-in for traditional Igbo society as a whole.[4] Walsh sees Okonkwo's downfall as a marker of the destruction of traditional Igbo society "because of the way in which the fundamental predicament of the society is lived through his life" (Walsh 1970, 52). JanMohamed, influenced by Jameson's work, follows Walsh in suggesting that Achebe makes "his heroes the embodiments of the fundamental structures and values of their cultures" (JanMohamed 1983, 161). On the other hand, the relationship between Okonkwo and his society is complex and problematic. It comes as no surprise, then, that the implications of the relationship between Okonkwo and his society have been the object of considerable critical disagreement. Eustace Palmer, for example, agrees that Okonkwo is "the personification of his society's values." Thus, "if he is plagued by a fear of failure and of weakness it is because his society puts such a premium on success" (Palmer 1972, 53). For Palmer, then,

---

[4] One might compare here Fredric Jameson's controversial suggestion that the protagonists of postcolonial literature can generally be viewed as "national allegories" whose personal experiences parallel the histories of the development of their nations (Jameson 1986). See Ahmad for a detailed critique of Jameson's argument (Ahmad 1992, 95–122).

Okonkwo's ultimate tragedy results from weaknesses that are the direct result of flaws in Igbo society. For other critics, Okonkwo's fall results not from the characteristics of Igbo society, but from the destruction of this society by British colonialism. Killam thus agrees that Okonkwo consolidates "the values most admired by Ibo peoples," but concludes that his fall occurs because colonialism disrupts these values and not from shortcomings in the values themselves (Killam 1977, 16).

Killam's reading is clearly more consonant with the overall theme of *Things Fall Apart* than is Palmer's. For one thing, Palmer (though himself an African) obviously reads the text from a purely Western, individualistic perspective. From this point of view, which privileges strong individuals who are willing to oppose conventional opinion, it is clearly a flaw for an individual to embody the mainstream values of his culture. On the other hand, Killam's reading is undermined by the fact that Okonkwo already seems headed for trouble even before Umuofia is aware of the British presence, perhaps because, in his quest for personal success, he is already more individualistic than most of his fellow villagers. Several times Okonkwo breaks fundamental rules of his society and then must be punished, culminating in his banishment from Umuofia at the end of the first part of the book.[5] Many critics argue that Okonkwo's fall occurs not because he embodies the values of his society, but precisely because he deviates from his society's norms of conduct. Biodun Jeyifo, for example, argues that Okonkwo is "doomed because of his rigid, superficial understanding—really misrecognition—of his culture" (Jeyifo 1991, 58). Similarly, Carroll believes that Okonkwo's successes are largely achieved through an inflexible focus on his goals, a focus that eventually sets him at odds with a society "remarkable for its flexibility" (Carroll 1990, 41). Finally, critics such as Ravenscroft and Ojinmah note that the Igbo society depicted by Achebe is characterized by a careful balancing of opposing values (particularly of masculine and feminine principles), while Okonkwo focuses strictly on the masculine side of his personality and thus fails to achieve this balance (Ravenscroft 1969, 13; Ojinmah 1991, 15–16).

Such gendered readings of Okonkwo's characteristics are central to many critical discussions of *Things Fall Apart.* Much of JanMohamed's discussion of Okonkwo's typicality focuses on the way Okonkwo "becomes an emblem of the masculine values of Igbo culture." But JanMohamed emphasizes that the culture itself balances masculine with feminine values. Okonkwo's rejection of the feminine aspects of his culture thus make him seem "rigid, harsh, and unfeeling in his pursuit of virility" (JanMohamed 1983, 164). Innes also emphasizes the balance between masculine and femi-

---

[5] For a succinct discussion of Okonkwo's offenses and subsequent punishments, see Obiechina 1975 (214–15).

nine values in Igbo culture, arguing that Okonkwo's tendency to categorize various activities as either masculine or feminine is typical of his society, but again pointing out that Okonkwo has less respect for feminine values than does his society as a whole (Innes 1990, 25–26). Several feminist critics, however, have pointed out that the society itself, at least as depicted by Achebe, is heavily oriented toward masculinity. While some value is placed on feminine virtues and activities, the values labeled by the society as masculine are consistently valued more highly than those labeled as feminine. In addition, the power structure of Igbo society, while decentered and in many ways democratic, is entirely dominated by males. Okonkwo's domination of his household thus becomes a microcosm of the domination of the society as a whole by patriarchal figures.

It is certainly the case that the leaders of Umuofia are all male. Moreover, these leaders are often shown exercising power directly over women. In one of the book's key demonstrations of the workings of justice in Umuofia, the village elders meet to adjudicate a marital dispute in which the woman Mgbafo has fled the household of her husband, Uzowulu, because he has repeatedly beaten her (sometimes severely) for nine years. The proceedings are restricted to males, and no women (including Mgbafo) are allowed inside the hut where they occur. Indeed, we are told that no woman has ever participated in such proceedings and that women know better than even to ask questions about them (p. 88). Uzowulu presents his case, asking that Mgbafo be ordered to return to him. Then, Mgbafo's brother argues that she should be allowed to remain with him and her other brothers apart from her abusive husband. The elders (some of whom seem to regard the case as too trivial to be worthy of their attention) order Uzowulu to offer a pot of wine to Mgbafo's brothers in restitution. They then order the brothers to return Mgbafo to her husband, refusing to cast blame on the abusive husband.

Stratton grants that Achebe's "masculinization" of Igbo society serves the positive function of countering the feminization of Africa so typical of narratives like those of Cary, Conrad, H. Rider Haggard, and other colonial writers. On the other hand, she also argues that Achebe may undermine colonialist racial stereotypes only at the expense of perpetuating gender stereotypes (Stratton 1994, 37). One could, of course, argue that Achebe is simply being realistic in his depiction of Igbo power relations, but Stratton is probably correct that he could have done more to question these relations in terms of gender.[6] After all, Achebe does an excellent job of deconstructing the hierarchical relationship between the races in colonial Africa, but Stratton is

---

[6] Achebe's presentation of traditional Igbo society as entirely male-centered may not be entirely realistic. See, for example, Ifi Amadiume (1987) for a discussion of the ways that society placed far more weight on feminine values than Achebe indicates.

probably justified in suggesting that, while Achebe effectively dismantles "ra-cial romances" such as Cary's *Mister Johnson*, he does little to prevent his book from becoming a sort of "gender romance" (Stratton 1994, 36). The decision in this marital dispute, for example, is not challenged in any way in the text and could even be taken as an example of the smooth, almost utopian, func-tioning of Umuofian society before the intrusion of colonialism. Indeed, Achebe's book sometimes suggests that one of the negative effects of colo-nialism was its disruption of the clear hierarchy of gender relations in Umuo-fia. For example, when the men of the village discuss the strange customs of some of their neighbors, Okonkwo mentions that some people are so pecu-liar that they consider children the property of their mothers rather than their fathers, as in any properly patriarchal society. His friend Machi responds that such a practice would be as inconceivable as a situation in which "the wom-an lies on top of the man when they are making the children." Obierika then links this reversal of gender roles to the arrival of Europeans. He suggests that such a sexual inversion would be "like the story of white men who, they say, are white like this piece of chalk" (p. 74).

It may also be significant in this regard that Okonkwo, when exiled from Umuofia in Part Two of *Things Fall Apart*, is sent to the home of his mother's family as punishment. And it is precisely in this locale, which for Okonkwo has clearly feminine resonances, that European culture makes its first signifi-cant intrusions into traditional Igbo life. The second part of the book also details the increasing inroads made by Christian missionaries, thus further increasing Okonkwo's sense of crisis about his own identity. Importantly, one of the converts won by the missionaries is Okonkwo's son Nwoye, whom Okonkwo comes to regard as degenerate and effeminate—that is, as a throw-back to his grandfather Unoka. Christianity is thus linked to femininity, again suggesting that the European impact on Igbo society included a disruption in the traditional gender hierarchy. Achebe suggests that it is typical of Igbo culture to view all aspects of life in terms of gendered categories. Recogniz-ing this tendency can help Western readers understand the significance of Okonkwo's exile, just as an appreciation of the communal nature of Igbo so-ciety can help us to see why Okonkwo's exile is so difficult for him. In Igbo society, individual identity is connected far more closely to participation in a community than it is in the West. Therefore, Okonkwo's separation from his community is far more difficult and traumatic for him than a similar separa-tion might be for a Western character.

This part of the book ends on a high note as Okonkwo prepares to re-turn to Umuofia and hosts a feast to thank his kinsmen for their kindness during his seven years of exile. This communal event presents traditional Igbo society at its best, but it is undermined by the reader's recognition that this way of life is already being eroded by the incursions of Christianity and

Western individualism. One of the elders of the clan ends the feast on a sad note, thanking Okonkwo for his hospitality, but gloomily acknowledging that the younger generations of Igbo are already losing their appreciation for the traditional bonds of kinship:

> You do not know what it is to speak with one voice. And what is the re-sult? An abominable religion has settled among you. A man can now leave his father and his brothers. He can curse the gods of his fathers and his ancestors, like a hunter's dog that suddenly goes mad and turns on his master. I fear for you; I fear for the clan (p. 167).

The obvious accuracy of this somber prediction adds a tragic irony to Okonkwo's attempts in Part Three of the book to rebuild his life in Umuo-fia and to regain his status as a leader of the community: the traditional life of the community is already doomed. In this part of the book, the Christian missionaries are joined by soldiers and bureaucrats as British colonial rule is established in Nigeria. This process culminates in Okonkwo's impulsive kill-ing of a messenger sent by the British to order the break-up of a meeting of Umuofia's leaders. The leaders are trying to decide upon a response to the recent detention and abuse of several elders of the community—including Okonkwo himself—by the British District Commissioner. The Commis-sioner then arrives with soldiers to arrest Okonkwo, only to find that Okonkwo (in radical violation of Igbo tradition) has hanged himself. Okonkwo, in this final example of the breakdown of Igbo communal life as a result of British colonialism, dies alone—and in a manner so repugnant to his fellow villagers that tradition does not allow them to bury him. That task must fall to the British. The Commissioner concludes that Okonkwo's story should make interesting reading, and might be worthy of a chapter, or at least a paragraph, in the book he himself is writing. Because this book, *The Pacification of the Primitive Tribes of the Lower Niger*, tells Okonkwo's story from the Commissioner's point of view, it serves as an emblem of the Africanist discourse Achebe seeks to overcome with *Things Fall Apart*, which tells Okonkwo's story in an African voice.

Achebe's novel stands as a direct refutation of Africanist discourse like the commissioner's *Pacification* report and makes it clear that colonialism brought not civilization but chaos and destruction. In its depictions of the British colonial administration and the missionary Smith (far more strident and uncompromising than his predecessor Brown) Achebe's book is sharply critical of the colonialism that shattered traditional Igbo life. Ernest Emenyonu calls attention to this aspect of Achebe's work when he argues that, "no matter how couched in proverbs, images and innuendoes, the in-tense virulence of Achebe's indictment of colonial diplomatic tactlessness and absurd human high-handedness cannot be lost on the perceptive read-er" (Emenyonu 1990, 83–84). This critical side of Achebe's project is achieved through a variety of complex strategies and goes well beyond mere description of the damage done by British colonialism to Igbo society. By situating itself in opposition to the depiction of relationships between Africa and Europe in such texts as *Heart of Darkness* or *Mister Johnson, Things Fall Apart* opens a complex literary dialogue that challenges not only the content of such texts, but also the fundamental rationalist, individualist, and historicist assumptions upon which those texts are constructed. Margaret Turner thus argues that "Chinua Achebe's trilogy, *Things Fall Apart, Arrow of God*, and *No Longer at Ease*, refutes Western standards of literature and Western ideology, in this case Hegel's universal and homogeneous state, by showing that both constitute aspects of the new colonialism" (Turner 1990, 32).

As Moses points out, sharp though his critique of colonialism may be, Achebe ultimately accepts the historical inevitability of modernization in a mode that shows a fundamental agreement with "the historicist legacy of Hegel's thinking" (Moses 1995, 108). Achebe's approach is again extremely complex. Just as he points out negative aspects of traditional Igbo society (such as the killing of twins and the treatment of certain members of the community—the *osu*—as total outcasts), so too does he suggest potentially positive developments related to the coming of Christianity and European civilization.[7] Indeed, in many cases the positive aspects of Westernization amount to direct reversals of abuses in Igbo society. Ultimately, however, *Things Fall Apart* demonstrates that even the negative aspects of Igbo society were part of an organic whole and that the disruptions brought about by their removal led to a collapse of the entire social structure. The book thus raises a number of profound questions not only about the nature and function of literature, but also about the nature of human societies and human cultural practices and the extent to which aspects of a given society are interwoven in complex and interdependent ways.

Historical Background
Nigeria, with a population of over ninety million (1993 estimate), is the most populous nation in Africa. It is also one of the largest, covering an area of approximately 357,000 square miles—somewhat larger than France and Great Britain combined. The Niger-Benue river system divides the country into three physically diverse sections. The hot, dry north is a heavily cultivated area of rolling savannahs located roughly fifteen hundred feet above sea level. Lake Chad, in the northeast, is one of the few large, permanent, standing bodies of water in the country, though its size varies with seasonal

---

[7] One might include the treatment of women in this list, though Achebe does not clearly identify the strictly patriarchal nature of the Igbo society depicted in *Things Fall Apart* as a shortcoming.

changes in rainfall. The southwest region contains both low-lying coastal plains and upland areas. The southeast region, consisting primarily of the delta of the Niger River, is largely covered by dense tropical forest. Nigeria's rich petroleum reserves are also located principally in this region. The new city of Abuja (designed and built beginning in the mid-1970s and located almost exactly in the middle of the country) became the capital in late 1991. The population of Abuja in 1992 was about 300,000, though it was growing rapidly. The largest city in Nigeria is the southwestern coastal city of Lagos, the former capital, with a population (1992 estimate) of over 1.3 million. Lagos is still the administrative and economic center of the country. The nearby city of Ibadan, with a population (1992 estimate) of nearly 1.3 million, is also a major commercial and intellectual center.

English is widely used in Nigeria in government, commerce, and education. In their everyday activities many of the inhabitants speak a form of "pidgin" English which preserves most of the basic grammatical features of English but incorporates a number of changes in syntax and vocabulary arising from the influence of local cultures. The more than 250 ethnic groups have their own languages as well. The largest of these groups are the Hausa and Fulani on the north, the Yoruba in the southwest, and the Igbo in the southeast. About half the total population, mostly in the north, are Muslim; about one-third of the population, almost all in the south, are Christian. Just over half of the adult population are literate, mostly in English. The economy of Nigeria is mostly agricultural. More than half the work force is engaged in farming (much of it subsistence farming), and a variety of crops are produced, including sorghum, millet, cassava, soybeans, groundnuts, cotton, maize, yams, rice, palm products, rice, and cacao. Goats, sheep, and cattle are raised as well. Periodic droughts frequently reduce agricultural production to the point that food must be imported. Hardwoods such as mahogany and ebony are produced in the forest regions, and there is some industry in the urban regions, though most manufactured products are imported. Nigeria is rich in mineral resources, producing iron, magnesium, niobium, tin, lead, and zinc. The major mineral resource, however, is petroleum: Nigeria is Africa's largest producer. Most of the petroleum reserves (estimated at about twenty billion barrels) are controlled by the government.

The people in what is now southern Nigeria had extensive contact with Europeans as long ago as the end of the fifteenth century, and the region has a rich history that goes back hundreds of years before that. The first centralized state in the region was Kanem-Bornu, probably founded in the eighth century A.D. Important states such as Oyo and Benin had arisen in the area by the fourteenth century, establishing a rich artistic tradition, especially in the production of bronze artifacts. By the seventeenth and eighteenth centuries, the area was one of the centers of a brutal slave trade in which millions of Nigerians were forcibly removed by European traders and brought to the Americas. Arab slave traders had also operated in the region earlier. The slave trade was abolished in the early nineteenth century, but European traders continued to visit the region, exchanging manufactured goods for local agricultural products.

The area occupied by modern Nigeria became one of the most important regions of British colonial power in Africa. Ceded to British control in the Berlin Conference of 1884–1885, the area was the object of extensive missionary activity in the late nineteenth century. British colonial rule was solidified through a massive program of "pacification" that lasted from 1900 to 1920, and the region was officially amalgamated as a single colony in 1914. The pacification program included the intentional destruction of important cultural sites and artifacts, including the great oracle of the Aro (an Igbo people). It also included the military conquest of peoples who resisted British rule. Villages were often subject to so-called punitive expeditions that amounted to massacres of the local population. For example, British-led troops slaughtered much of the population of the village of Ahiara in late 1905, an event echoed in the destruction of the fictional village of Abame in *Things Fall Apart*. The slaughter was precipitated by the killing of one J. F. Stewart, an Englishman traveling by bicycle in the area. This same killing was also the pretext for the massive Bende-Onitsha expedition into the interior of Nigeria, an expedition that included the destruction of an important oracle at Awka and that opened the way for more thorough British penetration of the region.

The British established an elaborate system of "indirect rule" that relied largely on African agents of the colonial government and on cooperative local rulers (often installed as puppets by the British) for its everyday operation, though all important decisions were made by the British governor. British rule led to a great deal of development, such as the building of roads and railways, but the system of indirect rule was an open invitation to corruption and abuse. Moreover, it often came into conflict with long-established local traditions. For example, the culture of the Igbo was based on discussion and decentralized, collective rule by groups of elders, no one of whom could be identified as the local ruler. When the British—bent on dealing with a single person as the leading power in a village—sought to establish such rulers, conflicts necessarily arose. Indeed, well-established social customs and traditions among the Igbo and other peoples in the region were so foreign to the customs and traditions of modern Britain that the British typically concluded that the indigenous peoples were mere savages without any legitimate culture or social structure. This belief was used to justify the various atrocities committed by the British during the period of pacification and to legitimate the continuation of British rule in the ensuing decades.

Nigeria finally gained independence from British rule on October 1, 1960. The new nation was divided into northern, western, and eastern administrative regions along the lines of the natural geographic division of the country. Nigeria became a republic in 1963, with Nnamdi Azikiwe as its first president. The early years of independence were marked by considerable political conflict and unrest, leading eventually to the January 1966 coup. A group of Igbo military officers took control of the government, placing Major General Johnson T. U. Aguiyi-Ironsi in charge of the new military regime. In July 1966, Ironsi was ousted and killed in another coup, this time led by Hausa officers. The new regime, headed by Lieutenant Colonel Yakubu Gowon, attempted to move toward civilian government, but internal troubles (especially the massacre of a number of Igbo living in the Hausa-dominated north) led to continuing instability. The dissatisfaction of the Igbo with their position in Nigeria led to the secession of the Eastern Region, led by Lieutenant Colonel Chukwuemeka Odumegwu Ojukwu. Ojukwu proclaimed the region the Republic of Biafra on May 30, 1967. A bloody civil war ensued, leading eventually to Biafra's surrender in January, 1970, and to the restoration of Nigeria's previous boundaries. In addition to massive casualties from the actual fighting, it is estimated that more than a million Igbo starved to death as a result of the war.

A worldwide boom in oil prices in the early 1970s led to an era of rising prosperity in Nigeria, marked by a massive government program of construction and industrialization, including the founding of the new capital of Abuja. On the other hand, the rapid influx of wealth was unevenly distributed and led to considerable corruption. By 1975, Gowon had still not restored civilian rule, and his regime was toppled in a coup led by General Murtala Muhammed and a group of officers who pledged to return the country to civilian rule as soon as possible. Muhammed was assassinated in an unsuccessful coup attempt a year later and replaced by General Olusegun Obasanjo. By the late 1970s the government had established increasingly close ties with the United States, and a new civilian government was installed, headed by President Alhaji Shehu Shagari and modeled on the American system. The new federal system was plagued by corruption and social disturbances. Shagari was reelected in 1983, but was overthrown in a violent military coup only a few months later. Another coup in 1985 instituted a military regime that held power until 1993, when a joint civilian-military government was installed and elections held. However, on November 17, 1993, General Sani Abacha seized control of the government in a bloodless coup and declared the elections void. Moshood K. O. Abiola, the apparent winner of the election, was jailed a year later when he declared himself president of Nigeria. At this writing Abacha is still in power, amid international outcries against the oppressive policies of his regime. He recently announced plans to hold new elections and to return Nigeria to civilian rule in 1998.

Biographical Background

Chinua Achebe is probably Africa's best known novelist, both in Africa and worldwide. He was born in 1930 in Ogidi, in eastern Nigeria and was originally christened Albert Chinualumogu Achebe. His father was a Christian evangelist and teacher, and his devoutly Christian parents had an intense sense of their difference from the non-Christians around them. Many of Achebe's neighbors and family members still adhered to traditional Igbo cultural and religious practices. Achebe was thus exposed at a very early age to the hybridity that informs postcolonial literature. Indeed, in his autobiographical essay "Named for Victoria, Queen of England," Achebe describes the principal experience of his childhood as one of being "at the crossroads of cultures":

> On one arm of the cross, we sang hymns and read the Bible night and day. On the other, my father's brother and his family, blinded by heathenism, offered food to idols. That was how it was supposed to be anyhow. But I knew without knowing why that it was too simple a way to describe what was going on (Achebe 1975, 119–20).

Achebe recalls that his parents looked down upon the "heathens" in their community who did not espouse Christianity, but he eventually came to wonder if "it isn't they who should have been looking down on us for our apostasy" (p. 115). In any case, the hybrid nature of Achebe's personal cultural background—which mirrors the hybrid experience of twentieth-century Igbo society as a whole—is a powerful informing factor in his work. As he grew older he began to read the various books that were in his parents' home, most of them either Christian religious tracts or works of European literature that reinforced his vague sense of European cultural superiority to Africa. Achebe was educated in a system designed and administered by the British colonial rulers of Nigeria, first at the local mission school, then at secondary school in the Government College in Umuahia, and finally at University College, Ibadan, where he received his B.A. in 1953.

Achebe's studies of Western literature in college convinced him of the need to develop more literature written from an African perspective and contributed greatly to his decision to become a writer. After graduation from University College, Achebe worked briefly as a producer for the Nigerian Broadcasting Corporation. While still working for the NBC he traveled to London where he studied broadcasting at the British Broadcasting Corporation. He also began writing his first novel during this period. This initial work eventually became two different novels. The first, *Things Fall Apart*, was published in 1958 and established Achebe as one of the important founding figures of the modern African novel in English. Achebe's second novel, *No Longer at Ease* (1994a), was published in 1960, the year of Nigerian independence. A sort of sequel to *Things Fall Apart* (the protagonist of the second book is the grandson of the protagonist of the first), *No Longer at Ease* describes the tensions in a 1950s Nigerian society moving toward independence from British rule.

Achebe continued to work with the Nigerian Broadcasting Corporation, becoming Director of External Broadcasting in 1961. In 1964 he published *Arrow of God*, his second novel about the early interaction between the cultures of the Igbo and the British. Set in the 1920s (slightly later than *Things Fall Apart*), *Arrow of God* describes a colonial Nigeria in which British political rule has been firmly established but in which many Igbo have still had relatively little contact with European culture. The villagers of this book continue to adhere to relatively traditional Igbo religious and cultural practices, but their lives are strongly informed by a sense that British control of Nigeria is firm and that they must learn to deal with the consequences of this alien rule.

In 1966 Achebe published *A Man of the People* (1989b), his first novel to be set in postcolonial Nigeria. A political satire that exposes the widespread corruption that plagued the new nation, *A Man of the People* marks a turn in Achebe's career from an attempt to recreate the past to a critical engagement with the present. At this point, the social and political instability that led to the Nigerian civil war caused Achebe and his family to flee from Lagos back to the Igbo territory in the east. The ensuing conflict caused a great disruption in Achebe's career. Achebe himself attempted to generate international support for the Biafran cause, serving as a sort of roving ambassador around the world. Concerned with the immediate disaster in Biafra and occupied with his work as an Igbo spokesman, Achebe found himself unable to sustain the effort required to write a novel and instead concentrated on writing shorter pieces such as essays and poems. *Beware, Soul Brother* (1972), a book of poems, was first published in 1971, and in 1972 Achebe was awarded the first Commonwealth Poetry Prize. His book of short stories, *Girls at War and Other Stories* (1972), was published in 1972 as well.

Achebe would not publish another novel until 1987, when *Anthills of the Savannah* (1988a) appeared, though a revised version of *Arrow of God* was issued in 1974 (Achebe 1989a). *Anthills of the Savannah* is Achebe's most formally intricate work, employing a complex nonlinear narrative form reminiscent of Western modernist novels but drawing upon African oral forms as well. Partially a meditation on the power and function of storytelling in society, the book is another satire of postcolonial politics, describing a military dictatorship in a fictional African nation (Kangan) that obviously resembles Nigeria. Clearly influenced by the events of the Nigerian civil war, the novel is a powerful indictment of the violence and corruption that have been part of the postcolonial histories of so many African nations. Together, Achebe's five novels constitute an extended fictional history of Nigeria from the moment of the first British colonial intrusion at the end of the nine-teenth century to the abuses of power that continue to plague Nigerian pol-itics at the end of the twentieth.

In the twenty-year period between the appearance of his fourth and fifth novels, Achebe spent a considerable amount of time teaching at univer-sities in the United States. He also remained involved in Nigerian politics, becoming the deputy national president of the People's Redemption Party in 1983 after turning down an offer to become the party's presidential can-didate in the elections of that year. His international reputation as a master of the craft of fiction continued to grow. His numerous awards included be-ing named an honorary fellow of the Modern Language Association of America in 1975 and a fellow of the British Royal Society of Literature in 1981. He is the only Nigerian to have twice received the Nigerian National Merit Award, his nation's highest honor for intellectual achievement. He has also been awarded more than twenty honorary degrees from universities in Africa, Europe, and America. Achebe's lectures and essays, many of which are published in the collections *Morning Yet on Creation Day* (1975) and *Hopes and Impediments* (1988c), have established him as a major spokesman for modern African culture and as an important leader in the effort to establish an African culture that escapes the domination of Western paradigms. As of this writing, Achebe and his wife live in Annandale-on-Hudson, New York, where they both teach at Bard College.

There is almost certainly more published criticism on Achebe's work than on that of any other African writer. A bibliography of works relevant to Achebe and his works published in Nigeria in 1990 listed 1,453 entries, 287 of which were written by Achebe himself. There are numerous full-length critical readings of Achebe's work (especially the novels), including those by David Carroll (1990), Simon Gikandi (1991), C. L. Innes (1990), G. D. Killam (1977), Benedict Chiaka Njoku (1984), Umelo Ojinmah (1991), and Arthur Ravenscroft (1969). Another important book-length study of Achebe is Robert Wren's *Achebe's World* (1980), which documents the histor-ical background of Achebe's work. Some of the numerous critical essays on Achebe's work are collected in the volumes edited by Innes and Bernth Lindfors (1978) and by Kirsten Holst Petersen and Anna Rutherford (1990). Most general studies of the African novel include extensive treatment of Achebe's work. Critical studies such as Obiechina's *Culture, Tradition and So-ciety in the West African Novel* (1975), JanMohamed's *Manichean Aesthetics* (1983), and Gikandi's *Reading the African Novel* (1987) feature discussions of Achebe's novels. Achebe's work is frequently taught in British and American university courses on literature, and the Modern Language Association has published a volume of essays detailing various approaches to teaching *Things Fall Apart* (Lindfors, ed. 1991).

Further Reading

Achebe, Chinua. 1984. *The Trouble with Nigeria*. London: Heinemann.

Asiegbu, Johnson U. J. 1984. *Nigeria and Its British Invaders, 1851–1920: A Thematic Documentary History*. New York: NOK International.

Ben-Amos, Paula. 1980. *The Art of Benin*. New York: Thames and Hudson.

Crowder, Michael. 1977. *The Story of Nigeria*. 4th ed. London: Faber.

———. 1979. *Nigeria: An Introduction to Its History*. London: Longman.

Diamond, Larry Jay. 1988. *Class, Ethnicity, and Democracy in Nigeria: The Failure of the First Republic*. Basingstoke, England: Macmillan.

Ekwe-Ekwe, Herbert. 1990. *The Biafra War: Nigeria and the Aftermath*. Lewiston, N.Y.: Mellen.

Isichei, Elizabeth. 1976. *A History of the Igbo People*. London: Macmillan.

———. 1983. *A History of Nigeria*. London: Longman.

Millar, Heather. 1996. *The Kingdom of Benin in West Africa*. New York: Benchmark.

Ogbalu, F. Chidozie, and E. Nolue Emenanjo. 1975. *Igbo Language and Culture*. Ibadan: Oxford University Press.

Olaniyan, Richard, ed. 1985. *Nigerian History and Culture*. Harlow, Essex: Longman.

Uchendu, V. C. 1965. *The Igbo of Southeast Nigeria*. New York: Holt, Rinehart, and Winston.

Chapter 4

Buchi Emecheta:
The Joys of Motherhood

Buchi Emecheta, more than any other writer, is responsible for bringing the Nigerian novel by women onto the stage of world literature (Ogunyemi 1996, 220). Her literary output is varied and prolific, but *The Joys of Motherhood* (1988b, first published in 1979) is certainly her best known and most widely discussed novel. It is also one of the most important novels ever written by an African woman. In its treatment of the oppression of women, *The Joys of Motherhood* is a central statement in Emecheta's extensive exploration of the complex relationship between racism and sexism within the context of the sweeping changes brought by colonialism. The book is typical of Emecheta's ability to treat complex issues in sensitive and accessible ways. It also raises fundamental questions about the role of women in African society—and the role of feminist criticism in the treatment of African literature.

The basic plot of *The Joys of Motherhood* is simple and straightforward. The protagonist, Nnu Ego, is born in the village of Ibuza, the daughter of the powerful and respected local chief, Nwokocha Agbadi, and his beautiful and defiant mistress, Ona. After Ona dies during the birth of a subsequent child, Nnu Ego grows up under the protection of her father. She becomes a beautiful young woman who has numerous suitors. Agbadi finally chooses a husband for her, and she is married to Amatokwu, from the village of Umo-Iso. When this marriage results in no children, Amatokwu takes an additional wife who becomes pregnant the first month. Nnu Ego tries to help tend the baby boy after it is born, but Amatokwu's increasingly abusive treatment finally leads Agbadi to take Nnu Ego back home. Agbadi then arranges another marriage for his daughter, this time to Nnaife Owulum, who lives in distant Lagos and works as a servant for the white Meers family. Nnu Ego travels to Lagos, where she finds her overweight husband rather unappealing, but she sees no alternative to the match. Nnu Ego endures her new husband's voracious sex-

ual appetite and the humiliation of his fawning attitude toward his employers. Meanwhile, she helps the family meet its expenses by working as a vendor of cigarettes and matches. She soon gives birth to a baby boy, but just as
she begins to enjoy her life, the boy suddenly dies, nearly driving Nnu Ego
to suicide. She recovers, however, and soon gives birth to another boy, Oshia.
As World War II approaches, the Meers return to England, leaving Nnaife un-
employed and forcing the family to live on Nnu Ego's meager income. Nnaife
finally finds work aboard a British ship and leaves home, with Nnu Ego again
pregnant. She gives birth to another boy, Adim, and Nnaife returns with
enough money to fund a lavish naming ceremony for the new child.

When Nnaife's older brother suddenly dies, however, Nnaife becomes
responsible for his brother's children and wives, one of whom, Adaku, comes
with her daughter to live in Lagos as Nnaife's second wife. Nnaife gets a job
as a grass cutter for the colonial railway company to help support his new
extended family. Nnu Ego resents Adaku's presence, and the two women do
not get along well. As the effects of World War II begin to be felt in Nigeria,
Nnu Ego gives birth to twin girls, and Adaku gives birth to a son who dies
only a few weeks later. Nnaife, who has grown increasingly abusive toward
both wives, is forcibly conscripted into the British army, leaving the women
to fend for themselves. Adaku begins to prosper as a seller of foods, but after
some male relatives insult her, she leaves home and defiantly resolves to become a prostitute. Her brief career in this role helps her earn the capital to
begin a thriving business, while the relatively traditional Nnu Ego struggles
to support herself and her four children from her own paltry income. Nnaife
finally returns, but uses much of his army pay to meet the bride price of a
new sixteen-year-old wife, Okpo. Nnu Ego gives birth to another set of
twin girls, but the life of the family is focused on her two sons, who receive
good educations and eventually go abroad to the United States and Canada.
After Nnaife is imprisoned for attacking the family of a Yoruba man who
seeks to marry his daughter Kehinde, Nnu Ego returns to Ibuza with Okpo
and the remaining small children. There, she is scorned by Nnaife's family,
who partially blame her for his conviction and imprisonment. He is soon
released, however, and returns to Ibuza, where he lives with Okpo. The rejected Nnu Ego declines rapidly and soon dies alone by the side of a road.
Her estranged sons return from abroad for her burial and erect a shrine in
her name (financed mostly by Oshia) "so that her grandchildren could ap-
peal to her should they be barren" (p. 224).

This simple story makes a number of points about the plight of women
in colonial Nigeria and about the impact of colonialism on Nigerian society, including the patriarchal nature of traditional Nigerian society, the masculine need for power and dominance, and the treatment of women as the
property of men. Central to the issue of women as property are the tradi-

tions of polygamy and of motherhood as the most valuable contribution that women can make to their society. At the same time, Emecheta suggests that traditional societies offered numerous opportunities to women that have been denied to them in modern Nigeria, which is influenced by European ideas that in many cases are detrimental to women. Finally, Emecheta supplements her criticisms of the oppression of women in both traditional and modern societies with several positive images of strong women who have been able to assert their independence nevertheless.

Emecheta's description of the patriarchal nature of traditional African society can be seen most clearly in her portrayal of Nnu Ego's father, Agbadi. "Cruel in his imperiousness" and a man who "ruled his family and children as if he were a god" (p. 15), Agbadi has much in common with Okonkwo, the protagonist of Achebe's *Things Fall Apart*. He can be extremely brutal even to his beloved Ona, as when he intentionally hurts her during sex so that she will cry out, thus impressing the neighbors with his masculine power (pp. 20–21). Such patriarchal behavior continues even in the more modern Lagos, as in the way Nnu Ego's sons are considered more valuable than her daughters. Oshia himself realizes his special position as the family's eldest son early on, and he quickly comes to understand that "he and his brother Adim were rare commodities, and that he being the oldest was rarer still" (p. 128). Indeed, the text suggests that modernization has introduced new ways in which sons are privileged over daughters, as when Nnu Ego is told that her daughters are most valuable because their bride prices can help pay for the modern education of her sons (p. 160). At the same time, the text also shows that colonialism violently disrupted the patriarchal structure of Igbo society. Nnu Ego's husband, Nnaife experiences special problems of his own as a result of the British colonial presence in Nigeria. In particular, Nnaife finds it very difficult to assume the godlike position held by his father-in-law, when he is forced to earn a living doing the laundry of the imperious Meers family in Lagos. Nnu Ego herself sometimes entertains thoughts that her first husband back in the village of Ibuza would never have allowed himself to be humiliated in such a way (p. 72). But Nnu Ego is assured by her neighbor Cordelia that Nnaife's position is typical in colonial Lagos. "Men here are too busy being white men's servants to be men," she tells Nnu Ego. "Their manhood has been taken away from them. The shame of it is that they don't know it. All they see is the money, shining white man's money" (p. 51).

Emecheta here indicates the corrupting effects of Western materialism on traditional African culture, a theme that figures prominently in her work. Nnaife is forced to assume a position relative to the British that his culture would regard as feminine, recalling Achebe's depiction of Okonkwo's father Unoka in *Things Fall Apart*. For example, Nnaife, like Unoka, sometimes neglects his financial responsibilities in order to spend his time playing his battered guitar. Much of the family's income must thus come from Nnu Ego's work, a situation that makes Nnaife even more insecure in his masculine power. When, after a period of unemployment, he gets the job as a grass cutter, his newly increased income makes him feel justified in abusing and even beating Nnu Ego (p. 117). Indeed, it is clear that the subservience forced upon Nnaife by the British encourages him to try to dominate Nnu Ego even more brutally than he otherwise might. He consistently attempts to assert his position as "lord and master" of his household. Nnaife's taking of multiple wives also represents an attempt to meet the expectations of masculine power set out for him by traditional Igbo society.

In short, if men are often household tyrants in traditional Igbo society, then colonialism, by challenging their traditional authority, may actually make them even more tyrannical. Similarly, Emecheta suggests that the treatment of women as the mere property of men in traditional society is not necessarily overcome by modernization. In one scene, Nnaife admonishes Nnu Ego for failing to show him the proper deference, to which she replies that such deference is demanded only in traditional Ibuza, not in modern Lagos. Nnaife angrily responds that, having paid the bride price, he is Nnu Ego's "owner," wherever they may be (p. 48). Girls and women are consistently regarded by their fathers and husbands as property in the book, and Emecheta presents other vivid images of the treatment of women as property. One of the most striking is the story of a slave woman who is forcibly buried along with Agbadi's just-deceased senior wife (p. 23). That this slave is quite literally regarded as property and that her life must be sacrificed in order to meet the requirements of tradition obviously make her fate merely a more overt version of that which awaits all women in this society.[1] In a scene replete with the kind of irony for which Emecheta has become widely known, the slave woman, thankful that Agbadi's son strikes her a mortal blow so that she will not have to be buried alive, promises to return as a member of Agbadi's family. The young Nnu Ego is subsequently identified as this slave woman reincarnate, making the link between the two women quite explicit.

Many of Emecheta's points are made in explicit and overtly didactic ways. Because she calls attention to issues that have not typically received enough attention in African literature or in critical discussions of that literature, her unashamedly didactic style seems justified. If her work sometimes seems to lack the subtlety and ambiguity often valued in Western aesthetics,

---

[1] Emecheta makes a similar point in *The Slave Girl,* which not only focuses specifically on the Igbo practice of domestic slavery, but also includes a virtually identical burial scene (Emecheta 1977, 62).

it is because her project demands direct statement, not because she lacks sophistication as a writer. Emecheta skillfully weaves a number of subtle complications into her simple plot, making *The Joys of Motherhood* a far more sophisticated treatment of its basic issues than is immediately obvious. For one thing, the book can be fully understood only when read in conjunction with a number of other texts. It clearly responds to texts by male African writers in which traditional society is depicted as a positive alternative to modern, Western society without extensive exploration of the role of gender issues. Thus, Florence Stratton argues that Emecheta's realistic portrayal of the plight of African women "counters the tendency toward gender romance in works like *Things Fall Apart*" (Stratton 1994, 116). In addition, Stratton points out that Emecheta's critique of the emphasis on motherhood in traditional society stands in direct opposition to works such as *Things Fall Apart*, Ekwensi's *Jagua Nana*, and Ngugi's *Petals of Blood* (p. 113). At the same time, *The Joys of Motherhood* establishes a positive intertextual relationship with other works by African women writers, particularly Flora Nwapa's *Efuru* (1966). Emecheta's book derives its title from a line in *Efuru* and resembles it in numerous ways.[2] Stratton notes that, "through its intertextuality with *Efuru*, *The Joys of Motherhood* confirms the existence of a female tradition in fiction" (p. 111).

Another complexity of *The Joys of Motherhood* arises from the fact that the book presents what seems to be a relatively realistic depiction of life in colonial Nigeria, but it does not function as a transparent representation of reality, as readers might expect in Western texts. Nnu Ego, for example, actually functions as the allegorical embodiment of many of the most important social issues that inform her historical context. This may account for the criticisms of her characterization made by readers who seem to want her to function as a realistic individual woman. Eustace Palmer (1983) criticizes Nnu Ego's passivity and weakness, arguing that she is seduced by the lure of modern ways but lacks the strength and insight to see through them. Tuzyline Jita Allen, meanwhile, complains that Nnu Ego's passivity is not believable in a woman with two strong and independent parents like Agbadi and Ona, arguing that this depiction makes Emecheta's book ineffective as a feminist critique of the treatment of women in traditional Igbo society. "Emecheta," Allen argues, "seems more interested in her heroine's suitability to an idea of African womanhood than in breaking the chains which the culture has forged" (Allan 1995, 108).

Such criticisms are problematic if one reads Nnu Ego as an allegorical embodiment of historical forces rather than as a distinct individual in the West-

---

[2] For a detailed comparison of *Efuru* and *The Joys of Motherhood*, see Andrade (1990, 95–102).

ern sense. Achebe is again valuable for comparison here. Emecheta's Nnu Ego is a female version of Achebe's Okonkwo, a typical representative of the traditional Igbo woman. It might also be argued that she takes conventional feminine behavior to an extreme, just as Okonkwo represents an exaggeration of Igbo expectations of masculine behavior. Nnu Ego is also much like Okonkwo in the sense that her difficulties can be attributed largely to her attempt to maintain traditional values within the context of the sweeping changes brought to Igbo society by colonialism. Nnu Ego suffers from the patriarchal aspects of both traditions, but her greatest difficulties result from the transition between the two. In a sense, she partakes of the worst of both worlds and suffers more than a woman might who was firmly situated in either.

Emecheta's characterization of Nnu Ego is enriched by the fact that *The Joys of Motherhood* presents two alternative visions of feminine behavior in Ona and Adaku. Ona's refusal to marry Agbadi and her sometimes fierce resistance to his advances stand in stark contrast to Nnu Ego's relatively docile acceptance of her arranged marriage to Nnaife. It is also important that the proud independence of Ona occurs within the context of traditional life in Ibuza, while Nnu Ego's marriage to Nnaife occurs in a modern Lagos dominated by the British. It is thus possible to read the contrast between Ona and her daughter Nnu Ego as a suggestion that African women often lost a great deal of independence and power as a result of colonization. Andrade concludes that *The Joys of Motherhood* follows Nwapa's *Efuru* in demonstrating that "pre-colonial Igbo women had more independence than their colonized descendants" (Andrade 1990, 101). Indeed, Emecheta's narrator makes this point quite explicitly when she suggests early in the text that Agbadi finds Ona's independence and even arrogance quite appealing and that "to regard a woman who is quiet and timid as desirable was something that came after his time, with Christianity and other changes" (p. 10). On the other hand, the contrast between Ona and Nnu Ego is complicated by the fact that Ona's independent behavior arises largely from her loyalty to her father, while Nnu Ego's acceptance of her marriage to Nnaife can also be seen as an act of loyalty to her own father. Emecheta thus refuses to idealize traditional Igbo society and makes the patriarchal orientation of that society clear, even as she reminds readers that women in that society had certain opportunities to attain dignity and respect that are denied to them in modern Nigeria. On the other hand, Emecheta's depiction of Nnu Ego's co-wife, Adaku, complicates the comparison between traditional and modern ways still further. Adaku manages to assert her economic independence within the opportunities that are available to her in modern Lagos and that no doubt would not have been available in traditional Ibuza.

Nnu Ego's work as a vendor is a traditional African feminine role, and many African societies expect women to maintain a certain amount of economic independence from their husbands. Adaku, however, takes this role to a new level, engaging in business practices that clearly reflect capitalism more than traditional African systems of exchange. As a result, she achieves an income that Nnu Ego cannot hope to match. On the other hand, Adaku's radical departure from the behavior dictated for women by traditional society causes her family and others in Ibuzu to deny her the support and respect she might otherwise have received. Adaku is also forced to resort to prostitution in order to take advantage of the new business opportunities available in Lagos. This can indicate that women still function as property even under capitalism. Indeed, modern European writers who have been critical of the way capitalism tends to reduce all human beings to commodities have often employed prostitution as a metaphor.

The contrasts among Nnu Ego, Ona, and Adaku are complicated further by the fact that Nnu Ego is not as passive and submissive as she sometimes appears. She occasionally resists Nnaife's domination quite vehemently. Moreover, she manages to survive extreme social and economic hardships within the alien environment of Lagos, largely through her own courage and hard work and often with no help from her husband whatsoever. In particular, she is able to support her family and keep it together during extended periods when Nnaife is absent and when she must serve as the head of the family and its only source of income. Moreover, Nnu Ego does not blindly accept the roles thrust upon her by traditional Igbo society. In fact, she learns a great deal from her experiences. After her second set of twin girls is born, Nnu Ego gloomily reflects on the value placed on sons in her society, wondering to herself when it will finally be possible for a woman to be "fulfilled in herself, a full human being, not anybody's appendage" (p. 186). Yet she complains that, given the values of patriarchal society, such a woman is almost impossible (p. 187).

Readers who choose to interpret *The Joys of Motherhood* within the conventions of Western realism have sometimes found this late turn in Nnu Ego's attitude problematic, arguing that it represents a sudden change that seems inconsistent with Nnu Ego's characterization elsewhere in the book. Thus, Allen argues, "So incongruous is this complaint/confession with the heroine's psychological portrait that one is inclined to suspect a voice-over rather than Nnu Ego's own voice" (Allen 1995, 111). Of course, if one does not see Nnu Ego as a realistic character in the Western sense, then there is no reason why her behavior should be psychologically consistent. She may become a sort of spokeswoman for Emecheta's own political ideas here, but she is in fact meant as an embodiment of ideas all along.

On the other hand, Nnu Ego's critique of patriarchy seems to represent a radical repudiation of her earlier acceptance of her plight, suggesting that she does not remain passive but grows and learns as a result of her experiences. Comparing *The Joys of Motherhood* to Bessie Head's *A Question of Power*, Nancy Topping Bazin concludes that the protagonists of both books "move away from innocence into an understanding of the patriarchal culture in which they live" (Bazin 1990, 45). This movement in Nnu Ego's understanding of her position as a woman in Nigerian society suggests an additional intertextual framework for reading the book. *The Joys of Motherhood* can be compared to the European genre of the bildungsroman or to the traditional African oral genre of the initiation story. The book thus inherently sets up cross-cultural dialogues between the European and African versions of the story of development. And this dialogue can lead to valuable insights. For example, Eileen Julien notes that the African initiation story is designed to "preserve an already extant order, to preach the virtues of continuity and conformity to an established set of truths" (Julien 1992, 95). She then argues that such characteristics set this genre apart from the bildungsroman, which she sees as more individualistic and open-ended. Julien also suggests that some African "novels of growth"—such as *The Joys of Motherhood*—are more dynamic and less authoritarian than the traditional story of initiation (p. 47).

In this sense, Emecheta's story would seem to resemble the European bildungsroman more than the African initiation story, though the fact that Emecheta's protagonist is female sets her book apart from most of the major bildungsromans and places it instead in the tradition of the female bildungsroman.[3] Emecheta's book also has a great deal in common with the proletarian bildungsroman, a genre especially popular during the depression years of the 1930s, in which a working-class character comes to recognize the injustices of capitalism, often declaring this recognition in moments of epiphany much like that of Nnu Ego. Indeed, these proletarian texts have often been criticized for the seemingly abrupt ways in which their protagonists reach enlightenment, recalling some of the criticisms of Emecheta's presentation of Nnu Ego's moment of insight. In both cases, however, such criticisms really amount to a charge that the texts deviate from the conventions of European bourgeois realism, a deviation that is not necessarily a flaw in texts that are written in opposition to the dominance of bourgeois ideology and that have an explicitly antibourgeois didactic purpose.

In any case, Nnu Ego's declaration provides a trenchant description of the role played by the glorification of motherhood (and especially of being a mother to sons) in traditional Igbo society. It also provides an overt critique of the complicity of women in this phenomenon, as well as an implicit intertextual critique of the romanticization of motherhood that sometimes occurs in the works of African male writers such as Achebe, Ekwensi, and

---

[3] For discussions of the female bildungsroman, see Bannet (1991) or the essays collected by Abel, Hirsch, and Langland (1983).

Ngugi. Carole Boyce Davies thus describes the book's purpose as being "to show the tragedy of woman's existence when it remains circumscribed by motherhood alone" (Davies 1986b, 253). Emecheta's title (which is from this point of view presumably ironic) tends to reinforce this way of reading the book. The book's ending also tends to support this reading. Countering her own earlier prediction that as a woman she would be unable to be free even in death, Nnu Ego seems to assert her independence posthumously when she refuses to answer the prayers of the young women who come to her shrine to ask for children. Bazin thus notes that, while Nnu Ego may begin to understand her oppression during her life, it is only in death that she is "free to take action by denying fertility to the young women. She knows that the continuous pressure to bear sons that drives them to her shrine will enslave them as it did her. Freedom for them must begin with rejecting the patriarchal glorification of motherhood" (Bazin 1990, 51).

Western feminist readers have been virtually unanimous in seeing *The Joys of Motherhood* as a critique of the emphasis on the mothering of sons in traditional Igbo society, an emphasis that leaves women little room to achieve a rewarding life outside their prescribed roles as wives and mothers. On the other hand, it is quite possible that such readers are in some cases projecting Western feminist concerns onto Emecheta's African text in an inappropriate way. Katherine Fishburn thus concludes in her extended study of Emecheta's work that Western feminist readings constitute a particularly clear example of the way in which differences in cultural perspective make it impossible for Western readers ever to achieve a complete understanding of African texts on their own terms. Noting that it is probably a mistake to read Emecheta's texts within the conventions of Western realism, Fishburn argues that we should consider the possibility that the title of *The Joys of Motherhood* is not ironic to Nnu Ego and most members of her society. From a traditional African point of view, Fishburn concludes, it is entirely likely that Nnu Ego's life would be regarded as successful because she is the mother of numerous children (and especially of two sons) (Fishburn 1995, 105). One might note, for example, Barbara Christian's reminder that for most women in traditional African societies "there is no worse misfortune . . . than being childless" (Christian 1985, 216).

Becoming a mother, especially the mother of sons, does in fact bring a great deal of joy to Nnu Ego. Nnu Ego regrets all along that her daughters are valued less than her sons. But she truly begins to suffer from her devotion to her sons only when they move away to the United States and Canada and decline to provide the support to their parents that would be expected of them by Igbo custom. One of the saddest developments of Nnu Ego's life is that these Westernized sons, who have been so important to her and for whom she has sacrificed so much, maintain virtually no contact with her after they leave Nigeria. For example, Nnu Ego learns of Oshia's marriage in America to a white woman only from rumors, and the marriage drives Nnu Ego to the point of mental instability (and eventually to death), repeating the loss she suffered earlier at the death of her first son. In short, Nnu Ego's tragedy may not be that she is forced into a traditional role as the mother of Oshia and Adim but that the impact of colonialism makes it impossible for her to assume that role fully. Her sons are lost to the West, as are so many elements of traditional Igbo life.

For Fishburn, readings of Emecheta's book as a searing critique of traditional practices like polygamy represent failures to consider such practices from an African point of view. To support her point, Fishburn cites critics such as Filomina Chioma Steady (1981) and Joseph Okpaku (1970), who have concluded from their studies of African cultural practices that polygamy was actually advantageous to women in numerous ways (Fishburn 1995, 113). Indeed, while Emecheta's novels often show the negative impact of polygamy on women, she herself does not see the practice as an unmitigated evil. For example, she suggested at the 1984 African Studies Asasociation meeting in California that traditional polygamy worked to the advantage of women in many ways, a position that caused her to be severely criticized (Davies 1986a, 9). And, in her essay "Feminism with a Small *F*," Emecheta explicitly states that, while polygamy is in many ways a form of oppression, some women in Nigeria now "make polygamy work for them" (Emecheta 1988a, 176).

Emecheta's essay warns against the interpretation of her writing strictly within the framework of Western feminism. She emphasizes that the lives of African women differ from those of Western women in important ways and that the concerns of African feminism can differ from those of Western feminism.[4] In particular, Emecheta warns against the denigration of motherhood in some versions of Western feminism, arguing that, while it is certainly true that women can be many things other than mothers, African feminists need to value and cherish the contributions of mothers (Emecheta 1988a, 180).

Emecheta's description of her position as "feminism with a small *f*" is reminiscent of the way the African-American writer Alice Walker refers to her own philosophy as "womanist" in order to distinguish it from white-dominated feminism.[5] Indeed, Emecheta's essay is particularly meaningful when read within the context of numerous recent critical warnings against the appropriation of the works of African women writers by (mostly white) Western feminist critics. Andrade, for example, notes that Western feminist

---

[4] See Steady (1981) for an extended attempt to formulate the outlines of an African feminist theory. See Davies for a brief presentation of some of the major characteristics of an African feminism (Davies 1986a, 8–10).

[5] Allan (1995) discusses some of the differences and similarities between feminism and womanism.

theory "neglects to examine its own inscription within a European system of thought which is saturated by imperialism" (Andrade 1990, 92). And Davies emphasizes that African feminists and Western feminists have different points of view not only because the roles of women in traditional African societies often differ substantially from those in Western societies, but also because issues of race and class may interact with issues of gender differently in contemporary Africa than in the West (Davies 1986a, 10–11).

Fishburn may thus be justified when she argues that Western feminist readings of *The Joys of Motherhood* as a critique of the oppression of women by men may not adequately account for the book's African cultural background. For Fishburn, the book is as much a critique of colonialism as of gender inequities in traditional Igbo society:

> Rather than seeing the novel as an account of the war between the sexes, might we not see it as a war between the past and the present—between the voices of tradition and those of modernization. Might we not see it, in short, as a war between Igbo and Western values (Fishburn 1995, 114)?

The role of women writers such as Emecheta in calling attention to the special problems of women in African society has been an important one. But one should beware of readings that tend to circumscribe texts such as *The Joys of Motherhood* within the realm of women's personal lives and thus lose sight of the public political issues that impact those lives.[6] Emecheta's book describes special gender-related problems that occur because of the impact of colonialism on traditional Igbo society. Precisely the same thing might be said about *Things Fall Apart*, except that the gender is different. But Achebe's book has most often been read as being about colonialism, while Emecheta's is supposedly about gender. This contrast may represent the traditional biases that see the woman's sphere as separate from the public world of political action and that see the masculine viewpoint as a baseline (and thus not affected by gender) and the feminine viewpoint as a gender-oriented deviation from the norm.

Of course, it is clearly not necessary to read *The Joys of Motherhood* as either a clash between genders or a clash between cultures. It can—and should—be read as both, just as Nnu Ego's personal suffering can be attributed both to certain aspects of traditional Igbo society and to the breakup of that society under the impact of colonialism. Emecheta's fiction often presents complex issues in ways that encourage readers to think carefully about various alternatives without necessarily choosing any of them as ultimately

---

[6] One might recall here Molara Ogundipe-Leslie's reminder that the political commitment of African women writers does not relate only to gender. An African woman writer is "committed in three ways: as a writer, as a woman and as a Third World person; and her biological womanhood is implicated in all three" (Ogundipe-Leslie 1987, 13).

preferable. For Western readers, this uncertainty often hinges on the interpretation of Emecheta's irony, and in this sense her novels are often reminiscent of the open-ended and ambiguous works that we associate with modernist writers such as Joseph Conrad or Virginia Woolf. Yet Emecheta's mode of posing questions rather than providing answers can also be linked to African oral traditions like that of "dilemma tales," which William Bascom describes as "prose narratives that leave the listeners with a choice among alternatives, such as which of the several characters has done the best, deserves a reward, or should win an argument or a case in court" (Bascom 1975, 1). However, as Lloyd Brown points out, in such tales "it is not necessarily assumed that the questions themselves can be answered or that the underlying moral and legal problems can be solved" (Brown 1981, 85). This description fits *The Joys of Motherhood* well, suggesting that Western readers should be cautious in jumping to the conclusion that the open-endedness of Emecheta's stories is of the same kind as that of the "inconclusive narratives" of Conrad's Charlie Marlow. Nevertheless, Emecheta's book can (with proper caution) be approached from both Western and African perspectives.

Historical Background

Buchi Emecheta, like Chinua Achebe, is a Nigerian postcolonial novelist, and the historical background of her novels is very similar to that of Achebe's novels. The reader is thus referred to Chapter 3 for historical background to Emecheta's work. It should be emphasized, however, that Emecheta sometimes differs substantially from Achebe in her use of this background. Emecheta's fiction grows out of many of the same events (especially colonialism and its aftermath), but responds to these events from a different point of view. In particular, Emecheta presents the colonial and postcolonial history of Nigeria from an avowedly feminine perspective, thus calling attention to certain aspects of African history that often receive little attention in the works of Achebe and other male African writers. In addition, certain specific events related to the history of women in Africa underlie Emecheta's fiction. For example, Susan Andrade notes the importance of the Women's War of 1929 as background to Emecheta's *The Joys of Motherhood* (Andrade 1990, 95–97). In this anticolonial insurrection (referred to by the British as the "Aba Riots"), tens of thousands of Igbo women mobilized to protest against the unfairness and corruption of the systems of taxation and jurisprudence installed by the colonial administration. That administration reacted violently, and more than fifty women were killed, though no men were killed or even seriously injured. Importantly, this event was not a singular aberration, but was conducted within a tradition of women's political activism that had long informed Igbo society. Thus Judith Van Allen notes that the Women's War exemplified the considerable political power of women

in traditional Igbo society, a power which was "expressed in their own political institutions—their 'meetings' (*mikiri* or *mitiri*), their market net-
works, their kinship groups, and their right to use strikes, boycotts and force
to effect their decisions" (Van Allen 1976). This power, however, was largely
eroded under colonialism, which shored up the political role of men in its
policies of indirect rule (p. 166). Incidents such as the Women's War show
that the impact of colonialism was often different for women than for men
Such incidents thus provide important background to the writings of African women novelists.

Biographical Background

Buchi Emecheta is probably Africa's best known and most widely read
woman novelist. She was born in 1944 in Lagos, though her parents were
from the Igbo village of Ibuza in southeastern Nigeria. Her parents were
nominally Christian, but they continued to adhere to many traditional Igbo
beliefs, presenting the young Emecheta with an inherently multiple, hybrid
cultural background. Indeed, her parents made sure that she spent a considerable part of her time back in Ibuza to stay in touch with traditional Igbo
culture. Meanwhile, as an Igbo growing up in Yoruba-dominated Lagos,
Emecheta was from the beginning something of an outsider. Her feeling of
marginality was greatly reinforced by her growing recognition, even as a
child, that Igbo tradition placed far more value on boys than on girls.
Emecheta was an African in world dominated by the West, an Igbo in a city
dominated by the Yoruba, and a female in a society dominated by males. This
experience of multiple marginality would continue throughout her life and
would become a major factor in her writing.

Emecheta devoted much of her time and energy to her education,
dreaming of becoming a writer even as a girl. Her ambitions, however, were
not encouraged, as when one of the teachers at her Methodist high school
rebuked her for the pride of her ambition and ordered her to pray for God's
forgiveness (Emecheta 1994b, 23). At age sixteen, Emecheta left school to be
married. Two years later, her husband left for London to pursue his own education. Emecheta, who by now had two young children, accompanied him.
In London, the family lived in abject poverty amid a climate of intense racial prejudice. They soon had three more children, and Emecheta, while still
caring for all of the children, worked to support the family so that her husband could concentrate on his studies. By age twenty-two Emecheta had
split with her husband and found herself alone in London with five young
children to support and care for. While working several different jobs, she
managed to continue her own education, eventually receiving a degree in
sociology. She also took up the writing of fiction. In 1972 she found a market for her writing when the journal *New Statesman* began to publish her

stories. In that same year, she published her first book, *In the Ditch* (1994c), and her career as a novelist was launched. Since that time she has been able to support herself entirely from her writing, thus becoming perhaps the first full-time professional African woman writer.

In the Ditch is essentially a collection of stories published in the *New Statesman*. It is a highly autobiographical work based on Emecheta's life after the breakup of her marriage as she struggled to support her five children and to pursue her own education and career. The protagonist of the book, Adah, similarly struggles against the poverty of her surroundings and the extreme racial prejudice of London society, both of which she eventually manages to overcome through her own determination and hard work, as well as through solidarity with the other women in her slum community. The book is thus relatively optimistic in outlook, partly because its publication marked such a positive achievement in Emecheta's own life. In her autobiography, *Head Above Water* (1994b), Emecheta expresses her sense of accomplishment at seeing her first book in print: "I had come a long way, and only people who have set their hearts on achieving something and eventually getting it will realize how one feels at a time like this" (Emecheta 1994b, 74). Emecheta's first book would be followed by many more. At this writing, she continues to live and work in London, though she has spent occasional periods in Nigeria, as when she taught at the University of Calabar from 1980 to 1981.

In the Ditch received a rather negative critical reception, partially because the background behind Adah's experiences was unclear. In her next book, *Second-Class Citizen* (1974), Emecheta supplies this background, going back to Adah's childhood in Nigeria. Adah is determined to receive a Western education, but she finds herself thwarted by traditional prejudices that would bar a girl from receiving such an education. Adah marries and moves to England, where she hopes to escape such prejudices, only to find that her problems are compounded by the racial and class prejudices that she encounters there. Meanwhile, her husband, Francis, struggles to maintain his patriarchal authority, sometimes treating her with considerable brutality. Gender remains the principal source of Adah's oppression, and much of the novel details her attempts to escape Francis's domination, which she finally does by the end of the book, setting up the situation where *In the Ditch* begins.

In *The Bride Price* (1976) Emecheta turns from autobiographical to historical fiction. Set in colonial Nigeria in the early 1950s, it tells the story of a young girl, Aku-nna, who is born in Lagos and lives there until age thirteen, when her father's death makes it necessary for her to move (with her mother and brother) back to the family's original home in the village of Ibuza. The book is set almost entirely in Ibuza, though it suggests the contrast between the modern urban society of Lagos and the relatively traditional

Igbo society of Ibuza that will become to be a major focus of Emecheta's fiction in her next several books. Aku-nna finds the traditional roles thrust upon women in Ibuza extremely oppressive. She enters a forbidden marriage with her schoolteacher, Chike, and moves with him to a larger town where they enjoy the benefits of Western civilization. They have a happy marriage, and Chike, the descendent of slaves and thus an outcast from Igbo society, is a positive figure who loves Aku-nna and encourages her in her education. But traditional society is not so easy to escape. Because of her elopement, Aku-nna's bride price has not been paid, and she eventually dies in childbirth after her stepfather places a traditional Igbo curse on her. As a result, she becomes a warning to any other Igbo girls who would defy tradition: "Every girl in Ibuza after Aku-nna's death was told her story, to reinforce the old taboos of the land" (p. 168). *The Bride Price* thus represents a sharp departure from the optimism of Emecheta's first two novels.

This somber note continues in *The Slave Girl* (1977), which moves further back in history to 1910, when its heroine, Ogbanje Ojebeta, is born. Ojebeta's early childhood is unusual because her parents cherish her and value the fact that she is a girl. But she is orphaned at age seven and sold into slavery by her brother for the sum of eight pounds. Much of the book describes her life as the domestic slave of Ma Palagada and represents a sharp critique of the practice of slavery in Igbo society. On the other hand, as the slave of the wealthy and relatively benign Ma Palagada, Ojebeta lives in material splendor far beyond what she could have hoped to experience in her village, thus suggesting the potential lures of materialism. Beautiful, intelligent, and independent, Ojebeta becomes interested in education and learns to read Igbo. Eventually, Ma Palagada dies, and Ojebeta returns to her village, only to find that freedom for women in Igbo society is not so easy to achieve:

> No woman or girl in Ibuza was free, except those who committed the abominable sin of prostitution or those who had been completely cast off or rejected by their people for offending one custom or another. A girl was owned, in particular, by her father or someone in place of her father (p. 157).

This theme is reinforced when Ojebeta marries an educated man who repays the eight pounds to Ma Palagada's son to free her officially from slavery, only to place her in a new form of domestic servitude as his wife. At the end of the novel, the once-proud Ojebeta seems broken, passively accepting her subservience to her husband.

Emecheta's next book, *The Joys of Motherhood* (first published in 1979), continues the theme of the oppression of women in traditional Igbo society, though the book's exploration of tensions between this society and the modernization brought by colonialism introduces substantial complications that suggest positive aspects of life in traditional society. This kind of confrontation between modern and traditional values continues in *The Double Yoke* (1983a), which is set in contemporary Nigeria and builds upon Emecheta's experiences at the University of Calabar. This book is something of a departure in that its central character, Ete Kamba, is male, though it also features a strong female protagonist in his fiancée, Nko. The main narrative is framed by Ete Kamba's experiences as a creative writing student in the class of "Miss Bulewao," an internationally known Nigerian writer who has returned from abroad. Indeed, the main narrative, which tells the story of his engagement and subsequent breakup with Nko, is written largely by Ete Kamba as an assignment for this class. The story details the difficulties faced by the intelligent Nko as she seeks a university education in modern Nigeria while struggling with the conventional expectations of feminine behavior in her village. Ete Kamba is proud to think that his future wife will be a university graduate, but he has difficulty overcoming traditional masculine possessiveness and a need to dominate and control his would-be wife.

When Ete Kamba wins a scholarship to the university, Nko is so happy for him that she finally submits to his sexual advances, but Ete Kamba later interprets this submission as a sign of loose morals and accuses her of being a prostitute. Nko also faces sexual discrimination and harassment at the university, where she is eventually forced to submit to the sexual advances of her professor to assure her success in school. But Nko is a proud and defiant figure who threatens to expose the professor unless he makes sure that she graduates with first-class honors. The engagement eventually breaks up when Ete Kamba discovers Nko's relationship with Professor Ikot. He swears never to speak to his former fiancée again. However, by the end of the book, Ete Kamba (partially due to the influence of Miss Bulewao) has learned some valuable lessons and begins to try to understand Nko's point of view. Having heard that Nko, now pregnant by the professor, is contemplating suicide after the death of her father, Ete Kamba returns with her to her village to provide comfort and support.

Ete Kamba's turn toward a more enlightened understanding of Nko can be taken as a response to criticisms that Emecheta, in her earlier books, presents men in terms of negative stereotypes. *Destination Biafra* (1982) also represents something of a new turn in Emecheta's writing in its introduction of Debbie Ogedemgbe, a Western-educated heroine whose intelligence and bravery (she enlists in the federal army during the Biafran War) make her perhaps the strongest female character in all of Emecheta's fiction. This book, based on the events of the war, is a work of historical fiction, and Debbie is presented as a representative figure who not only seeks to mediate the rift between Nigeria and Biafra but also transcends the boundaries of race, class, gender, and ethnic group. Because of the intense political issues involved in the war itself, *Destination Biafra* may be Emecheta's most openly political novel. The book explores the difficult issues that lay behind the war and presents some powerful descriptions of the suffering of the Nigerian people on both sides of the conflict. It is also particularly critical of the role played by the British in exacerbating the conflict. To a certain extent, however, *Destination Biafra* focuses above all on sexual politics and on Debbie's relationship with various male figures in the text.

Emecheta extends the range of her work still further in *The Rape of Shavi* (1985, first published in 1983), a parable of cross-cultural exchange told in a mode of fantasy and science fiction. A group of Westerners flee England in an experimental aircraft, trying to escape what they believe to be an impending nuclear holocaust. But the craft crashes in the Sahara Desert, where the survivors discover the secluded community of Shavi, which has had no contact with the West and therefore maintains traditional African values and customs. The resulting comparison of Western and African values works very much to the advantage of the latter. Thus, *The Rape of Shavi* contrasts with the criticisms of traditional Igbo society in some of Emecheta's earlier work. The people of Shavi live a peaceful life and their society operates smoothly through communal sharing, dignity, and justice, though they do experience considerable hardships, particularly from the shortage of water in the arid region where they live. Their society is nominally patriarchal, but the women of Shavi exercise considerable power, especially through the strong element of solidarity and cooperation that unites them. By the end of the book, however, Shavi is in ruins, their once-idyllic society devastated by the effects of their contact with the West. This ending thus serves not only as a critique of the alienation and greed that inform life in the capitalist West, but also of these same tendencies in postcolonial Nigeria, a motif that is also a central focus of Emecheta's brief 1982 novel *Naira Power*.

In *The Family* (1990, also published as *Gwendolen*), Emecheta returns to the London immigrant community that was the focus of her first two books. However, the protagonist, Gwendolen Brillianton, is not an African but a black West Indian, thus extending Emecheta's exploration of racial and sexual oppression to the African diaspora. The book also treats important issues such as incest and interracial relationships. It begins in Jamaica, where Gwendolen lives with her grandmother after her parents have gone to London to live. At age nine, the young Gwendolen is raped by her Uncle Johnny. When she reveals her experience, she is declared wicked by the people of her village, making her life there even more miserable. Later Gwendolen moves to London, where her parents need her to help care for her three younger siblings. She suffers more poverty and abuse, eventually becoming pregnant at age sixteen by her own father. Gwendolen then suffers the hatred of her mother and hovers near madness. The father eventually commits suicide, and Gwendolen is never entirely reconciled with her mother. She does, however, begin to take control of her life and to establish supportive relationships, including a friendship with a white former boyfriend, who helps her care for her daughter, Iyamide.

In *Kehinde* (1994d) Emecheta tells the story of a relatively traditional Nigerian woman who lives for many years in London with her husband, Albert. She stays there with their children when Albert returns to Lagos in the 1970s to take advantage of opportunities available in the oil boom. By the time Kehinde finally makes her way back to Nigeria, she finds that Albert has taken another wife. She also finds that, after two decades in London, she no longer seems to fit in in Nigeria. She eventually returns to London and works at various jobs until she is able to complete her college education and receive a degree in sociology. More importantly, she succeeds in forging a sense of her own identity despite the confusions caused by the conflict between her traditional Igbo upbringing and her life in modern London.

In addition to these major novels and her autobiography, Emecheta has published a number of children's books, including *Titch the Cat* (1979), *Nowhere to Play* (1980), *The Moonlight Bride* (1983b, first published in 1980), and *The Wrestling Match* (1983d, first published in 1980). Her work has probably received more critical attention than that of any other African woman writer. However, the relative shortage of published criticism of her work in comparison to male writers (such as her countryman Achebe) indicates a lack of critical attention to African women writers that has only recently begun to be corrected. There is to date only one book-length study devoted to the work of Emecheta, Katherine Fishburn's *Reading Buchi Emecheta* (1995). There are, however, numerous critical essays on Emecheta's work, including one compilation edited by Marie Umeh (1995). Emecheta also figures prominently in most critical discussions of African women's writing. While some (mostly male) critics have been particularly disparaging of her treatment of male characters, by and large Emecheta's work has been treated positively by critics. Katherine Frank summarizes Emecheta's importance to African literature when she notes that, as a whole, "Emecheta's novels compose the most exhaustive and moving portrayal extant of the African women, an unparalleled portrayal in African fiction and with few equals in other literatures as well" (Frank 1982, 477).

Further Reading
See the suggestions for further reading at the end of Chapter 3.

Chapter 5

Ayi Kwei Armah: The Beautyful Ones Are Not Yet Born

The Beautyful Ones Are Not Yet Born (1969) focuses on the failure of postcolonial Ghanaian society, under the leadership of Kwame Nkrumah, to live up to the utopian hopes generated by the Nkrumah-led independence movement in the 1950s, despite the leadership of Kwame Nkrumah. The book gloomily concludes that the coming of independence brought little improvement in the lives of most Ghanaian people. "The sons of the nation were now in charge," the narrator tells us early in the book, but the most striking aspect of this phenomenon is "how completely the new thing took after the old" (p. 10). Indeed, the book is filled with such images of neocolonialism, suggesting that independence has led not to the liberation of utopia, but to the enslavement of a new form of colonial domination. The book, in its focus on the disappointment of utopian dreams, has much in common with the Western genre of dystopian fiction.[1] Thus, S. A. Gakwandi has compared the tone and atmosphere pervading Armah's text to those of George Orwell's *Nineteen Eighty-Four*, one of the central texts of Western dystopian fiction (Gakwandi 1992, 102–3). Armah creates this atmosphere by using a number of striking images and motifs. The real texture of everyday life in postcolonial Ghana is characterized through imagery involving corruption, decay, garbage, and excrement. On the other hand, the false promises presented by the rhetoric of Nkrumahism and the lure of Western commodity culture are represented by images of brightness and cleanliness that turn out to obscure an even more thorough corruption underneath.

---

[1] For a general discussion of this genre, see Booker (1994). On the adaptation of this genre to African literature, see Booker (1995).

The central image of this corrupt brightness is the "gleam," a metaphor for the almost hypnotic lure of Western commodities that enthralls the Ghanaian populace with fantasies of wealth they can never hope to achieve except through dishonesty. To some extent, the gleam is a literal, physical phenomenon. Material symbols of Western wealth (such as the Atlantic-Caprice tourist hotel) are painted in dazzling white and bathed in bright light. But this brightness merely obscures the exploitation and injustice that allow such wealth to exist amid the general poverty of Ghana. Armah's presentation of the gleam inverts the traditional Western image structure in which whiteness and light are associated with good, blackness and dark with evil. In addition, the use of the gleam in both a literal and a figurative sense exemplifies a technique that Armah uses throughout the book in which the two senses are conflated. Thus moral corruption and physical rot become inextricably intertwined. The gleam, as Lazarus discusses at some length, is a complex ideological construct that conditions the fundamental attitude toward reality of almost all of the characters in the book (Lazarus 1990, 56–66). By focusing the attention of the impoverished masses on the possibility (however remote) of future wealth, the gleam diverts their attention from their current suffering and helps to ensure that they will take no effective action to change the system.

The plot of *The Beautyful Ones* largely involves the efforts of the protagonist (simply called "the man") to resist the lure of the gleam in the face of pressure from his family and friends to succumb. And the lure is a powerful one. Viewing the Atlantic-Caprice early in the book, the man recognizes its attractions: "The gleam, in moments of honesty, had a power to produce a disturbing ambiguity within. It would be good to say that the gleam never did attract. It would be good, but it would be far from the truth" (p. 10). The pressure to succumb is made all the greater by the man's realization that the gleam has conquered virtually everyone else in Ghana, including his own family. He is thus made to feel an alien in his home, "the land of the loved ones," where "it was only the heroes of the gleam who did not feel that they were strangers" (p. 35). By the end of the book, however, the man's wife, Oyo, comes to appreciate his integrity in the face of the gleam, especially after she sees the ignominious fall and flight of the corrupt government minister Koomson, the book's central image of an individual whose life is entirely consumed with the pursuit of the gleam.

While concentrating on public political and social issues in postcolonial Ghana, *The Beautyful Ones* presents these issues primarily through their impact on the lives of individual characters. Central among these is the nameless protagonist, whom Fraser sees as a very positive figure, informed by an "acute and sensitive intelligence" and a "stubborn refusal to compromise on basic principles, an integrity of intention which exposes him to general obloquy and familial contempt" (Fraser 1980, 16). Lazarus similarly sees the man as a positive character, listing his virtues as "moral perspicacity," "social integrity," and "self-discipline" (Lazarus 1990, 72). Moreover, Lazarus believes that the man's efforts to resist corruption are not entirely futile and that he scores several small victories that suggest a bit of hope amid the generally bleak prospects presented by the novel (p. 74). Other critics see the man more negatively. Wright, for one, sees no suggestion of optimism in Armah's depiction of the man, while Leonard Kibera believes that the man does not successfully resist corruption (Kibera 1992, 97), and S. A. Gakwandi sees the man as weak and more interested in his own survival than in moral integrity (Gakwandi 1992, 111).

On the one hand, the lack of a name tends to make Armah's "man" seem typical of the citizenry of postcolonial Ghana. On the other hand, while the man's life does seem quite ordinary (he is a petty railway clerk who works at his banal job to support his wife and two children), he is not really presented as typical of the Ghanaian populace. Indeed, most of the other characters (including his wife Oyo) seem to find his refusal to participate in the corruption around him to be a kind of aberrant behavior. Fraser thus argues that, while the man could conceivably be taken as a sort of Everyman figure, it is the corrupt minister Koomson, rather than the man, who epitomizes the national moral outlook of Ghana: his "ideals correspond to the triumphant average" (Fraser 1980, 17). Given the man's apparent uniqueness in his society, his namelessness might suggest that he is the only character who maintains a genuine humanity amid the dehumanizing conditions in which he lives. Richard Priebe thus notes that the man "carries a tragic potential, for we are made to feel the dignity of this struggle with forces that overwhelmingly contrive against human dignity. He is . . . the only person in the context of the novel who is struggling to maintain his humanity" (Priebe 1976, 112–13).

The namelessness of the man is striking and significant, especially because, as Kofu Anyidoho notes, the names of characters are generally of great importance in Armah's work (Anyidoho 1992, 36–37). Indeed, names are quite generally significant in West African culture: "The name has an ontological significance in the thinking of traditional Africans. The name is the man and the man is the name" (Obiechina 1975, 82). The man's lack of a name may then indicate his lack of any genuine identity whatsoever. From this perspective, it is also interesting that Armah uses names (and indeed language in general) to indicate the general falseness of the society depicted in his book. Thus, when the man wanders into an affluent residential section, he notes that the new African bourgeoisie have not only moved into the houses once occupied by their European predecessors, but have even modified their names to take on a more European sound (p. 126).[2]

---

[2] In another example of linguistic decay, characters like Koomson use proverbs (a crucial component of traditional African oral culture) in debased and inappropriate ways (Obiechina 1975, 180).

Another important nameless character in *The Beautyful Ones* is the man's friend Teacher, a frustrated former Nkrumahist intellectual who has retreated into seclusion to escape the corrupt society that he finds around him. Actually, the characters of Teacher and the man tend to merge to a certain extent, further illustrating the anti-individualist nature of Armah's characterization. In the scene where the two converse, Teacher is frequently referred to as "the naked man," and many readers have trouble distinguishing between the two speakers. Again, the sixth chapter is a long monologue in which Teacher relates his experiences in the anticolonial independence movement and his growing sense of despair in the wake of Ghanaian national independence. But the point of view in this chapter frequently fluctuates between that of Teacher and that of the man. Finally, at the end of the book the man encounters a woman on the beach whom he recognizes as Maanan—an old friend of Teacher whom the man himself has probably never met.[3]

Teacher can thus be seen as an image of what the man might have become if he had continued his education rather than starting a family.[4] Labeled by profession rather than by name, Teacher can also be taken as a representative character whose alienation and despair are typical of many postcolonial intellectuals. Such alienated intellectuals are important figures in all of Armah's early novels (one thinks of Baako Onipa in *Fragments* and Modin Dofu and Solo Nkonum in *Why Are We So Blest?*), no doubt bespeaking some of his own frustrations as an intellectual in postcolonial Ghana. Indeed, it is tempting to see the Teacher as a spokesman for Armah himself, and some critics have done so. Moreover, this view of Teacher seems to be reinforced by the fact that the sixth chapter, dominated by Teacher, diagnoses the ills of postcolonial Ghana in a vein very reminiscent of Frantz Fanon, one of the major influences on all of Armah's work. Thus Griffiths argues that this chapter "dramatizes by image and scene Fanon's analysis of bourgeois corruption and psychic disturbance" (Griffiths 1992, 84).

Teacher, however, is not merely a spokesman for the positions espoused by Fanon. In his cynicism and despair, he is also an embodiment of the postcolonial decadence that Fanon warns against. In particular, his withdrawal from the world is precisely the opposite of the intense engagement with the everyday life of the people that Fanon sees as crucial to the function of intellectuals in postcolonial societies. For Fanon, the "native intellectual" must "return to the people" and through his contact with popular life learn to provide intellectual leadership in the ongoing struggle against cultural imperialism in the postcolonial era (Fanon 1968, 47). Thus, Fanon approvingly

---

[3] See Griffiths (1992, 82).

[4] Similarly, Koomson can be read as a suggestion of what might have become of the man if he had succumbed to the temptation of corruption and unscrupulous ambition.

quotes an address delivered by Sékou Touré at the 1959 Congress of Black Writers and Artists in Rome, in which Touré notes that the intellectual

> must be an element of that popular energy which is entirely called forth for the freeing, the progress, and the happiness of Africa. There is no place outside the fight for the artist or for the intellectual who is not himself concerned with and completely at one with the people in the great battle of Africa and of suffering humanity (quoted in Fanon 1968, 206).

In short, as Lazarus points out, a careful reading shows that *The Beautyful Ones* ultimately rejects Teacher's escapist reaction to the troubles of postcolonial Ghana, seeing it as a form of "living death" (Lazarus 1990, 72).

Teacher describes himself as "one of the dead people, the walking dead" (p. 61). Images of the living dead are in fact quite central to Armah's depiction of postcolonial Ghana, as are nightmare images of rotting and decay. Armah's Ghana is littered with garbage and excrement, which the man encounters at virtually every turn. Early in the book, for example, he comes upon what had once been a gleaming white waste container, still bearing the legend "KEEP YOUR COUNTRY CLEAN BY KEEPING YOUR CITY CLEAN" (p. 7). But this empty slogan turns out to be merely another example of linguistic decay in postcolonial Ghana, a sample of the empty rhetoric of the Nkrumah administration. The waste receptacle itself signifies the rather feeble and inconsequential efforts of the government to "clean up" postcolonial Ghana. The people have done their part, dutifully depositing their rubbish. But, because the government never empties the contents, the once sparkling container is overflowing with rotting garbage, the legend almost totally obscured. The box itself is barely visible, nearly buried beneath the mound of refuse that surrounds it.

The man next proceeds to the building ("the Block") where he is employed at the railway offices. This building, despite its "squat massiveness" was once intended to be beautiful. Each of its bricks is imprinted with a design resembling the petal of a hibiscus flower, and the bricks themselves are carefully laid. A closer look, however, shows that these original good intentions have gone badly to seed. The building, constructed in 1927, is by 1966 covered with multiple coats of paint and plaster that not only obscure the flower designs but also only partially conceal the dirt and grime over which they have been haphazardly applied. The overall effect is one of "lumpy heaviness," and the building becomes little more than a decaying remnant of colonial days, a sign that things are getting worse, rather than better, in postcolonial Ghana (pp. 10–11). Inside the building, the man slowly mounts a stairway. Its banister is one of the book's most striking and effective images. The decaying wooden rail, looking like a "very long piece of diseased skin," is covered by ancient coats of cracking and peeling paint; it seems that for many years "different kinds of wood and floor polish" have been used in a hopeless attempt to cover the rot (p. 12).

The banister thus symbolically indicts the policies of the Nkrumahist regime in Ghana. The government had not attempted to create a genuinely new society; rather it merely covered over colonial rot with ineffectual layers of postcolonial polish. Further, this banister serves as the book's most powerful image of hopelessness and futility. Despite the efforts at painting and polishing, the narrator tells us,

> the wood underneath would win and win till the end of time. Of that there was no doubt possible, only the pain of hope perennially doomed to disappointment.... In the natural course of things it would always take the newness of the different kinds of polish and the vaunted cleansing power of the chemicals in them, and it would convert all to victorious filth (p. 12).

Of course, this image does not necessarily indicate that progress is impossible in Ghana but simply that any genuine progress requires radical and revolutionary transformation, not mere surface repairs: this banister needs to be replaced, not polished. Further, the ultimate and inevitable triumph of the wood might even be taken as an optimistic suggestion that the technological civilization of the West will ultimately succumb to the more nature-oriented culture of Africa—the decay of the wood as an entirely natural process contrasts dramatically with the unnatural rot of postcolonial Ghanaian society.

In any case, the banister image suggests that the changes undertaken in Nkrumah's Ghana were, in fact, superficial, despite the socialist rhetoric of the regime. Armah expresses this feeling quite clearly in his essay "African Socialism: Utopian or Scientific?" where he argues that in Africa socialism has often been a mere "sloganeering gimmick" that has not sought to bring genuine revolutionary change (Armah 1967, 27). Indeed, postcolonial African regimes, despite their frequent recourse to the revolutionary rhetoric of socialism, have typically sunk into an "arrestingly vulgar, premature decadence" that prevents such change (p. 28). Armah recommends the work of Fanon as an alternative to Nkrumah and as an example of the kind of revolutionary thought that African socialism needs to draw upon (pp. 29–30).

This recommendation comes as no surprise: the model of decadent African socialism presented by Armah in this essay is taken almost directly from Fanon. The same can be said for the overall vision of *The Beautyful Ones,* and Lazarus is certainly correct when he argues that "above all ... *The Beautyful Ones* needs to be read in light of Fanon's classic essay on 'The Pitfalls of National Consciousness'" (Lazarus 1990, 55). In this essay, Fanon warns against the potential for disaster in postcolonial African nations if those nations simply replace the colonial bourgeoisie by an African bourgeoisie, while leaving the basic class structure of the societies still in place. In particular, Fanon argues that the African bourgeoisie lack the historical energy that had enabled the European bourgeoisie to defeat their feudal-aristocratic predecessors and to sweep into power in Europe in the seventeenth to nineteenth centuries. The African bourgeoisie are mere imitators of their Western masters, who were already decadent when they colonized Africa in the late nineteenth century. According to Fanon, the African bourgeoisie thus

> follows the Western bourgeoisie along its path of negation and decadence without ever having emulated it in its first stages of exploration and invention. . . . It is already senile before it has come to know the petulance, the fearlessness, or the will to succeed of youth (Fanon 1968, 153).

The bourgeoisie, decadent before their time, can never lead Africa in the building of an energetic new society and thus, for Fanon, must be displaced from positions of power at all costs.

Teacher invokes this same premature decadence when he rails against African leaders who were "old before they had even been born into power and ready only for the grave" (p. 81). Armah presents a striking image of premature decadence when Teacher describes a picture he saw in his school days in a book of "freaks and oddities." This particular picture was of a seven-year-old child already grown gray with premature old age. This "old manchild . . . had been born with all the features of a human baby, but within seven years it had completed the cycle from babyhood to infancy to youth, to maturity and old age, and in its seventh year it had died a natural death" (p. 63). This manchild joins the dazzling Atlantic-Caprice, the overflowing rubbish container, and the decaying wooden banister as excellent examples of Armah's ability to represent abstract ideas through strikingly concrete visual images. The premature aging of this child clearly serves as a generalized image of the premature decadence that Fanon decries in *The Wretched of the Earth*. It also serves as a specific image of the death of the dream of Nkrumahism, identifying that death with Nkrumah's ascension to the lifetime presidency in 1964, seven years after independence.

This image of the death of the original Nkrumahist dream is linked with another historical event. The book suggests that the 1966 military coup in which Nkrumah was deposed was an event of little consequence to the Ghanaian populace and was unlikely to lead to any real improvement in conditions. This combination suggests an air of hopelessness and despair that again recalls dystopian works like Orwell's *Nineteen Eighty-Four*. Wright thus emphasizes the dystopian nature of the text in a number of articles (1990, 1992a) and in his chapter on *The Beautyful Ones* in *Ayi Kwei Armah's Africa* (1989). He argues that the book is bleak and pessimistic throughout and that in the end it presents "no Utopias, prospective or retrospective" (Wright 1989, 135). Numerous critics have concluded that Armah's attitude toward his native Ghana is one of pure negativity and disgust. In this sense, he has been compared to V. S. Naipaul, against whom similar charges have frequently been leveled. Kibera makes such a comparison and also suggests that Armah's political message in *The Beautyful Ones* is dogmatic and simplistic (Kibera 1992, 98–99).

The first of these charges, however, can be countered by the fact that numerous aspects of the book can in fact be taken to suggest possible sources of hope. As Fraser argues, the book subtly extends its historical scope beyond the 1960s by setting this period against "a backdrop of centuries of oppression, a recurring cycle of despair" (Fraser 1980, 26).[5] But, lest this suggestion of the long legacy of corruption and oppression in Ghana be taken as a sign that things can never improve, Fraser also notes that characters like Teacher and the man are still able to "discern the original wholesomeness that lies somewhere beneath the festering refuse" (p. 27). If this wholesomeness can still be discerned, it can perhaps be recovered. In addition, the book's title certainly suggests a coming future in which the "beautyful ones" will be born at last: the title is taken from a legend the man sees on the back of a bus that surrounds a picture of a flower, a traditional symbol of rebirth (p. 183).[6] This image, meanwhile, links up with Teacher's earlier reminder that "out of the decay and the dung there is always a new flowering" (p. 85). Noting such images, Lazarus concludes that, like the leftist dramatist Bertolt Brecht, Armah seeks "to describe the preconditions of and prevailing constraints to change. The novel is formulated upon the premise that it is only by knowing one's world, by seeing it for what it is, that one can ever genuinely aspire to bring about its revolutionary transformation" (Lazarus 1990, 48).

For many, the frequent use of excremental imagery in *The Beautyful Ones* has been taken as a sign of the book's negativity. Harold Collins argues that Armah's references to excrement indicate disgust and are chosen because "of all man's works and creations his excrement is most disgusting" (Collins 1971, 42). But Armah's symbolic use of excrement is surely more complicated than Collins indicates. For example, the book clearly draws a parallel between the production of excrement as a result of the consumption of food and the production of garbage as a result of the consumption of Western commodities. But, again, the first of these processes is natural, the second unnatural. This suggests that Armah is commenting on the commodity culture of Western capitalism by employing excremental imagery to subvert official pretentiousness and seriousness. Mikhail Bakhtin describes a similar use of excremental imagery in the work of François Rabelais. Bakhtin pays particular attention to Rabelais's treatment of the "grotesque" body, of the aspects of human life (like sex and excrement) associated with the "material bodily lower stratum"

---

[5] Fraser, incidentally, also compares Armah to Naipaul, but suggests that both writers have perhaps been criticized unfairly for what is really nothing more than "a determination to see things straight" (Fraser 1980, 15).

[6] Compare here the scene near the end of Maxim Gorky's autobiographical *My Universities*, in which the enlightened peasant Barinov tells the young Gorky, "Evil men are the truth, but where are the good ones? Not even invented yet, oh no!" (Gorky 1979, 157).

that call attention to the status of human beings as physical creatures living in a physical world. Bakhtin notes traditional attempts to view the body as a seamless classical whole by denying excremental, sexual, and other processes that emphasize the dynamic interaction between body and world; he then suggests that these attempts represent a denial of history. But the "unfinished and open body (dying, bringing forth and being born) is not separated from the world by clearly defined boundaries; it is blended with the world, with animals, with objects" (Bakhtin 1984b, 26–27). Moreover, the dynamic nature of this blending and of the carnivalesque representation of body functions in Rabelais thrusts the subject directly into the contemporaneous flow of history: "The material bodily lower stratum and the entire system of degradation, turnovers, and travesties presented this essential relation to time and to social and historical transformation" (p. 81). In short, the transfer of physical material from the interior of the body into the outside world (and vice versa) provides a graphic reminder that human beings are part of that world and undermines the Kantian duality of subject and object that underlies the alienated relationship between individuals and their surroundings in the modern Western world.

In addition, Bakhtin suggests that traditional attempts to taxonomize the body into "high" and "low" segments represent the oppression of marginal social groups by dominant ones in class society. According to Bakhtin, Rabelais's explicit focus on the "material lower bodily stratum" undermines this movement with its transgressive challenge to the usual hierarchical privileging of the "high" parts of the body over the "low"—while simultaneously calling attention to the fact that the same physical processes occur in the bodies of both kings and beggars. In this way, Rabelais's excremental images demonstrate the artificiality of social hierarchies and provide a metaphor for political revolution. Thus Holquist concludes that "Bakhtin's carnival . . . is revolution itself" (Holquist 1984, xviii). At times, Armah hints that his excremental imagery is also meant to subvert official hierarchies. For example, he describes the lowly "shitman" who cleans the latrines at the Block early in the morning before anyone else arrives; he follows this description with a sardonic reference to the biblical prediction that in the coming new order "the last shall be first" (p. 104). This statement both challenges the official seriousness of the Bible and also uses the biblical passage to suggest a possible inversion of the existing power structure. And there is certainly a carnivalesque aspect to Koomson's fate: after the coup that thrusts him from power, he is reduced to escaping arrest by crawling out (head first, in another sign of carnivalesque inversion) through the latrine next to the man's house (pp. 168–69). Even Wright, who sees the book's vision as almost entirely negative, finds Armah's excremental imagery "exuberant" and argues that it functions as a "leveling metaphor, bringing the Koomsons back to the filth and squalor out of which they have corruptly carved a niche of cleanness and prosperity" (Wright 1990, 30; Wright 1992a, 31).[7]

At the same time, Wright notes the simplicity of Armah's political vision, arguing that only the inventiveness of Armah's language saves *The Beautyful Ones* from "the cartoonlike banality of its political themes" (Wright 1990, 30). Similarly, Gakwandi complains of the "shoddiness of Armah's political sentiments" (Gakwandi 1992, 108). Such critics are part of a long Western tradition of prejudice against political statements of any kind in literature. According to this tradition (exemplified by American New Criticism), *all* political sentiments are shoddy, and all political themes are banal. But in postcolonial Ghana (or postcolonial Africa in general), politics is a very real and palpable part of the texture of everyday life. Any literary representation of postcolonial life that ignores politics would be irresponsible and unrealistic at best. In addition, it is useful to recall that *The Beautyful Ones* is a work of satire. Satire as a genre works through methods of simplification and emphasis that call attention to specific ills that might otherwise be obscured by the complexities of everyday life. From this point of view, the political statement made by Armah's book is not simplistic, but simply focused. Finally, it might also be useful to consider Armah's pointed critique of neocolonialism within the context of the "abuse" tradition, a very well developed aspect of African oral culture in which an opponent's defects are outlined in colorful (and often highly exaggerated) fashion in order to make a point. The abuse tradition often focuses on physical attributes of an opponent to call attention to intellectual or moral shortcomings. One thinks here of Armah's description of Koomson's obesity, flatulence, and body odor as signs of the minister's political corruption and moral decay. Thus, reading *The Beautyful Ones* through either the Western genre of satire or the African genre of abuse (or, preferably, both) justifies the stark political oppositions of the book as literary strategy rather than philosophical simplicity. Ultimately, Armah's book is powerful and aesthetically successful not despite his political engagement but because of it.

Historical Background
The Republic of Ghana is a nation with a population of just over fifteen million (1990) covering an area of approximately 92,000 square miles, most of which is low fertile plains and scrubland. Its capital is Accra, a city of approximately one million inhabitants located on the southern coast. The official national language is English, though five other languages have official

---

[7] Elsewhere, Wright emphasizes the specifically African nature of Armah's excremental imagery, noting that it owes a great deal to the "graphic and grotesque hyperbole of the traditional griot" (Wright 1989, 82).

status in various regions. Most common among these languages is Akan, spoken by the Ashanti, who comprise about half of the total population. Two-thirds of Ghana's population live in small rural villages. Over sixty percent of the inhabitants are Christians (located principally in the south and in urban areas), while just over twenty percent ascribe to traditional African religions and just under twenty percent are Muslims (located principally in the north). Approximately thirty percent of the adult population are literate, mostly in English. Ghana has little industry. Most manufactured goods are imported from abroad, as are much of the staple food supply and most of the crude petroleum. Ghana's agricultural products include cocoa, coffee, timber, bananas, kola nuts, and palm oil. It also produces gold, industrial diamonds, manganese, and some petroleum. The per capita GNP (1989) is about $380.

The name Ghana derives from a powerful African empire that flourished between the Sahara Desert and the headwaters of the Niger and Senegal Rivers from the fourth to the thirteenth century A.D. The central region of what is now Ghana was also the center of the Ashanti Empire, which grew in wealth and power from the thirteenth to the nineteenth century. The Ashanti were defeated in a series of wars with the invading British, who annexed the Ashanti lands to the British Gold Coast colony in 1901. Ghana became independent on March 6, 1957, thus becoming the first British African colony to gain independence (with the exception of South Africa). As a result, and especially because of the leadership of Kwame Nkrumah, Ghana became a model for other postcolonial nations in Africa. Ghana thus has a long and eventful history that can provide important material for postcolonial writers who seek to contribute to the development of positive and viable cultural identities for their new nations.

Central to the history of the founding of Ghana is Kwame Nkrumah, one of the towering figures of the African anticolonial independence movements of the 1950s. Nkrumah was born in Nkroful in 1909. His father was a goldsmith, his mother a petty trader in the village market. He was educated in mission schools, graduated from Achimota College in 1930, and became a teacher. Because of his brilliance as a student, he was able to go the United States for further education in 1935. He graduated from Lincoln University in Pennsylvania in 1939, then earned master's degrees from Lincoln and the University of Pennsylvania. But his education in America went well beyond the classroom; he learned a great deal from the long African-American tradition of struggle against white domination, both in his extensive interactions with African-Americans and in his readings of thinkers like W. E. B. Du Bois. He then studied at the London School of Economics, where he met the numerous revolutionary activists who lived in London at that time, including George Padmore and C. L. R. James. By the time he returned to Ghana in 1947, Nkrumah was a committed Marxist-socialist, dedicated to ending colonial rule in Africa. In 1949, he founded the Convention People's Party, whose activities led to his imprisonment by the British in 1950. He was released in 1951 when his party swept the general elections, culminating a four-year nonviolent revolution against colonial rule that must be counted among the great political accomplishments of the century. Nkrumah became prime minister under the colonial government in 1952, and the next five years saw the gradual dismantling of a colonial system that had once seemed insurmountable. During the 1950s, Nkrumah became a well-known African intellectual and political leader and a leading spokesman for pan-Africanism—the idea of African unity against colonial oppression as opposed to individual national struggles for independence. In 1957 he became the first leader of independent Ghana. In 1960 after the institution of a republican system, he became the first president and ruled the nation as a one-party socialist state modeled to a certain extent on the example of the Soviet Union.

As the leader of postcolonial Ghana, Nkrumah made gestures toward African unity by effecting a loose union with Guinea in 1959 and with Mali in 1960. Meanwhile, poverty and corruption in Ghanaian society led to increasing unrest, and Nkrumah's rule became increasingly authoritarian in response. In 1964 he became president for life, growing more and more distant from the general population amid a cult of personality that continually emphasized his greatness. In an event that provides one of the central plot elements of *The Beautyful Ones*, Nkrumah was deposed in a military coup on February 24, 1966. He went into exile in Guinea, then in Romania, where he died in 1972. Ghana, meanwhile, continued to be troubled. The government was returned to civilian control in 1969, but continuing social discontent and economic decline led to another coup in January 1972. A subsequent military coup (led by Flight-Lieutenant Jerry Rawlings) again overturned the government in 1979; the failed policies of the new civilian government installed in 1979 led to another coup (also led by Rawlings) in 1981, after which Rawlings himself remained in control of the government as chair of the Provisional National Defense Council. During the 1980s the economy showed significant signs of growth, and in 1992 Rawlings easily won a democratic multiparty presidential election.

Biographical Background
Ayi Kwei Armah was born in 1939 to Fante-speaking parents in Takoradi in the British colony of the Gold Coast. He received secondary education just outside of Accra at Achimota College, by then widely respected as one of the finest secondary schools in Africa. The political atmosphere at Achimota, Nkrumah's alma mater, was highly charged and contributed greatly to Armah's later development. In 1959, after working briefly for Radio Ghana,

Armah traveled to the United States, where he spent a year at Groton School, an exclusive preparatory school in Massachusetts. He entered Harvard University in the fall of 1960, intending to major in literature but eventually shifting his focus to the social sciences. According to Armah himself, this change was partially motivated by an attempt to come to grips with the assassination of the Congolese anticolonialist leader Patrice Lumumba in 1961, and it shows the intense concern with social and political issues that would come to characterize all of Armah's fiction (Armah 1985a, 1752). Armah's sense of political commitment was further energized by the atmosphere of increasing political activism he encountered in the United States, especially among African Americans. Figures such as Marcus Garvey and Malcolm X were especially important influences during this period. By 1963, Armah had decided not to complete his degree at Harvard and returned to Ghana to participate in the process of revolutionary change he hoped was underway there.

The Beautyful Ones Are Not Yet Born, Armah's first novel, was published in 1968, and it is clear that Armah's early enthusiasm over the prospects of postcolonial Ghana had already been colored by an extreme skepticism toward the conditions he observed around him. Indeed, all of Armah's first three novels—*The Beautyful Ones, Fragments* (1970), and *Why Are We So Blest?* (1974, first published in 1972)—are highly critical of the ills of postcolonial Ghanaian society. *Fragments* focuses on the experiences of Baako Onipa, a young Ghanaian intellectual who returns from his schooling in the United States to find a society rife with corruption and enthralled by the lure of Western commodity culture. Frustrated by his family's disappointment that he did not return wealthy from the United States and disillusioned by his experiences working as a television producer for Ghanavision, Baako eventually suffers a nervous breakdown. The depiction of Ghanaian society in *Fragments* is bleak, though there are positive elements in Armah's presentation of Baako's grandmother and of Juana, an African-American psychiatrist from Puerto Rico working in Ghana. *Why Are We So Blest?* is informed by an even more pessimistic vision, suggesting that the corruption associated in Armah's earlier books with postcolonial African societies has infected even supposedly revolutionary African anticolonialist movements. The book revolves around Modin Dofu, an American-educated African intellectual who comes back to Africa with his white American girlfriend, hoping to join the anticolonial revolution in "Congheria" (a sort of amalgam of Algeria and the Congo). Much of the book, however, is narrated by Solo Nkonum, another African intellectual, who has become completely cynical about the possibilities of successful revolutionary change and who learns of Modin's murder by a group of French soldiers. Armah's political vision during the period of these early novels is clearly expressed in essays such as "African Socialism:

Utopian or Scientific?" (1967), where he expresses his disappointment with the failure of postcolonial African societies to fulfill the utopian expectations created by the rhetoric of the anticolonial independence movements. He is particularly critical of one-time heroes of anticolonialism such as Ghana's Nkrumah and the Senegalese poet and politician Léopold Senghor (one of the founders of the Négritude movement and president of Senegal from 1960 to 1980). Armah also makes clear in this essay his sympathy with the kinds of socialist ideals originally espoused by Karl Marx and Friedrich Engels, though Frantz Fanon emerges as the most important influence on Armah's thought.

Armah's next two novels turn to the Ghanaian past for inspiration in the project to build a better future. As a result they are much more affirmative in tone than the three earlier novels of postcolonialism. *Two Thousand Seasons* (1979b, first published in 1973) employs a narrative voice reminiscent of traditional Akan oral narratives to tell the story of Ghana from the original migration of the Ashanti to the area, through the intrusions of Arab slave traders and European colonizers, and into the contemporary postcolonial era. The book points out the role of foreign invaders in the breakdown of the traditional African "way" of reciprocity and communal cooperation. It also acknowledges the complicity of the Africans themselves in this breakdown. However, it also suggests great hope for a utopian future that would take its inspiration from the traditions of the past. *The Healers* (1979a) is based on events leading to the fall of the Ashanti Empire in the 1860s and 1870s, focusing especially on the second Anglo-Ashanti war of 1873–1874. It is thus far more focused than the sweeping historical narrative that informs *Two Thousand Seasons*, though it continues to employ narrative techniques reminiscent of traditional oral storytelling. Armah's latest novel, *Osiris Rising,*(1995) was published in Africa in 1995 after years of silence. This novel builds upon the Isis–Osiris myth to address many of the concerns of Armah's earlier work, including African history, the possibility of a better African future, and the relationship between Africa and African Americans.

Armah is widely recognized as one Africa's most important writers. As a result, his work has received extensive critical attention, including three book-length studies. Robert Fraser's brief book was the first of these and still provides an accessible introduction to Armah's work (Fraser 1980). Derek Wright's *Ayi Kwei Armah's Africa: The Sources of His Fiction* (1989) is more extensive and is particularly useful for its explorations of the backgrounds of Armah's books in traditional African culture. Neil Lazarus's *Resistance in Postcolonial African Fiction* (1990) is probably the most sophisticated study of Armah's work, placing it within the broader context of African anticolonial resistance and the postcolonial aftermath. Fraser's book is particularly affirmative of Armah's project, while Lazarus is uncomfortable with some of the political positions taken by Armah in his later novels, and Wright is at times downright hostile to Armah's positions. All agree, however, that Armah is an important and gifted writer. A number of the many published essays on Armah's work have been conveniently gathered in a collection edited by Wright (1992b).

Further Reading

Bretton, Henry L. 1967. *The Rise and Fall of Kwame Nkrumah: A Study of Personal Rule in Africa*. New York: Praeger.

Davidson, Basil. 1989. *Black Star: A View of the Life and Times of Kwame Nkrumah*. Boulder, Colo.: Westview Press.

Davidson, Basil, and Paul Strand. 1976. *Ghana: An African Portrait*. Millerton, N.Y.: Aperture.

Edgerton, Robert B. 1995. *The Fall of the Asante Empire: The Hundred-Year War for Africa's Gold Coast*. New York: Free Press.

Fitch, Robert, and Mary Oppenheimer. 1966. *Ghana: End of an Illusion*. New York: Monthly Review Press.

James, C. L. R. 1977. *Nkrumah and the Ghana Revolution*. London: Allison and Busby.

Jones, Trevor. 1976. *Ghana's First Republic, 1960–1966: The Pursuit of the Political Kingdom*. London: Methuen.

Kellner, Douglas. 1987. *Kwame Nkrumah*. New York: Chelsea House.

Marable, Manning. 1987. *African and Caribbean Politics: From Kwame Nkrumah to the Grenada Revolution*. London: Verso.

Nkrumah, Kwame. 1965. *Consciencism: Philosophy and Ideology for Decolonization and Development with Particular Reference to the African Revolution*. New York: Monthly Review Press.

———. 1966. *Neo-colonialism: The Last Stage of Imperialism*. New York: International Publishers.

———. 1968. *Ghana: The Autobiography of Kwame Nkrumah*. New York: International Publishers.

———. 1970. *Class Struggle in Africa*. New York: International Publishers.

Wilks, Ivor. 1993. *Forests of Gold: Essays on the Akan and the Kingdom of Asante*. Athens: Ohio University Press.

brief book is an excellent example of the broad scope of Aidoo's concerns. Chimalum Nwankwo compares Aidoo to writers such as Ngugi wa Thiong'o and Ousmane Sembène in terms of her ability to deal with "so many problems" and to remain aware that "a campaign for social justice is meaningful only when all disadvantaged people in human society receive undiscriminating attention" (Nwankwo 1986, 155).

"Into a Bad Dream" begins with several pages of visually striking typographic experimentation and sets the tone for the book in terms of both form and content. This section immediately introduces many of the important issues of the book, particularly the problem of the ongoing neocolonial domination of Africa by the West. The narrator begins with a complaint about the difficulty of arguing with "a nigger who is a 'moderate'" and who accepts the bourgeois values inherited from Europe by postcolonial African societies. Particularly troublesome, continues the narrator, is the "academic-pseudo-intellectual" whose Western education leaves him indoctrinated in modes of thought that imply the fundamental superiority of Western culture. Such intellectuals believe that the only road to progress in Africa is the European road, based on the concepts of "universal truth, universal art, universal literature and the Gross National Product." The narrator calls such intellectuals "dogs" whose masters are in the West, making clear her disdain for their Eurocentric modes of thought. She also directly links such Western bourgeois ideas with the image of the slave forts that still stand in Ghana and other parts of Africa as reminders of past atrocities committed against Africans in the name of European cultural and economic progress. To continue to accept the superiority of Western ideas, she clearly implies, is to continue the legacy of slavery and colonialism into the postcolonial present (p. 6).

This aspect of Aidoo's text clearly echoes the warnings of Frantz Fanon in *The Wretched of the Earth* that decolonization would not lead to liberation for the African people if this process merely involved the replacement of a ruling colonial white bourgeoisie by a new postcolonial black bourgeoisie with basically the same values. Many of Aidoo's descriptions of postcolonial Ghanaian society in *Our Sister Killjoy* reinforce this point, leading the narrator to conclude (using capital letters for emphasis) that life in Ghana in the 1960s, Nkrumah or no Nkrumah, is "JUST LIKE THE GOOD OLD DAYS / BEFORE INDEPENDENCE," except, of course, that rich Africans now join rich Europeans and Americans in reaping the benefits of the exploitation of Africa and its people (p. 56).

Perhaps the most striking scene in the first section of *Our Sister Killjoy* involves Sissie's attendance at a cocktail party at the home of the German ambassador in preparation for her departure for Germany. There she encounters many of the accoutrements of upper-class European civilization for the first time. She also meets Sammy, a fellow Ghanaian who seems to have

Chapter 6

Ama Ata Aidoo:
Our Sister Killjoy

Ama Ata Aidoo, in an introduction she wrote to one edition of Armah's *The Beautyful Ones Are Not Yet Born*, emphasizes the tradition of feminine independence in Ghana, a tradition that obviously underlies her own work in important ways. Aidoo argues that Western models of the oppression of women by men are not adequate to describe the situation in Ghana (Aidoo 1969, x). This same insight informs much of Aidoo's creative writing, including *Our Sister Killjoy* (1994b), which focuses on the experiences of Sissie, a young Ghanaian woman who pursues her education in Ghana, receives a government grant to attend an international program in Germany, then returns to Ghana via England. But Sissie's private experience is used to make a number of important political points, leading Kofi Owusu to proclaim that Aidoo's book is an important "contribution to ongoing attempts to rescue the African woman from the fringes of African literature and restore flesh, blood, voice and credibility to her" (Owusu 1990, 342). As C. L. Innes puts it, "The dilemma of the woman who has views of her own, and the determination not to dissociate the personal and the political become the central concerns of Aidoo's novel" (Innes 1992, 138).

The book is divided into four parts, each with its own subtitle. "Into a Bad Dream" is set in Ghana and describes Sissie's preparation to leave for Germany. "The Plums" is set in Germany and details Sissie's reaction to German culture and her relationship with Marija, a lonely German housewife. "From Our Sister Killjoy" describes Sissie's stopover in England and her meetings with African expatriates living there, including her lover. The last section, "A Love Letter," consists primarily of Sissie's farewell letter to this lover, written aboard the plane on her way back to Ghana. Together, these sections show how a number of crucial issues relating to colonialism, neocolonialism, and gender affect Sissie's consciousness. Indeed, this relativel been chosen specifically to assure her that "going to Europe was altogether more like a dress rehearsal for a journey to paradise" (p. 9). Sammy thus functions as an image of the modern African who has succumbed to the dazzling lure of Western commodities, mistaking superior Western material wealth for moral and cultural superiority. Sissie, not surprisingly, reacts to Sammy's performance with discomfort, as she will continue to react to the numerous Sammys she will meet on her travels (p. 9). After the party, Sissie departs for Germany aboard a South African airliner, where she is asked to move to the rear with the other black passengers, even though she has a first-class ticket. She thus experiences early on the kind of racial consciousness that will inform all of her stay in Europe. Waiting for a train in Frankfurt, she overhears a German woman calling the attention of her young daughter to "das Schwartze Mädchen," making Sissie feel like an exotic species of animal on display before the inquiring gaze of Europe (p. 12). The section ends as Sissie bemoans the fact that "someone somewhere would always see in any kind of difference, an excuse to be mean." She then notes that the racial difference of Africans has traditionally been used as an excuse for European brutalization and exploitation (p. 13).

"The Plums" focuses on Sissie's relationship with Marija, a German woman who speaks almost no English and who is so woefully ignorant of other peoples and cultures that she initially thinks Sissie may be from India; when she is told that Sissie is from Ghana, she asks if that is near Canada (pp. 19, 24). She is also quite surprised to learn that when Sissie was in Christian school in Ghana, she was given the name Mary, a name that is quite common in European nations but is decidedly un-African. That Sissie has been forced to accept a European name functions as an image of the continuing impact on Ghanaian culture of Christian missionaries who believe that

> For a child to grow up
> To be a
> Heaven-worthy individual,
> He had
> To have
> Above all, a
> Christian name (p. 25).

On the other hand, it is also significant that Sissie has rejected this name, along with its resonances of conventional feminine purity and "being a lady" (p. 24). Meanwhile, Sissie, alone in a foreign land, turns out to have more in common with Marija than the similarity in their names. Marija, too, is alone, though she has a husband and infant son. The son, Adolf, is too young to provide much company, and the husband, also named Adolf, seems to be away at work all the time, attempting to earn enough to provide material comforts for his family. He thus becomes the typical commodified Western man, whose only life is his work. But Marija has no opportunity to explore her genuine human potential: she may enjoy the comforts of a Western middle-class lifestyle, but she has little to do except tend her garden and dream, like Flaubert's Emma Bovary, of someday living vicariously through her son (p. 60).

The material comforts of the West are symbolized in the book particularly by food, and Sissie is continually amazed at the abundance of food of various kinds available in Germany. Marija, attempting to make contact with Sissie though the two do not have a common language, continually offers her food. The title of this section, in fact, derives from the plump Bavarian plums (symbols of European abundance) that Marija brings to Sissie by the bagful. These plums indicate a contrast between European wealth and African poverty. Thus, while Europe produces a vast variety of luxury products for its own consumption, Ghana in the era of neocolonialism is forced to scavenge for leftovers. This once proud territory now "picks tiny bits of / Undigested food from the / Offal of the industrial world" (p. 53). But these plums, which Marija grows in her own rather Edenic garden, can also be taken as symbols of forbidden fruit, in particular lesbian sexuality: the friendship of Marija and Sissie gradually deepens until a crucial scene in which Marija finally makes a sexual advance, which the surprised Sissie repels almost by reflex.

In its frank and sensitive treatment of lesbian sexuality, *Our Sister Killjoy* breaks new ground in the African novel. However, Marija's sexual advance also has a pathetic aspect and shows how far Europeans must go to try to achieve any sort of human contact amid the alienating consequences of modern capitalism. In the aftermath of this abortive sexual encounter, Marija cries silently to herself, and Sissie suddenly realizes just how lonely her new friend really is. In particular, she realizes that in the individualistic milieu of Europe, Marija experiences a depth of loneliness that goes far beyond the loneliness that anyone in a communal society (like those of precolonial Africa) would ever be likely to feel. Sissie also realizes that much of her revulsion at Marija's advance comes from a horror of lesbianism instilled in her (and her culture) by the teachings of Christian missionaries, for whom such a relationship would amount to a "C-r-i-m-e / A Sin / S-o-d-o-m-y" (p. 67). On the other hand, as Nwankwo suggests, Sissie's rejection of Marija's advance can clearly be taken as a symbol of the "gap between the European female and African female's response" (Nwankwo 1986, 157). These women have much in common and should be able to band together, but the legacy of colonialism creates a racial and cultural split that is very difficult to overcome.

In addition, the text suggests that the kind of intense sense of loneliness and lack of fulfillment through personal relationships that Marija feels may have been a major motivation for colonial expansion as Europeans, seeking to fill the void at the heart of their lives, attempted to compensate by conquering most of the rest of the world (pp. 65–66). Sissie thus ponders the injustice of the fact that the entire world has had to pay so dearly for the fundamental unhappiness of Europeans. One can also detect a hint in Aidoo's text that the monstrous project of colonialism was dehumanizing to the European colonizers as well as their victims, and thus made the colonizers all the more unhappy (p. 66). Aidoo also uses the German setting to supplement the personal story of Marija's loneliness with numerous reminders of some of the more violent and horrifying aspects of European history. In particular (as the names of Marija's husband and son make clear), the text resounds with reminders of the Nazi past. Indeed, Sissie herself is intensely aware of the Nazi legacy of the beautiful German countryside she is visiting. When she and her fellow participants in the international camp plant pine trees in a German forest, they are supervised by a group of German women, all wearing black. This makes Sissie wonder if they are all widows of husbands killed "Building the walls of / The Third Reich," that is, in World War II (p. 36). The narrator reminds us that Marija, in walking the Bavarian countryside, is "Walking / Where the / Führer's feet had trod" (p. 48). Marija urges Sissie to visit Munich, which Marija proudly sees as the heart of her Bavarian culture. Sissie, however, refuses because this city was the site of the beginning of Hitler's rise to political power:

> Munich, Marija,
> Is
> The Original Adolf of the pub-brawls
> and mobsters who were looking for
> a
> Führer (p. 81).

Of course, Aidoo is perfectly well aware that African history has had its own violent episodes, and the narrator at one point even suggests that the Nazis for her are reminiscent of the "Abome kings of Dahomey" (p. 37). Aidoo also attempts to provide a broader historical background in her depiction of the drive to control others that she sees as central to Western civilization. In particular, the pastoral German setting of "The Plums" is dominated not only by memories of the racial hatred of Nazism, but also by a giant medieval castle that recalls the slave forts of Ghana and serves as a reminder that oppression in Europe predates Hitler by a considerable margin. This castle, one of the largest in all of Germany, is beautiful and impressive, but we are not allowed to forget that it originally stood as a symbol of a feudal lord's power over his vassals, a power that included the traditional right to deflower virgins under his rule before their wedding nights:

> How many
> Virgins has
> Our Sovereign Lord and Master

Unvirgined on their nuptial nights
For their young husbands in
Red-eyed
Teeth-gnashing
Agony (p. 19).

The castle thus carries reminders of a long legacy of European domination and oppression based on class and gender, a list to which race was added in the nineteenth century. And this legacy cannot be erased by the fact that the castle has now been converted into a youth hostel to house Sissie and her fellow campers.

Aidoo continues this highly symbolic evocation of place in "From Our Sister Killjoy" when Sissie travels to England, "her colonial home" (p. 85). Indeed, Sissie is almost overwhelmed by reminders of the legacy of colonialism during her stay on English soil, a reaction that causes her to earn the label of "killjoy" because she is consequently unable to enjoy the creature comforts offered by modern England. For one thing, many of the Africans she encounters are too poor to enjoy most of these comforts. Sissie is clearly embarrassed by the poverty of most Africans living in England, where they can afford to wear nothing but "cheap plastic versions of the latest middle-class fashions" (p. 89). She is also disturbed that so many of the black people she sees in England are either highly-trained professionals or students, neither of whom seem to have any intention of returning to Africa. Indeed, the major thrust of this section of the book is a biting criticism of African intellectuals who travel to the West to study, then decide to stay, enjoying the material rewards available there rather than bringing their new knowledge and training back to Africa.

Aidoo suggests that these Africans are not only depriving their own people of the benefits of their services, but they are also playing into the hands of a Western neocolonial educational system that is designed not only to create a "brain drain" by luring Africa's best and brightest to the West, but also to help the West maintain its economic and cultural domination of post-colonial Africa. For the narrator African expatriate intellectuals have betrayed their African heritage, selling out for a few crumbs of Western material wealth (p. 86). These intellectuals cannot contribute meaningfully to the development of a postcolonial African cultural identity that escapes the legacy of the colonial past because they have gone too far in accepting the superiority of Western education and culture.

Medicine is central to this motif and Aidoo is critical throughout *Our Sister Killjoy* of talented African doctors who decide to practice in the West rather than returning to Africa where their services are so sorely needed. Also important to the discussion of medicine is Sissie's encounter with her lover and his relative, Kunle. Kunle has been in England for seven years and seems entirely enthralled by the achievements of Western technology. In particular, he is completely uninterested in discussing the civil war then raging in Nigeria, instead preferring to speak enthusiastically of what he sees as the very positive implications of recent news from South Africa that Dr. Christiaan Barnard has successfully transplanted the heart of a black donor into a white recipient. For Kunle, this new medical technology represents an important advance in the human ability to fight disease. Moreover, he finds it particularly encouraging that the heart of a black African is now beating in the chest of a white man in South Africa, believing that this is "the type of development that can solve the question of apartheid" (p. 96). For Sissie, however, Barnard's operation represents not a step toward racial understanding, but a horrifying movement toward the use of black people as sources of spare parts for whites, thus opening a whole new range of possibilities for exploitation. The narrator clearly sides with Sissie, pointing out Barnard's own boast that the frequent violent deaths of blacks in South Africa make their hearts particularly easy to come by for use in transplants (p. 100).

The discussion of Barnard's work allows Aidoo to focus on a number of issues that are crucial to her text, so much so that Caroline Rooney argues that the story of this heart transplant is, in fact, very much at the heart of the book (Rooney 1992, 102). Both Sissie and her friend wonder how many Nazi-like experiments on human subjects (no doubt black) were performed by Barnard before this successful operation. But Kunle, ever the believer in science and the supporter of the "Christian Doctor," assures them that any prior experiments must have been done on animals like dogs and cats, rather than on people. Neither Sissie nor her friend are convinced, though this claim does cause Sissie to think that experiments with animals might cause outrage in the West, where dogs and cats often seem to be treated better than human beings, and certainly better than *black* human beings. She thus envisions a letter to her brother back in Ghana in which she explains that the West is a land where "men would sit at table and eat with animals, and yet would rather die than shake the hands of other men." Indeed, in this land "they treat animals like human beings and some human beings like animals because they are not / Dumb enough" (p. 99). Because of their radical sense of alienation from their fellow human beings, Sissie concludes, Westerners can feel comfortable only in relationships where they are clearly dominant, as in a relationship with a pet—or a member of a subjugated class, race, or gender.

Aidoo echoes descriptions of the ideology of science that have been made by Marxist cultural critics such as Max Horkheimer and Theodor Adorno (1972), especially by placing this diagnosis within the context of a discussion of scientific research. Moreover, she calls attention to the fact that technology was crucial to the European colonial domination of most of the rest of the world in the late nineteenth and early twentieth centuries. Science was an important justification for that domination. Europeans, confident that their scientific outlook was superior to the more spiritual approach to reality that they encountered in most of the societies they colonized, could congratulate themselves on bringing enlightenment to the "dark places of the earth." Medicine was central to this phenomenon, and Aidoo's text raises a number of important questions about whether Western science and medicine were in fact always an unequivocal blessing to colonized peoples.

In "A Love Letter," Sissie tries to explain her position to her (now former) lover, who has decided to stay in England, a decision that Sissie cannot accept. Medicine is again central to this explanation: Sissie tells her former lover about her encounter with a gifted African surgeon who attempted to convince her (and perhaps himself) that he had good reasons to remain in the West. For one thing, the surgeon told her, his spreading international fame would help to overcome negative stereotypes of Africans, thus convincing the rest of the world of "our worth" (p. 129). For another, the kind of work he did was so technically advanced that facilities to do it were simply unavailable in Africa. His choice, then, was between working on the cutting edge of research in the West and working as an ordinary, underequipped physician in Africa. For him, this choice was clear, and for Sissie it is as well—except that Sissie has no doubt that he would be more valuable treating patients at home than doing research in England (p. 130).

This section of the book includes some of Aidoo's most biting condemnations of colonialism, partially because the narrator of the earlier sections takes a more distant and ironic attitude toward her subject matter than Sissie does in this section. Sissie complains that the ruthless expansion of Western civilization around the globe "chokes all life and even eliminates whole races of people in its path" (p. 112). Thinking of the exploitation of Africa that is still going on, even in the supposedly postcolonial era, she curses "all those who steal continents" and is particularly contemptuous of the ongoing cultural imperialism which lies at the heart of the "brain drain." Sissie also comments on the universalizing tendency of Western thought, which dictates that "literature, art, culture, all information" should obey absolute rules that are the same in all societies. These rules, of course, are Western, and the claim to universality really amounts to nothing more than a belief that Africans should disavow their traditional cultures in favor of Western models (p. 121). Language is central to this disavowal, and the fourth section of *Our Sister Killjoy* appropriately begins with a meditation on language. As she record her thoughts in English, Sissie becomes intensely aware of the irony of the fact that she is using the language of the very colonizers she is railing against, a language "that enslaved me, and therefore, the messengers of my mind always come shackled" (p. 112). Aidoo here shows her awareness of the language question that has become so important in African literature and, indeed, in all postcolonial literature. Aidoo herself clearly has a sense of working in an alien medium when she writes in English, though it is certainly the case that she manipulates that medium in very effective ways. *Our Sister Killjoy* makes a number of very explicit political points about the damaging impact of colonialism on both African and Western societies (and about the special suffering of women as a result of colonialism). And the effectiveness of Aidoo's political statement is enhanced by the highly poetic manner in which she presents these ideas. As Odamtten notes, "Aidoo's works have always been original and challenging, especially in her insistence on mingling the formal elements and aesthetics of orature and the concerns of contemporary Ghana, Africa, and its diaspora with the impact of Western imperialism" (Odamtten 1994, 117).

The most obvious example of literary technique in *Our Sister Killjoy* is Aidoo's mixture of prose and poetry, using poetry not only to emphasize certain ideas but also to introduce the feel of an oral performance into the text. This mixture of modes shows not only how the novel as a genre can incorporate the features of other genres but also how African writers can shape the novel to their own purposes. Many critics have remarked the innovative nature of Aidoo's text. Sara Chetin characterizes the book as "an African woman writer's dilemma tale—directed at an African audience but written within a Western structure that deviates from the conventional, unified shape of the novel" (Chetin 1993, 146). As Innes puts it, the highly innovative formal technique of *Our Sister Killjoy* "revises the form and conventions of the novel as they have been handed down from British writers and, more specifically, rewrites Conrad's *Heart of Darkness*, as the archetypal European novel 'about' Africa" (Innes 1992, 139–40). Indeed, there is a rich dialogue between Aidoo's novel and Conrad's. For example, the two novels can be compared not only in terms of content but also in terms of their use of a complex narrative voice. In Conrad's novel, a frame narrator relates a story that has been told to him (and several others) by Charlie Marlow, the book's protagonist. In this way, Conrad not only highlights the event of storytelling, but also creates a rhetorical structure that is extremely complex: what the reader actually reads is Conrad's version of the narrator's version of Marlow's story, so the information gets to us third-hand, as it were, and in at least three combined voices. A similar effect occurs in *Our Sister Killjoy*. The fourth section, narrated directly in Sissie's voice, creates a sort of dialogue between Sissie's voice and that of the third-person narrator of the other three sections. In addition, the third-person narrator's point of view is very much like (but not necessarily identical to) Sissie's. Indeed, the voices of narrator and protagonist often merge into a sort of chorus in the first three sections, in the mode generally described as "indirect free style"— a mode of narration in which a third-person narrator speaks in ways that clearly reflect the point of view of one or more characters in the text while still reflecting the narrator's point of view. As Hernadi has pointed out, narration presented in indirect free style is inherently dialogic, because it allows the narrator and character to speak simultaneously (Hernadi 1972, 36).

McHale suggests that indirect free style is a "characteristic Modernist device," and this mode of narration is indeed often associated with the works of modern Western writers from Flaubert to Pynchon (McHale 1979, 87). The complex narrative voicing of *Our Sister Killjoy* thus recalls not only *Heart of Darkness* but also any number of other Western modernist texts. On the other hand, the narrative technique of Aidoo's works is also clearly related to that of the traditional African storyteller, so that her works have an unusual ability to provide "a literate audience with a close approximation of the experience one receives as a participant in an oral storytelling session" (Hill-Lubin 1989, 223–24). That the narrative voice of *Our Sister Killjoy* can be reminiscent of both Western modernism and traditional African storytelling suggests certain parallels between the two forms, one of which reacts against the bourgeois traditions of nineteenth-century European aesthetics and one of which predates and evolves independently of that aesthetics. But the similarity of *Our Sister Killjoy* to works of Western modernism indicates the pitfalls of interpreting African texts from a purely Western perspective. Aidoo's narrative voice has much in common with the narrative voices of modernist texts, and the experimental, poetic form of Aidoo's book is also clearly reminiscent of many works of Western modernism. The Western reader could thus easily place Aidoo's text within the conventions of Western modernism. But such a placement would do considerable violence to the text by depriving it of the energies it derives from African oral narrative and by diminishing its ability to maintain a critical voice outside the control of Western perspectives. In short, such readers would be in danger of applying Western aesthetic principles in the very mode of universalization that Aidoo so strongly criticizes in *Our Sister Killjoy*.

Historical Background

Ama Ata Aidoo, like her friend Ayi Kwei Armah, is a Ghanaian postcolonial novelist, and the historical background of her novels is thus very similar to that of Armah's novels. The reader is referred to Chapter 5 for historical background to Aidoo's work. Of course, Aidoo's perspective on Ghanaian history sometimes differs from Armah's. Aidoo builds upon the colonial and postcolonial history of Ghana from an avowedly feminine perspective, calling attention to certain aspects of African history that often receive little attention in the works of male African writers. Especially important here is the fact that many traditional Ghanaian societies (especially that of the Akan) were matrilineal in nature and therefore differed in important ways from the patriarchal societies of either Africa or Europe.

When the British began to extend their involvement in Ghana in the nineteenth century, they encountered widespread cultural practices that granted women considerably more social and economic autonomy than they had back in England. For example, it was quite typical in traditional Ghanaian society for a woman to be expected to be financially independent, even when married. Colonization disrupted this tradition in a number of ways. The British established an extensive system of education that offered considerably more educational opportunities to boys than to girls, creating opportunities for men that were denied to women. But women continued to pursue economic opportunities, especially as independent retail traders. Aidoo emphasizes the Ghanaian tradition of female independence and argues that Western models for the oppression of women by men are often

> ridiculous . . . especially in the area of exactly what the African woman is, the assumption on the part of most Westerners being that the poor African woman was a downtrodden wretch until the European missionary brought her Christianity, civilization and emancipation. This may apply in certain areas of Africa, but certainly, for most Ghanaian women, the question of their emancipation is not really a problem to discuss since it has always been ensured by the system anyway. Nor is this an idealized view. It is there for anyone who is prepared to observe a society instead of imposing on it his own prejudices and syndromes (Aidoo 1969, x).

Thus, while it may be true that in Ghana women were traditionally not considered to have fulfilled themselves fully as women unless they were mothers, it is also true that "real" women were expected to maintain their economic independence from men. Aidoo's work, which often deals with the special problems encountered by educated women in modern Ghana, treats these problems in ways that clearly suggest the relevance of the earlier Ghanaian tradition of women's independence.

Biographical Background

Aidoo was born in the Gold Coast colony (in what is now central Ghana) in 1940. Like so many African novelists, she grew up in a complex cultural environment that mixed indigenous traditions with practices imposed by the colonial rulers. In particular, her early education was in colonial schools where boys were generally given preferential treatment, though she was fortunate that both of her parents strongly believed in the value of educating girls as well as boys. Aidoo did well in school and eventually attended the University of Ghana in Legon in the early years of Ghanaian independence. The system there was still dominated by Western models, but Aidoo's growing sophistication allowed her to begin to imagine ways of going beyond that aesthetic tradition, as she began to ponder the possibility of becoming a writer. She was particularly influenced by the work of the Ghanaian playwright Efua Sutherland, who drew upon traditional forms of storytelling and other oral cultural traditions.

After graduation, Aidoo served as a junior research fellow at the Institute of African Studies at the University of Ghana from 1964 to 1966. She continued her studies of African oral cultural traditions, strongly influenced by the pan-Africanist and socialist ideas that were of wide currency in Africa (especially in Nkrumah-led Ghana) during those years. Vincent Odamtten, in his book-length study of Aidoo's writing, emphasizes the important influence of the exciting atmosphere in Ghana in the mid-1960s (Odamtten 1994, 10). Indeed, the important Caribbean thinker C. L. R. James described Ghana as "the center of the world revolutionary struggle" during this period (James 1977, 164). It was also during this same period that Aidoo made her debut as an author with the 1965 publication of her play, *The Dilemma of a Ghost* (1995). This play, which deals with the relationship between a Ghanaian man and an African-American woman, sets the tone for the treatment of complex and sensitive issues that characterizes all of Aidoo's writing. Moreover, as Mildred Hill-Lubin points out, this play is one of only a few African works that deal with relationships between Africans and African-Americans (Hill-Lubin 1982, 191).

The Dilemma of a Ghost draws upon a complex combination of African and Western literary models, and the formal construction of the play mirrors its theme of cross-cultural relationships. Aidoo's second play, *Anowa* (1995, first published in 1970), also draws upon the dilemma tale tradition, but draws even more obviously upon other African sources; it is based on a folk legend that Aidoo heard from her mother, a legend derived from events in West Africa in the nineteenth century. The play details Anowa's efforts to establish her independence within a variety of confining social structures. First, she escapes her family to marry the ambitious Kofi Ako, of whom her family disapproves. Then, she becomes increasingly alienated from Kofi because of his all-consuming greed, especially when he resorts increasingly to slave-keeping as a source of income. She finally declares her independence from Kofi's domination, publicly charging that his acquisitiveness serves as a substitute for sex and as a mask for his sexual impotence. The humiliated Kofi commits suicide, and Anowa is independent at last. The play thus deals directly with important feminist issues, but it does so within the context of a critical treatment of the impact of colonialism on Ghana, especially the Bond Treaty, which opened the way to increasing British domination in the 1870s.

Between these two plays, Aidoo wrote her first novel, *Our Sister Killjoy*, which was copyrighted in 1966 and thus gives Aidoo some claim to being the first English-language woman novelist in West Africa. However, Aidoo's novel was not published until 1977, by which time women such as Flora Nwapa and Buchi Emecheta were established as novelists. In the intervening years, Aidoo concentrated largely on the writing of poems and short stories. Many of the early stories were published in the collection *No Sweetness*

Here (1994a). These stories draw upon West African oral storytelling traditions and—in intense and often highly poetic ways—deal with the dilemmas of individuals faced with the complexities of life amid the dramatic changes wrought in Ghanaian society by the experience of colonialism and its postcolonial aftermath. All of the stories focus on the attempts of individuals to establish a stable sense of their own subjective identities within a society whose cultural identity is highly unstable.

A second book of stories, *"The Eagle and the Chickens" and Other Stories*, was published in 1987, and volumes of Aidoo's poems appeared in 1985 (*Someone Talking to Sometime*) and 1992 (*"An Angry Letter in January" and Other Poems*). Aidoo's talents as a poet are also crucial to *Our Sister Killjoy*, which is written largely in verse. Like Aidoo's stories, the highly poetic *Our Sister Killjoy* draws on African oral traditions, though its formal innovation and emphasis on the subjective experience of the title character are reminiscent of the works of Western modernist writers such as Virginia Woolf. At the same time, Aidoo manages to treat the private concerns of her protagonist within a broadly public political framework. Indeed, Aidoo has emphasized her concentration on issues that go beyond the private concerns of individuals.

On the other hand, the title of Aidoo's second novel, *Changes* (1993, first published in 1991), might thus refer to her own career because it focuses specifically on the private life of the protagonist, Esi Sekyi, especially her relationships with her husband Oko and her lover (and subsequent husband) Ali Kondey. Aidoo herself acknowledges this seeming shift in emphasis, beginning the text with a reference to her own statement that she had more important things to write about than "lovers in Accra." In fact *Changes* does not represent a reversal in Aidoo's interests but merely an extension of them. Just as many Western feminists have emphasized the political nature of private relationships (often touting the slogan "The personal is the political"), Aidoo also makes a number of political points in her story of Esi's private loves. As Aidoo states in an interview with Maya Jaggi, "I've grown to see that life is not just politics or the liberation struggle, or even economics: love *is* political, and everything is intertwined" (Aidoo 1991, 17). The book does, in fact, address a number of crucial political issues, including the complex combination of modern Western social practices with the continuing influence of Muslim and indigenous African traditions that informs life in contemporary Ghana. For example, *Changes* treats the issue of polygamy in a complex and sensitive way, showing that the practice has both advantages and disadvantages for women.

Aidoo's work, like that of other African women writers, is only beginning to receive the kind of critical attention that it clearly deserves. Indeed, Aidoo addresses traditional lack of critical attention to African women's writing in her essay, "To Be an African Woman Writer" (1988), in which she excoriates critics—mostly male— for treating the works of African women writers in condescending ways, if at all. She then reviews the works of a number of important women writers (including herself) who have received insufficient critical attention. Odamtten's *The Art of Ama Ata Aidoo* (1994) is the first book-length study of Aidoo's writing and thus marks a positive milestone in critical attention to her work. Odamtten's book presents detailed discussions of all of Aidoo's major texts and is especially valuable for its delineation of continuities in Aidoo's career despite the unusual stylistic and generic diversity of her work. Numerous critical essays have been published on Aidoo's work, and most major treatments of African women writers include discussions of her work.

Further Reading
See the suggestions for further reading at the end of Chapter 5.

Chapter 7

Nadine Gordimer:
Burger's Daughter

Gordimer's fiction tracks the history of South Africa from the early years of apartheid through its demise and aftermath. Indeed, despite the impressive technical accomplishment of Gordimer's fiction—an accomplishment that has drawn considerable praise from Western critics—Stephen Clingman argues that the most important characteristic of Gordimer's fiction is its intense engagement with its historical context, marked by Gordimer's ability to "maintain an extraordinarily close observation of the world in which she lives" (Clingman 1986, 7). In this sense, Gordimer's novels are paradigmatic of the genre as a whole, which is distinguished precisely by its ability to establish and maintain a "zone of direct contact with developing reality" (Bakhtin 1981, 39). *Burger's Daughter* (1980a), one of Gordimer's better known and most respected novels, is one of the most representative in this sense. Events such as the Sharpeville and Soweto massacres inform the narrative of the book in crucial ways, and the life of Gordimer's protagonist, Rosa Burger, is inextricably intertwined with the history of South Africa, especially the history of resistance to apartheid. Indeed, *Burger's Daughter* can be seen as a complex, dialogic combination of two of the most important European novelistic genres: in telling the story of the growth and maturation of Rosa Burger, the book clearly participates in the tradition of the bildungsroman; in connecting the experience of its characters to the history of South Africa, the book recalls the great European historical novels of the nineteenth century. This combination of genres, with their respective emphases on "private" and "public" life, parallels what numerous critics have identified as the most important aspect of both the style and the content of *Burger's Daughter*—its attempt to establish a productive dialogue between public and private realms of experience.

This public-private dialogue is established in the first scene of the *Burger's Daughter*, which is presented in a series of segments with different narrative voices. In this scene we are introduced to fourteen-year-old Rosa as she waits outside a South African prison with a group of people who have come to deliver clothing and other items to some of the prisoners. The first narrator is a rather detached, journalistic, third-person voice that introduces Rosa simply as "the schoolgirl." We soon learn, however, that this schoolgirl's participation in this public political event has a strong personal dimension—she has come to bring a quilt and hot-water bottle to her mother, Cathy Burger, who is being held in the prison for her antiapartheid activities. The second section fills in more details about Rosa and her background, and is again related in a distant, reportorial voice. The third section, presented as a diary entry by one of the demonstrators outside the prison, is more personal, but still describes Rosa in a relatively detached way, though the diarist expresses admiration for young Rosa's support for her parents' political activities. The fourth section, a single sentence, gives us Rosa's own first-person perspective, but looking back from some undefined later perspective. It shows her awareness of being a public figure who is constantly on display—as a source of inspiration to the opponents of apartheid and as an object of surveillance to the South African secret police: "When they saw me outside the prison," she asks, "what did they see?" (p. 13). The fifth section then presents the book's first instance of extended first-person narration by Rosa, filling in a number of private details about the preceding public scene, including the fact that Rosa was at the time suffering from early-puberty menstrual cramps.

This first scene serves as a microcosm of the text: the major issues are put into place in this relatively brief introductory scene. Most obviously, Rosa and her parents are identified and placed within the historical context of resistance to apartheid. We learn that the communist leader Lionel Burger is a prominent opponent of apartheid, that Cathy is an important dissident as well, and that Rosa has had to assume unusual responsibility in her young life because of her parents' frequent arrests and imprisonment. Secondly, Rosa undergoes extremely private personal experiences even while she participates in this public political event—the first of many demonstrations in the book that private and public experience do not occur in separate realms but are closely interconnected. The style and narrative technique of the rest of the text are anticipated as well. In particular, the alternation of narrative voices—particularly the shifts between third-person voices that give various "public" points of view and the more private perspective of a first-person voice—is continued throughout the text.

A similar alternation occurs in the text's plot, which moves through three major sections. The first section deals primarily with the historical and political situation in South Africa and with the attempts of the Burgers and their circle to change that situation. Among other things, it narrates the history of leftist politics in South Africa, focusing in particular on Lionel's final trial, which leads to a life sentence and to his death in prison. This section might be seen as public in its orientation, though Gordimer continues to focus on Rosa and how she is personally affected by the oppressive South African political system and the Burgers' opposition to that system. In the second section, Rosa, unable to deal any longer with the abject political realities of apartheid South Africa, flees to the south of France, where she seeks personal happiness in the carefree lifestyle of Lionel's first wife, Katya. This section is primarily private. In the third section, Rosa realizes that her flight was irresponsible and returns to South Africa to do what she can to help the situation there. One might, then, view this third section as a resolution of the conflict between public and private orientations. Indeed, critics have argued that the plot structure of the novel is dialectical in the Hegelian sense. That is, they believe the plot moves from the thesis of public responsibility in the first section, to the antithesis of the search for personal happiness in the second section, to a synthesis of these emphases in the third section.[1] Although this model of the plot may be helpful, the public and private spheres are actually interwoven throughout the text. Thus, in the first and most public section, Rosa's first-person speeches are addressed to her lover, the apolitical Conrad, an almost allegorical representative of the private sphere, whose relationship to Rosa is personal. The second, mostly private section revolves around Katya, but Katya is a former communist, and hints of politics creep in, even in the sun-and-fun world of the French Riviera. In addition, the dialogic combination of bildungsroman and historical novel infuses the entire text.

In the same way, the book's shifts between first- and third-person narrative voices extend the dialogue between public and private spheres, but the interaction among these voices also demonstrates that the relationship between the public and private spheres in *Burger's Daughter* is more complex than a simple opposition. As Stephen Clingman points out, there are several distinctively different third-person voices that assume different tones and attitudes in the text (Clingman 1986, 190). Even Rosa's first-person voice varies as the text proceeds. In particular, she addresses her narration to a different listener in each of the book's three main sections: her monologues in the first section are addressed to Conrad; in the second section she addresses Katya; in the third Rosa speaks to her dead father. Indeed, these sections are more properly described as second-person narratives, and it is clear that Rosa's narration is strongly affected by her addressees' points of view. As Bakhtin and other language theorists argue, linguistic utterances are constituted not only by speakers, but also by listeners and by the context in which the utterance is spoken. For Bakhtin, "an essential (constitutive) marker of the utterance is its quality of being directed to someone, its *addressivity*" (Bakhtin 1986, 95).

---

[1] For a clear elaboration of this argument, see Peck (1989).

In *Burger's Daughter* even the most impersonal third-person passages bear the marks of distinctively individual speakers, while even the most personal first-person speeches are delivered in a specific social context, in dialogue with other people. The complex narrative voicing of *Burger's Daughter*, like the book as a whole, does not so much enact an opposition between public and private spheres as suggest that these spheres are always interrelated. Neither exists independently of the other. This point is extremely important. Many Marxist critics have seen the creation of a sense of separation between public and private life to be one of the central effects of capitalism and one of the crucial tools through which the bourgeoisie maintain their power in capitalist society. In particular, Georg Lukács sees the separation between public and private life under capitalism as the most important example of the fragmentation of social life he associates with "reification"—the inevitable effect of capitalism in which all aspects of life, including human beings and human relationships, are reduced to the status of objects. Reification emphasizes private experience, which draws energies away from the public world of politics and thus weakens any attempt to oppose the current structure of power. But, by separating private life from the public world, reification leads to an impoverishment of private life as well.[2]

In addition, the separation between public and private makes it difficult for individuals to think historically, so Gordimer's insistence on a genuine historical perspective in her novels can be taken as a form of resistance to this separation and to reification in general. (The concept of reification is of obvious relevance in South Africa, where the system of apartheid enforced social fragmentation in a particularly overt and damaging way.) Lukács himself emphasizes the relevance of this concept to literature. He argues that one of the major characteristics of the great bourgeois realist novels of the early nineteenth century is their ability to maintain an intimate connection between the public and private spheres, a connection that helped the bourgeoisie to maintain their sense of historical mission and thus to sweep to power, supplanting the aristocracy as the ruling class of Europe. For Lukács, one of the most important signs of the growing decadence of later bourgeois literature is the increasing inability of texts to reflect this sense of connection. *Burger's Daughter* can thus be seen as an attempt to recover some of the energies of the early-nineteenth-century novels praised by Lukács, a suggestion that gains support from the fact that Gordimer has identified Lukács as one of the major influences on her work.

For Lukács, the great realist novelists achieve their connection between public and private realms primarily through the technique of "typicality," that is, through the creation of characters who are both distinct individuals

---

[2] For Lukács's major statement on reification, see Lukács (1971).

and "typical" representatives of large historical forces, thus embodying private and public energies in a single figure. For example, he praises such writers as Walter Scott and Leo Tolstoy for creating "characters in whom personal and social-historical fates closely conjoin" (Lukács 1983, 285). Clingman notes that such typification is common in Gordimer's writing, especially in *Burger's Daughter*, where Rosa is the clearest example of Gordimer's creation of "typical" characters (Clingman 1986, 173). Rosa might be seen as the lo cus of contention among these forces, as the place where the confrontation between public and private forces is played out. Rosa's very name identifies her as a point of confluence of the private and the public. Christened "Rosemarie," but called "Rosa," she is named for both her grandmother Marie Burger (a private connection) and the important communist thinker and revolutionary activist Rosa Luxemburg (a public connection).

Lionel Burger represents South African communism, but he is also a more complex figure. It is not really fair to follow Richard Peck and see Burger as a figure of "dehumanized radicalism" whose "doctrinaire communism" functions as the polar opposite of Conrad's "uncommitted solipsism" (Peck 1989, 26). Indeed, Peck's vision of Burger may be as much a product of Cold War stereotypes (which typically assume that any committed leftist is by definition dehumanized and doctrinaire) as of anything in Gordimer's text. Gordimer goes out of her way to demonstrate in *Burger's Daughter* that the history of the South African Communist Party is, as Clingman puts it, "a proud one" (Clingman 1986, 173). In this sense, it is important that her main historical source on communism in South African seems to have been the essay "South Africa—No Middle Road," by the leading South African communist Joe Slovo (Clingman 1986, 186–87).[3]

Gordimer is careful to make Burger a figure of genuine compassion and humanity who has a successful professional career and a rich personal life, with many important personal relationships despite his devotion to his political cause. Far from adopting a rigid and doctrinaire "party line," the Burgers and their associates are willing to adapt their beliefs to historical circumstances and, in particular, to the special situation in apartheid South Africa. Rosa herself makes it clear that the communism of her parents was carefully tailored to "local conditions" rather than simply modeled on Soviet or Chinese positions. Further, Rosa insists on the particularly personal, human nature of the Burgers' communism:

---

[3] Slovo, who preceded Chris Hani as General Secretary of the South African Communist Party, was the first white to become a member of the executive committee of the African National Congress. A close ally of Nelson Mandela, Slovo was one of the principal architects of the reconciliation plan through which apartheid was officially ended. He was named Minister of Housing in Mandela's first cabinet. Slovo survived an assassination attempt in January 1994, but died of cancer in January 1995.

> Lionel—my mother and father—people in that house, had a connection
> with blacks that was completely personal. In this way, their Communism
> was the antithesis of anti-individualism. . . . The political activities and at-
> titudes in that house came from the inside outwards (p. 172).

Lionel Burger's humanity is further reinforced by the fact that he is not
merely a generalized figure of abstract political ideas, but seems to have been
based largely on Bram Fischer. Fischer was an important South African communist whose antiapartheid activities (extensive enough to cause some to
compare him to Mandela) led his own imprisonment for life in 1966.[4]
Gordimer clearly respects Fischer, as she shows in essays such as "Why Did
Bram Fischer Choose Jail?" (Gordimer 1989, 68–78). Indeed, Gordimer's
deep admiration for Fischer's political commitment and genuinely warm
humanity make it highly unlikely that she intends Burger to be seen as anything other than admirable.[5] In addition, any reading of Burger as a one-di-
mensional extremist is also undermined not only by the etymology of his
name, but also by the fact that he (like Fischer) is an Afrikaner, thus compli-
cating any simple Manichean vision of South African politics, in which Afrikaners would surely be aligned with apartheid.

In short, Burger is a genuinely "typical" figure, embodying both public
and private forces. The relative richness of Burger's characterization, meanwhile, suggests the relative richness of his communist social vision, which
inherently seeks to establish links between the public and private worlds.
That the affluent Afrikaner Burger is the text's central figure opposing both
capitalism and apartheid also indicates the complexities of South African
politics. As a Marxist, Burger understands that history is driven primarily by
economic conflict between classes. As a South African, he knows that race,
not class, is the most obvious source of division and conflict in his society.
In South Africa, as in the United States, race and class are closely interrelated. Clingman's suggestion that under apartheid "lines of class and race coincide" is probably a slight exaggeration, but it is true that in apartheid South
Africa whites were likely to occupy professional and management positions,
while blacks could hope at best for positions as workers (Clingman 1986,
15). Burger understands this situation quite well, and further understands
that racism arises primarily as an attempt to justify and maintain the class
structure of South African society. In this sense, he again resembles Fischer,
who, according to Gordimer "sees the colour problem in South Africa as
basically an economic one: the white man's fear of losing his job to the over-
whelming numbers of Africans" (Gordimer 1989, 73).

---

[4] For a discussion of some other possible models for various aspects of Burger's character, see
Leeuwenburg (1985).

[5] For details of Fischer's life and beliefs, see Mitchison (1973).

But Burger's insight into the economic origins of apartheid goes beyond a recognition that whites in South Africa seek to maintain their privileged position by oppressing blacks. In particular, Burger (like Gordimer) recognizes that racism in South Africa (and elsewhere) is a historical phenomenon with roots that go back to the days of slavery. Burger's insight resembles the suggestions by numerous scholars that slavery and capitalism are intimately related. For example, contrary to the conventional belief that slavery was made possible by racism, Walter Rodney argues that racism was made thinkable merely by economic necessity, and that racism was a product of slavery rather than the other way around: "Having been utterly dependent on African labour, Europeans at home and abroad found it necessary to rationalize that exploitation in racist terms as well" (Rodney 1972, 99). Similarly, Eric Williams emphasizes the economic motivation for slavery as a form of cheap labor and concludes that "racial differences made it easier to justify and rationalize Negro slavery" (E. Williams 1944, 18). Finally, the African political leader Kwame Nkrumah has argued that "it was only with the capitalist economic penetration that the master-servant relationship emerged, and with it, racism" (Nkrumah 1970, 29).

Apartheid can be seen as a particularly brutal form of capitalism. It is, however, a particularly *colonial* form of capitalism. While the economic structure of South Africa resembles that of western Europe or North America in many ways, the overt physical violence with which South African whites maintained their political and economic dominance under apartheid was highly uncharacteristic of capitalist systems. The bourgeoisie typically maintain their power primarily through subtle techniques of psychological manipulation, and the exigencies of a market economy require that workers have the freedom to move from one job to another, marketing their labor like any other commodity. Antonio Gramsci argued that the European bourgeoisie gained and maintained their power through a process of "hegemony," a network of political and cultural practices designed to convince the more numerous "subaltern" classes to accede willingly to bourgeois authority as natural and proper.[6] Hegemony is a complex and plural strategy that is, by definition, never fully successful, making it necessary to keep the police and the military in the background in case of emergency. Such emergencies seldom occur in the metropolitan centers of Europe, but they were more frequent in the colonies, where hegemonic practices of power were supplemented by brute force, theatrical display, and other techniques held over from the era of feudal-aristocratic rule in Europe. Despite complex cultural interchanges and the Europeanization of certain members of the indigenous

---

[6] Gordimer is familiar with Gramsci's ideas; She employs a quotation from his work as the epigraph to *July's People* (Gordimer 1982a).

elite, most colonized peoples would never mistake the position and attitudes of the British bourgeoisie for their own because of the radical racial and cultural Manicheanism of the colonial situation.

The subtleties with which the ruling classes in Europe exercise their power are largely designed to make the class structure of capitalist society invisible. In the colonial situation, however, lines of class are supplemented by the more visible lines of race, and as a result power is exercised in far more overt ways. In an observation clearly relevant to apartheid, Frantz Fanon has noted that colonial regimes, marked by strict lines of racial difference, consistently relied far more on physical force as a technique of power than did the ruling regimes in Europe (Fanon 1968, 38). Indeed, though South Africa was the first African colony to obtain its ostensible independence from European colonial rule, the result was essentially an internal colonialism, with South African whites treating blacks as colonial subjects.[7] As Michel Foucault has emphasized in his history of power in Europe in *Discipline and Punish* (1979), techniques of domination based on overt physical violence were quite characteristic of Europe in the Middle Ages, but these techniques were supplanted by more subtle methods of manipulation and persuasion. Foucault notes that the feudal aristocracy exercised their power on the physical bodies of the citizenry, often through spectacular displays that demonstrated the aristocracy's ability to dominate the bodies of its subjects, up to and including the taking of their lives. Foucault traces the evolution of punishment techniques into the modern bourgeois era, noting the decline in public tortures and executions. He insists, however, that this decline represented a movement toward greater efficiency in the control of the populace (through "disciplinary" techniques designed to obtain "voluntary" obedience) rather than a drive toward increased humanity and justice in the use of power. Both apartheid and colonialism, then, represent distortions of the historical process by creating a fundamentally bourgeois economic system that is maintained largely via feudal social structure and practices of power.[8] Gordimer acknowledges this contradiction: in a passionate speech delivered in court just before receiving his life sentence, Burger explains that the historical roots of apartheid lie in this very distortion of the historical process (p. 25).

In the larger sense, this recognition of the contradictions that lie at the heart of apartheid (and colonialism) is critical to understanding the events

---

[7] In his discussion of Gordimer's fiction, JanMohamed emphasizes these parallels, noting that under apartheid the "fundamental socio-political-economic structure is still the same as was that of other colonies" (JanMohamed 1983, 79).

[8] For an extensive study of this aspect of colonialism in the context of British India, see Booker (1997).

narrated in *Burger's Daughter*. Moreover, Gordimer's insistence on historical vision in her works implies a recognition that to understand apartheid one must understand its historical roots. As Clingman points out, Gordimer's books also respond quite directly to the specific historical conditions that existed in South Africa at the time they were written. *Burger's Daughter* thus responds to events in the middle and late 1970s, especially to the rise of the Black Consciousness movement and the resulting disturbances in Soweto. In this movement, black leaders such as Steve Biko insisted that the struggle for liberation in South Africa was a struggle for the liberation of the indigenous population from oppression by white colonial settlers. In this sense, the Black Consciousness movement directly repudiated the multiracialist ideology long espoused by the African National Congress (ANC), insisting that the ANC rhetoric of cooperation between the races was likely to perpetuate the existing system of oppression. Crucial here for Gordimer's book is the fact that the Black Consciousness movement traces its roots to the Pan-African Congress (PAC), a dissident group that withdrew from the ANC not only because of the ANC's multiracialist emphasis but also because they believed that the ANC was dominated by (mostly white) communists.

This antagonism between the Black Consciousness movement and South African communism is fundamental as background to all of *Burger's Daughter*, though it is most vividly enacted in two crucial scenes. In the first, the communist supporter Orde Greer presents a version of the Marxist interpretation of South African history and is bitterly rejected by the young black radical Duma Dhladhla, who instead espouses the Black Consciousness position that the idea of class struggle is "white nonsense" in South Africa, where "the white workers belong to the exploiting class and take part in the suppression of blacks" (p. 163). An even more powerful presentation of the ideology of Black Consciousness occurs late in the book in the crucial telephone conversation between Rosa and Zwelinzima Vulindlela, a black man who, as a boy, lived in the Burger home and was regarded as a member of the family. Rosa's idyllic memories of their childhood together are shattered when Vulindlela expresses his resentment of Burger's fame, when so many blacks (including his own father) have made similar valiant sacrifices in the cause of opposition to apartheid. Moreover, he accuses Rosa and her family of subtly racist paternalistic attitudes toward blacks in terms so bitter that Rosa is made physically ill.

Indeed, the key dialectical opposition in *Burger's Daughter* is not between Burger's politics and Conrad's individualism. The latter is, in fact, rejected so categorically by the text (and, eventually, by Rosa) that it plays little role in the final resolution of the plot. The real opposition in the text is between the communism of Burger and the Black Consciousness of Vulindlela and Dhladhla. Gordimer treats both of these positions with considerable respect, establishing a dialogue between the two that ultimately privileges neither. In particular, the book is informed by both an essentially Marxist historical vision and a recognition that the special situation of apartheid South Africa introduces complications that this vision cannot encompass. The dialectical "synthesis" of the book thus involves not only Rosa's ultimate ability to understand that the public and the private can be reconciled, but also Rosa's decision, in the last section of the book, to continue to pursue the ideals espoused by her parents despite her acknowledgement of the validity of many of the arguments of Black Consciousness proponents.[9]

In this sense, while much of *Burger's Daughter* can be best appreciated by reading the book within the context of Lukács's comments on realism (and especially on the historical novel), it is also important to understand the ways Gordimer goes beyond Lukács. These include not only the content of her book but also the style, which incorporates many of the self-conscious metafictional features of modernism even as it remains within a fundamentally realist matrix. For Dominic Head, the combination of modernism and realism is central to Gordimer's writing and may mark this writing as postmodern (Head 1995, 193). One can also see Gordimer's combination of realism and modernism as another aspect of her attempt to link the public and private realms—to transcend the private emphasis of modernism by combining it with the social and historical vision of realism.

Among other things, the use of multiple narrative voices in *Burger's Daughter* contributes to this project. For Head, one of the primary ways Gordimer engages with history is in her examination of the way both public history and private individual identities are constructed via "ideological discursive practices" (Head 1995, 110). For example, by showing that events or people may appear differently when described from different perspectives, Gordimer comments on the textuality of all history, suggesting that fiction and history are related discourses. In her treatment of Rosa's development, Gordimer also comments on the textuality of individual identity. The text's representation of Rosa demonstrates, according to Karen Halil, that "subjectivity is a discursive process constructed by conflicting and often oppressive discourses which, through their very intersections, allow for the possibility of resistance" (Halil 1994, 44). On the other hand, Gordimer eschews the most overt metafictional techniques of postmodernist writers such Robert Coover or Gilbert Sorrentino. Instead, the textuality of Gordimer's work is generally quite subtle, mirroring the subtlety with which language and texts help to shape the cultural identities of societies and the personal identities of individuals. For example, as Clingman points out, one of Gordimer's cen-

---

[9] This reconciliation is represented particularly in the utopian image of multiracial solidarity between Rosa and her fellow prisoners at the end of the book.

tral techniques in *Burger's Daughter* involves the extensive use of unattributed quotations to create a sort of textual collage (Clingman 1986, 186–87).
Gordimer quotes extensively from Joe Slovo's essay (noted above) and from
such thinkers as Marx and Lenin without identifying the sources of this
material. This strategy may have been designed partly to evade the South
African censors, but such quotation also makes the point that authors do not
produce texts from their own original thoughts, but from material provided
to them by other texts, as emphasized by poststructuralists thinkers such as
Foucault, Roland Barthes, and Julia Kristeva. As Kristeva succinctly puts it,
"any text is constructed as a mosaic of quotations; any text is the absorption
and transformation of another" (Kristeva 1980, 66).

Because Gordimer quotes primarily from Marxist thinkers, one could
see her use of unattributed quotation as an acknowledgment of their belief
in collective action and rejection of individualism. As Clingman points out,
Gordimer's appropriation of texts by other writers "overrides the conventions of bourgeois property relations" (Clingman 1986, 187). In this sense,
her writing resembles that of the Marxist dramatist Bertolt Brecht. As Keith
Dickson notes, "Brecht's magpie method of composition borders at times on
plagiarism" (Dickson 1978, 192). But this "plagiarism" is largely the point of
Brecht's technique, which is designed both to mock the typical bourgeois
emphasis on ownership and to challenge the hegemony of a Western literary tradition that has long provided cultural underpinnings for the economic
and political machinations of capitalism. Brecht's method of quotation, like
Gordimer's, is often quite subtle, but he also calls attention to this technique
at times. For example, many of Brecht's plays are adaptations of well-known
dramatic works. Late in *Burger's Daughter*, Gordimer provides a similarly overt
example. Recalling Bakhtin's description of the way novels often gain dialogic energy by incorporating material from other genres, Gordimer quotes
the text of a pamphlet produced by the Soweto Students Representative
Council, a Black Consciousness group (pp. 346–47).[10] This use of an actual
political document sets up a dialogic connection between this real-world
pamphlet and the fictional world of Gordimer's novel, breaking down the
perceived barrier between politics and literature that, in bourgeois ideology,
exemplifies the separation of public and private realms. As Jameson puts it,
the "working distinction between cultural texts that are social and political
and those that are not becomes something worse than an error: namely, a

---

[10] This organization was officially banned on October 19, 1977, the date of Rosa Burger's arrest. Gordimer's overt quotation of this pamphlet can be taken as an act of provocation to the
South African government and as a political statement in its own right. Indeed, as JanMohamed puts it, the publication of *Burger's Daughter* "constitutes an actual socio-political act which
could have relatively harsh consequences for the author" (JanMohamed 1983, 139).

symptom and a reinforcement of the reification and privatization of contemporary life" (Jameson 1981, 20). Indeed, Gordimer's use of this pamphlet combines with her more subtle appropriation of other historical and political texts to provide a central example of the engagement with history by which she seeks to overcome the bourgeois notion that literature exists in its own realm, separated from the social world.[11]

In *Burger's Daughter* Gordimer engages in a direct dialogue with the events of South African history. By focusing this dialogue on the consequences of apartheid and on the history of antiapartheid resistance, Gordimer makes a powerful statement against apartheid and a powerful statement in favor of the political relevance of literature. In addition, by intentionally constructing texts like *Burger's Daughter* to represent reality in ways that call attention to the process of representation, Gordimer calls attention to the ways in which language and discourse contribute to making the world rather than simply describing it. *Burger's Daughter* thus enacts a dialogue not only between literature and history, but between realism and modernism, just as it combines the genres of the historical novel and the bildungsroman. That is, the book achieves a particularly effective combination between subjective and objective modes of narration and between public and private realms of experience. Thus, Robert Boyers sees *Burger's Daughter* as one of the most successful political novels of our time because it establishes an unusually rich connection between private and public life. For Boyers, Gordimer has

> reconceived the very idea of private experience and created a form that can accommodate microscopic details of individual behavior and sentiment without suggesting for a moment that individuals are cut off from the collective consciousness and political situations characteristic of their societies (Boyers 1984, 63).

Historical Background

The Republic of South Africa, with a population of approximately forty-one million (1994), covers an area of more than 471,000 square miles, which makes it more than five times the size of Great Britain and nearly twice the size of Texas. Geographically, South Africa has three main regions: a great plateau of rolling grassland in the nation's interior (the veld); a belt of mountains that rims the plateau on the east, south, and west; and a coastal region between these mountains and the oceans. Before 1994 the country was divided into four provinces: Cape Province in the south, Natal in the east,

---

[11] Gordimer also addresses the bourgeois notion that art is separate from politics in her depiction of the disengaged Conrad, a literature student, and in her description of the paintings of Bonnard, which seem entirely unaffected by historical events (pp. 286–87).

Orange Free State in the center, and Transvaal in the northeast. Until the early 1990s, the country also recognized a number of pseudoindependent "homelands" (somewhat equivalent to the reservations set aside for Native Americans in the United States), where most of the nation's black majority population resided. However, with the end of apartheid, these homelands (including four that were recognized by South Africa—though not by the United Nations or any other country—as independent states in the late 1970s and early 1980s) were reabsorbed into South Africa proper after the 1994 elections. The provincial organization was also changed, and the republic now consists of nine provinces: Eastern Cape, Northern Cape, Western Cape, Northern Transvaal, Mpumalanga, North West, Orange Free State, KwaZulu-Natal, and Gauteng.

For many years, Cape Town served as the seat of the legislative branch of the government, Pretoria as the seat of the administrative branch, and Bloemfontein as the seat of the judicial branch. After the 1994 elections, however, Pretoria was made the official capital. About sixty percent of the population lives in cities, the largest of which are Johannesburg and Cape Town, each with a population of nearly two million. Durban and Pretoria each have populations of just over one million, and Port Elizabeth has a population of nearly one million. These urban areas are the centers of South Africa's manufacturing industry, which produces automobiles, chemicals, textiles, shoes and clothing, food products, and iron, steel, and other metallic alloys. Though less than one-fifth of the land is suitable for farming and water supply is a constant problem throughout the country, South Africa is largely self-sufficient in its production of food, importing little except wheat and coffee. Cane sugar, corn, fruit, vegetables, and other crops are exported in significant amounts. There is also a major fishing industry in the coastal regions, and cattle and sheep are widely raised.

South Africa possesses extremely rich mineral resources, including about three-fourths of the world's known reserves of chromium and vanadium, nearly two-thirds of the world's gold reserves, and over ninety percent of the world's platinum and manganese. South Africa is also the world's largest producer of gem-quality and industrial diamonds, and many other minerals (including coal, uranium, asbestos, nickel, phosphates, copper, zinc, antimony, and lead) are produced in large quantities as well. South Africa has few petroleum reserves, but the country contains the world's only commercial plants producing oil from coal. These plants are able to meet most of the nation's needs for gasoline and other petroleum products.

South Africa is a racially diverse society that is still struggling to overcome the brutal legacy of apartheid. In the early 1990s, the black population was nearly thirty million, or about seventy-five percent of the total. Moreover, this population was growing rapidly, while the numbers of the other major ethnic groups were relatively stable. In the traditional classification scheme used under apartheid, these other major groups included whites (approximately fourteen percent of the total), "coloureds" (persons of mixed race, about nine percent), and Asians (mostly immigrants or descendants of immigrants from India, about three percent). (Modern South Africa does not recognize these racial divisions.) The white population includes two major subgroups, one descended from British colonial settlers and one (the Afrikaners) descended from the early Boer settlers from the Netherlands. Under apartheid, the black population was divided into ten major groups: the Zulu, Xhosa, Tswana, Pedi, Southern Sotho, Shangaan, Swazi, Venda, and Ndebele. About sixty percent of the white population speaks Afrikaans (a derivative of Dutch, Flemish, and Malay) as their first language, while the remaining white population is English-speaking. Most of the coloured population speak Afrikaans, while most of the Asians speak English. In this multilingual society, of course, it is common for individuals to speak several languages at least to some extent. The principal religion is Christianity, though there are observers of traditional African religions among the black population and Hindus and Muslims among the Asians.

The San people were the first inhabitants of South Africa and have been in the region for thousands of years. The Khoikhoi migrated south into the region about two thousand years ago. Bantu speakers, ancestors of most of the current-day black population, moved into the northern part of what is now South Africa by the eighth century. The Portuguese navigator Bartolomeu Dias became the first European to round the Cape of Good Hope (the southern tip of Africa) in 1488, and Portuguese ships, seeking trade in the Orient, followed his route for the next several decades. During this period, there was relatively little contact with the interior, though Portuguese sailors who were shipwrecked and forced to come ashore reported contact with Bantu speakers by the middle of the sixteenth century. The first permanent European settlement in the cape region was established at Table Bay by a group of Dutch settlers led by Jan van Riebeeck in 1652. The European population gradually grew through the late seventeenth century, and settlers began to penetrate the interior, trading with the Khoikhoi and San peoples they encountered. In the eighteenth century, European settlers increasingly began to farm and graze cattle in the interior, leading to conflicts with the Bantu speakers, who were already using the same land for the same purposes.

The British seized the cape region from the Dutch in 1795, though their possession was not recognized by the Dutch until 1815, when the British officially bought the region and established a colonial administration there. In 1820, the British colonial government imposed a buffer zone between the European (mostly Boer) and African farmers to reduce the clashes between them. The Boers increasingly resented British rule, eventually beginning a large scale movement into the interior to escape British control (The Great Trek of 1836–1843). They moved, with their cattle and possessions, to the areas now known as the Orange Free State, Transvaal, Natal, and Mozambique and established lives virtually independent of South Africa's British colonial administration, while waging wars against the people (mostly Zulu) they encountered in these regions. The British unsuccessfully attempted to assert their control over these regions in the first Boer War (1880–1881), and the fiercely individualistic Boers grew increasingly distant from the British government.

In the meantime, the British—like the Boers—had waged significant battles against the Zulu. After the Zulu king Cetshwayo refused to acknowledge British sovereignty over the Zulu territories of Natal, the British launched an all-out campaign against the Zulu in 1878. The Zulu initially scored a number of victories, but British military superiority finally won out, and the Zulu surrendered in July, 1879. Continuing Zulu resistance eventually led to direct British annexation of the Zululand in 1887 and to the incorporation of the Zululand into Natal in 1897. The British, led especially by the ambitious Cecil J. Rhodes, who became Prime Minister of Cape Colony in 1890, continued to extend their control over South Africa through the 1890s. The discovery of large deposits of gold in the Transvaal in the 1890s increased the British resolve to control the region, and the Boers were finally defeated by the British in the Boer War of 1899–1902, one of the most brutal conflicts in the history of European colonial expansion in Africa. Indeed, the British resorted to a number of extremely brutal and oppressive measures (such as the imprisonment of Boer women and children in concentration camps) to squelch the surprisingly fierce resistance of the Boers.[12]

By 1910 the British had established the Union of South Africa, with dominion status within the British Empire. This union, consisting of the provinces of the Cape of Good Hope, Natal, the Free Orange State , and the Transvaal, granted considerable concessions to the Boers, and the Boer leader Louis Botha became the first prime minister. In 1914, Botha put down a minor Boer revolt against South African participation in World War I. South African troops occupied German South West Africa (present-day Namibia) and fought elsewhere in Africa and in France. After the war, the Union of South Africa retained control of South West Africa. Boer leaders maintained a great deal of political power in South Africa in the next two decades, during most of which the Boer nationalist leader J. B. M. Hertzog was prime minister. Boer nationalist agitation led to South Africa's independence from British rule through the Declaration of 1926 and the Statute of Westminster

---

[12] As many as 28,000 Boer civilians, most of them under the age of sixteen, apparently perished in the British concentration camps (Warwick 1983, 1).

in 1931. In 1939, Hertzog opposed South African participation in World War II, but parliamentary support for the war effort led to Hertzog's removal. His one-time associate Jan Smuts (who had been prime minister from 1919 to 1924) became the prime minister and led South Africa into active support of the Allies in the war.

Smuts remained in power until 1948, when his United Party lost the national elections to the Boer Nationalist Party, which proceeded to implement the extremist program of racial segregation that would eventually become known as apartheid. Under this program, South Africans were strictly classified according to their racial background as white, coloured, or "native" (later called Bantu or African). Racially mixed marriages were outlawed and separate residential, business, and public areas and facilities were designated for each race. Those traveling outside their own racial area were required to obtain government permits (known as passes), and an elaborate system of rules and classifications assured that only whites had access to the best jobs and educational opportunities. Nonwhites were largely disenfranchised and denied any meaningful participation in the national government. Virtually all economic resources remained in white control, and the majority nonwhite population either worked for white bosses or lived in abject poverty in strictly enclosed ethnic enclaves.

The system of apartheid remained in place for the next several decades. Modifications in the 1950s and 1960s strengthened the separation of the races and the official white domination of the country. Meanwhile, South Africa, despite its despotic apartheid regime, carried on active relations with the democratic nations of the West, which were hesitant to oppose the staunchly anticommunist South African regime. Indeed, South Africa, with its well-developed industrial base and its rich mineral reserves, carried on an active trade with Britain, Japan, Germany, the United States, and other leading capitalist nations. In 1960, a peaceful protest against the apartheid pass laws at Sharpeville (near Johannesburg) became a symbol of resistance when police opened fire on the unarmed crowd, killing seventy and wounding nearly two hundred others. Subsequently, a growing resistance movement gained more and more support in the West. South Africa's repressive racial policies led to the nation's expulsion from the British Commonwealth in 1961, and popular protests in Britain, the United States, and elsewhere gradually led to the diplomatic and economic isolation of South Africa. Many companies withdrew their South African investments, and by the late 1970s South Africa was under extreme pressure to revise its apartheid policies.

Still, the Nationalist Party maintained control of the South African government, and leaders such as the former Nazi sympathizer B. J. Vorster (who was prime minister from 1966 to 1978) worked to further white control and to suppress black dissent. Most opposition leaders (including Nelson Mandela, leader of the outlawed African National Congress, the most important opposition party) were either in jail or exile by the end of the 1960s. Beginning in the 1970s, South Africa attempted to solidify segregation by containing much of the black population in "homelands" that were declared independent of the rest of the country—and that contained few of the nation's rich natural resources. The Vorster regime gave significant military assistance to white regimes in the neighboring countries of Angola, Mozambique, and Rhodesia in an unsuccessful attempt to quell black liberation movements in those countries.

By 1976, internal opposition to apartheid had erupted into widespread violence, beginning with an open student-led rebellion in the township of Soweto, near Johannesburg. More than 600 blacks were killed in the subsequent government reaction to this and other rebellions, and the 1977 death of black leader Steve Biko in police custody further increased tensions. In 1978, P. W. Botha, Vorster's successor as prime minister, took a few tentative steps toward reform. A new constitution was adopted in 1984 that eased certain of the restrictions imposed by apartheid and established separate legislatures for whites, coloureds, and Asians, though not for blacks. In 1988, South Africa agreed to relinquish control of South West Africa, after considerable attempts to suppress the independence movement there.

On the other hand, P.W. Botha continued to support the basic tenets of apartheid and to launch military strikes against insurgent South African groups in exile in neighboring countries, even as international pressure to end apartheid (including an economic boycott originally called for by Mandela) began to mount. Indeed, most of the reforms of the 1980s were merely cosmetic, and brutal suppression of opposition to the ruling apartheid regime continued throughout the decade. Opponents of the government were continually harassed, arrested, tortured, and even murdered. Peaceful demonstrations were disrupted by police violence. An official state of emergency was declared in 1985, giving the police extraordinary powers to quell opposition to the government. In 1989, however, F. W. de Klerk became prime minister and began to work in earnest to dismantle the system of apartheid. In 1990, the state of emergency was lifted, and political parties such as the African National Congress and the South African Communist Party, banned for decades, were again legalized. ANC leader Mandela was released from prison after serving twenty-seven years of a life sentence for treason and began to work with de Klerk to prepare the country for a transition to majority rule. More than one hundred pieces of legislation relating to apartheid were repealed, and by the end of 1991 a constitutional convention met to draw up an interim constitution.

The transitional period of the early 1990s was marred by continuing police violence, attacks on blacks by Boer extremists, ethnic violence among blacks (especially between the Xhosa and Zulu peoples), and violent clashes between rival black political factions (especially between the ANC and the Inkatha Freedom Party, led by Zulu chief Mangosuthu Buthelezi). In April, 1993, Chris Hani, leader of the South African Communist Party and former military head of Spear of the Nation (a guerrilla group associated with the ANC), was assassinated by white right-wing extremists. The death of this much beloved leader led to expressions not only of mourning but of outrage. The South African police had refused to provide protection for him even though they had been warned that he might be in danger. Clashes between police and demonstrators escalated, to the point that de Klerk declared the country on the verge of racial war. When Oliver Tambo, the much-respected long-time chairman of the ANC, died of a stroke a mere two weeks after Hani's assassination, fears of further instability arose. However, Mandela urged calm, and order was maintained. Before the year was out Mandela and de Klerk had been jointly awarded the Nobel Peace Prize, announcing the full acceptance of the new South Africa by the international community. National elections in April 1994 allowed full black participation and were dominated by the ANC; Mandela was easily elected the first president of the new nation, which continues at this writing to struggle toward democracy and equality. The police, military, and other government institutions have officially been integrated, but the white and nonwhite populations still live separately and the economic gap between the two groups remains large. The social, cultural, and psychic scars of decades of apartheid continue to haunt the nation and its people.

Biographical Background
Nadine Gordimer was born in November 1923, in the mining town of Springs in the Transvaal. Her father was a Jewish immigrant from Lithuania, her mother an immigrant from England. Taken out of school at the age of eleven, Gordimer was largely educated at home by her mother. She became interested in writing as a young girl and published her first story by the age of fifteen. Later, she attended the University of the Witwatersrand for a year, but she was mostly self-educated. The young Gordimer read widely, and she became increasingly aware of the injustices of the apartheid system in which she lived. In particular, she became intensely aware of what she herself would come to call the "great South African lie," a mass delusion in which millions of South African whites were able to ignore the obvious fact that blacks were human beings. This awareness would eventually become central to her writing—which often presents powerful criticisms of apartheid—and to her life, which was devoted to opposition to the injustices that she saw around her. A supporter of the African National Congress, Gordimer worked tirelessly against the censorship that often prevailed in South Africa, advocating the right to free expression for all citizens of the country, regardless of race.

Gordimer's first novel, *The Lying Days*, was published in 1953. This book, a somewhat autobiographical bildungsroman, traces the development of its female protagonist, Helen Shaw, from her early childhood in a mining town to bohemian young adulthood in a Johannesburg caught up in the turmoil of the early years of apartheid. The novel, like most of Gordimer's early work, focuses on the damaging and dehumanizing impact of racism on the lives of white South Africans. However, *The Lying Days*, like *A World of Strangers* (1958), and *Occasion for Loving* (1960b), treats conditions in South Africa in a mode of relatively light satire. Gordimer's sense of political commitment grows more urgent in her later work as her outrage grows more emphatic. Novels such as *The Late Bourgeois World* (1982b, first published in 1966), *A Guest of Honour* (1970), and *The Conservationist* (1975) criticize social conditions in South Africa in increasingly strong terms, though they continue to concentrate on the damaging effects of apartheid on whites. For example, *The Conservationist* (winner of the 1974 Booker Prize and the first novel by an African writer to win that award) is a probing examination of the psychological alienation of its protagonist, the white businessman Mehring. Emotionally estranged from friends, family, and lovers, Mehring tries to regain a sense of his humanity through contact with nature on a farm he purchases outside Johannesburg, but political conditions in South Africa make this project impossible.

In *Burger's Daughter* (first published in 1979), Gordimer takes a more radical stance in her treatment of the antiapartheid activities of South African communists. While *Burger's Daughter* and *The Conservationist* are informed by an atmosphere of impending upheaval, this sense of historical crisis becomes the central motif of *July's People* (1982a), an imaginative study of a future South Africa. A black revolution has toppled white rule, and the formerly prosperous white Smales family fears that they may be the target of racial violence in the postrevolutionary chaos. Their loyal black servant, Mwawate (whom they call July), leads them to his village for safety, where they find themselves in the midst of a culture they do not understand. Their sense of inferiority and confusion serves as a commentary on how July and other blacks had long felt in the white-dominated urban regions of South Africa. Gordimer also comments on the power of white propaganda: the village chief is terrified of the revolution, which he assumes (after years of official anticommunist hysteria) to have been the work of Cuban and Russian agitators. The chief begs Bam Smales to use his gun to protect the village from the communists, whom he believes will soon come to take control.

A strong sense of political commitment continues to inform novels such as *A Sport of Nature* (1988) and *My Son's Story* (1991b). Gordimer also begins to meditate on the potential for a postapartheid cultural identity for South Africa and postapartheid personal identities for South Africans.

Gordimer's first postapartheid novel is *None to Accompany Me* (1994). Here she traces the attempts of several South Africans (both black and white) to develop a new national identity while at the same time seeking to revise their own personal identities, which had long been shaped by apartheid and their resistance to it.

Gordimer is also an accomplished writer of short stories and has published numerous story collections, including *Face to Face* (1949), *The Soft Voice of the Serpent* (1954), *Six Feet of the Country* (1956), *Friday's Footprint and Other Stories* (1960a), *Livingstone's Companions* (1972), *A Soldier's Embrace* (1980b), *Jump and Other Stories* (1991a), and *Why Haven't You Written* (1992). Many of her finest stories are collected in *Selected Stories* (1983). She has also published influential essays and criticism, many of which are included in *The Black Interpreters* (1973) and *The Essential Gesture: Writing, Politics, Places* (1989). *Writing and Being* (1995) contains many of her most recent statements on literature and politics. Together, her fiction, commentary, and political commitment have made her one of the world's best known and most respected literary figures. She has won numerous literary prizes and awards, culminating in the Nobel Prize for literature in 1991, a recognition that was greeted with enthusiastic approval worldwide.

Gordimer's work has received a great deal of critical attention. Numerous general studies of African literature feature discussions of her work, and essays on her work are published widely in scholarly journals. Some of these essays are collected in *Critical Essays on Nadine Gordimer*, edited by Rowland Smith (1990), and *The Later Fiction of Nadine Gordimer*, edited by Bruce King (1993). Gordimer's writing has also been the subject of numerous theses and dissertations, and book-length critical discussions of her work have been published in a variety of countries and languages. Some of the leading studies in English include those by Stephen Clingman (1986), John Cooke (1985), Andrew Ettin (1993), Dominic Head (1995), Judie Newman (1988), and Kathrin Wagner (1994).

Further Reading

Biko, Steve. 1978. *I Write What I Like: Steve Biko, a Selection of His Writings*. Ed. Aelred Stubbs. New York: Harper and Row.

Davidson, Basil, Joe Slovo, and A. R. Wilkinson. 1976. *Southern Africa: The New Politics of Revolution*. Harmondsworth, Middlesex: Penguin.

Fredrickson, George M. 1981. *White Supremacy: A Comparative Study in American and South African History*. New York: Oxford University Press.

———. 1995. *Black Liberation: A Comparative History of Black Ideologies in the United States and South Africa*. New York: Oxford University Press.

Johns, Sheridan, and R. Hunt Davis, eds. 1991. *Mandela, Tambo, and the African National Congress*. New York: Oxford University Press.

Lemon, Anthony, ed. 1994. *The Geography of Change in South Africa.* New York: Wiley.

Mandela, Nelson. 1994. *Long Walk to Freedom: The Autobiography of Nelson Mandela.* Boston: Little, Brown.

Moleah, Alfred T. 1993. *South Africa: Colonialism, Apartheid, and African Dispossession.* Wilmington, Del.: Disa Press.

Moodie, D. T. 1975. *The Rise of Afrikanerdom: Power, Apartheid, and the Afrikaner Civil Religion.* Berkeley: University of California Press.

Omer-Cooper, J. D. 1994. *History of South Africa.* 2d ed. London: James Currey.

Ottaway, David. 1993. *Chained Together: Mandela, De Klerk, and the Struggle to Remake South Africa.* New York: Times Books.

Pakenham, Thomas. 1979. *The Boer War.* New York: Random House.

Pascoe, Elaine. 1992. *South Africa: Troubled Land.* 2d ed. New York: F. Watts.

Paton, Jonathan. 1990. *The Land and People of South Africa.* New York: HarperCollins.

Ross, Robert. 1993. *Beyond the Pale: Essays on the History of Colonial South Africa.* Middletown, Conn.: Wesleyan University Press.

Thompson, Leonard. 1990. *A History of South Africa.* New Haven, Conn.: Yale University Press.

Woods, Donald. 1981. *Asking for Trouble: Autobiography of a Banned Journalist.* New York: Atheneum.

———. 1991. *Biko.* 3d ed. New York: Holt.

Chapter 8

▼▼▼▼▼▼▼▼▼▼

Alex La Guma:
In the Fog
of the Seasons' End

The political commitment central to all of La Guma's work is not unusual in African literature, but *In the Fog of the Seasons' End* (1972), in its elaboration of the possibilities for armed resistance to apartheid, represents a step toward the advocacy of violent revolution that is distinctive in African literature and a significant turning point in La Guma's career. The book focuses on the activities of a secret underground organization dedicated to the destruction of apartheid in South Africa. Its two principal protagonists are the "coloured" operative Beukes, who gives up a happy personal life to devote himself to revolutionary activity, and the black organizer Elias Tekwane, who is captured by the South African police, tortured, and beaten to death. La Guma refuses to romanticize revolutionary activity, showing starkly the sacrifices that must be made in the interest of a cause whose ultimate success is by no means certain. Tekwane's fate is gruesome; Beukes's work is more tedious than glamorous, although he is forced to endure extreme physical and mental hardship in the course of his day-to-day political activities. At the same time, *In the Fog of the Seasons' End* does contain a strong utopian dimension. During his torture, Tekwane refuses to reveal any information the police can use against the movement. Meanwhile, partially because of Tekwane's heroic silence, Beukes escapes from the police and succeeds in smuggling three other revolutionaries out of South Africa for military training for a possible all-out war against apartheid.

Most of the events in *In the Fog of the Seasons' End* involve the Beukes's efforts to distribute antiapartheid pamphlets and otherwise work against the system while avoiding the South African secret police. In the course of these activities, Beukes frequently recalls earlier happy times spent with his wife

Frances, though Beukes has not seen Frances or their young child since he was forced underground. Beukes sometimes longs simply to lead a normal, peaceful life with his family, apart from the dangerous world of revolutionary politics, but he also knows that as a coloured South African, he can never do so. He is willing to sacrifice his personal life for the movement because he knows that the destruction of apartheid is crucial to any hope he and his family might have of living a life free of oppression and humiliation.

If it is through Beukes that La Guma gives us a glimpse of the daily lives of those who worked in the underground resistance to apartheid, it is through the story of Tekwane that La Guma presents the brutal realities that made such resistance necessary. We are first introduced to Tekwane in Chapter 6, which briefly summarizes his childhood, including the death of his father in a mining accident. This chapter also outlines Tekwane's growing awareness of the racism of his society and of the intense regimentation of the lives of nonwhites in South Africa. They live their lives in a servitude whose bonds are "entangled chains of infinite regulations, its rivets are driven in with rubber stamps, and scratchy pens in the offices of the Native Commissioners are like branding irons which leave scars for life" (p. 80). Central to this bureaucratic nightmare is the system of government passes, which all adult nonwhite South Africans must carry when they travel outside their home areas. In Chapter 12, we see the hardships experienced by Tekwane, now in his forties and living in a squalid, prison-like single-man's barracks in a black "location." There, he recalls an earlier humiliating experience when he applied for a pass to travel from his home to the city, where he wanted to work to help feed his family and alleviate the labor shortage brought about by World War II. To receive the pass, the young Tekwane had to undergo a humiliating interrogation in which a white official, aided by a black clerk, determined Tekwane's age by examining his genitals. He was assigned the age of twenty, though he was actually seventeen. This modification of Tekwane's age is only another of the many ways in which the lives of nonwhite South Africans were controlled and manipulated under apartheid. Tekwane's first name, for example, is not really Elias, but the African name of his great grandfather.[1] The biblical name Elias was given to him by a white missionary who found the African name too difficult to pronounce.

The absurdity (and inhumanity) of the pass system is highlighted by La Guma in a scene in Chapter 6 where an abusive South African policeman interrogates a nonwhite South African. The man attempts to be cooperative,

---

[1] One might compare the events related in Elie Wiesel's autobiographical novel, *Night* (1987), in which the prisoners in Nazi prison camps are assigned arbitrary ages and given numbers that replace their names. The apartheid regime in South Africa has, in fact, frequently been compared to Nazi Germany. La Guma's Beukes himself makes the connection (p. 131).

but he finds that no matter how hard he tries, he can never fully please his interrogator. After an almost endless series of questions, the policeman concludes the interview with a brutal reminder of the realities of life under apartheid:

> "If these things are not followed with care, then into the prison with you or all permits cancelled so that you cease to exist. You will be nothing, nobody, in fact you will be decreated. You . . . you will be as nothing, perhaps even less than nothing" (p. 82).

The man interrogated in this scene might be Tekwane, but he is not specifically identified, suggesting that nonwhites were never viewed as individuals under apartheid but were seen merely as members of a racial group. La Guma achieves a similar effect by beginning his book with a prologue that describes the brutal torture/interrogation of an unnamed black prisoner by the South African police. It is only in chapter 17, nearly at the end of the book, that we return to this scene, with the prisoner now identified as Tekwane. This method of presentation makes it clear that Tekwane's case is not unique and that his experience, however horrifying, is that of many nonwhites in South Africa. JanMohamed identifies this aspect of La Guma's fiction as crucially important:

> While each black, "Coloured," or Indian person in South Africa is intuitively aware of himself as a unique being, the white society that controls him recognizes and treats him only as a generic being, as a "kaffir" (devil), as an interchangeable unit of a homogeneous group (JanMohamed 1983, 228).

This motif in La Guma's work functions largely as a commentary on the racism of South African society under apartheid. On the other hand, from La Guma's Marxist point of view, this reduction of individuals to interchangeable things is a particularly brutal and overt example of the ways in which individuals are inevitably reduced to the status of commodities under capitalism. Tekwane, the most theoretically sophisticated of the major characters in *In the Fog of the Seasons' End*, is perfectly well aware that there is more than racism at stake in apartheid. There is also a strong economic motivation behind the system. Tekwane thus realizes as he watches a crowd of blacks standing outside a government labor bureau hoping to be assigned menial jobs, that these men, like himself, are oppressed at least as much because of their class as their skin color. "We are not only humbled as Blacks," he thinks to himself, "but also as workers; our blackness is only a pretext" (p. 131).

Tekwane (like La Guma) believes that South African workers must band together to oppose their exploitation by their rich bosses. Indeed, La Guma is careful to make the revolutionary movement in *In the Fog of the Seasons' End* multiracial, emphasizing that its members belong to a common class rather than a common race and that their ultimate struggle is against the class structure of capitalism, of which apartheid is but a particularly perverse and brutal form.[2] La Guma thus emphasizes the need for the development of a strong proletarian class consciousness, that is, of a sense of solidarity and common interest among workers of whatever race. In this sense, La Guma's work recalls that of Frantz Fanon, who insists that any genuine liberation from the brutal racial inequities of colonialism (of which apartheid is an extension) requires a complete transformation not simply of racial power structures, but of class structure. As JanMohamed puts it, the "major imperative" of La Guma's fiction is a search for viable, nonexploitative communities that will allow their members to escape the oppression they have experienced under apartheid, and JanMohamed identifies the "mutual care, concern, and respect" of the members of the underground movement in *In the Fog of the Seasons' End* as an important example of such a community (JanMohamed 1983, 255). The movement, in short, represents an important step toward the development of a viable proletarian class consciousness that can lead to a class-based revolution.

In this sense, La Guma's fiction is extremely complex. It is, in fact, what Marxist thinkers refer to as dialectical. That is, it draws its conclusions only after a careful delineation and consideration of opposing alternatives. On the one hand, nonwhite South Africans are brutalized and dehumanized by a system that treats them as members of a racial group rather than as individuals. On the other hand, their only hope for emancipation lies in their ability to act not as individuals, but as members of a group. There is, however, no contradiction in this position. For one thing, the first kind of group involves race, while the second involves class; and class, in the Marxist vision, is a temporary category that will cease to exist after the successful establishment of socialism. For another, racism involves a genuine obliteration of individuality and humanity, while class solidarity creates a nurturing social context within which the individual can thrive and grow, reaching his or her own potential as a human being. As Emmanuel Ngara notes, La Guma's characters "tend to be 'types' rather than individuals" (Ngara 1985, 92). But literary characters are never literally individuals: they are textual constructs with specific narrative functions. And the function of the "types" portrayed by La Guma is to convey the large historical forces that impinge upon individuals in the real world, much in the mode praised by the Hungarian Marxist theorist Georg Lukács.

As many Marxist critics have pointed out, the individualistic rhetoric of Western bourgeois ideology is merely a disguise for the thorough subjection of the individual through the operation of complex ideological practices.

---

[2] See Chandramohan (1992) for an extended discussion of the "trans-ethnicity" of La Guma's vision.

Central to this idea is the Marxist notion that individuals exist as human beings only within a certain social context in which they become who they are through interaction with others. As a result, individuals assume their identities in ways that are greatly determined by their context. As Marx puts it in a famous passage in *The German Ideology*, "Life is not determined by consciousness, but consciousness by life" (Marx and Engels 1978, 155). Socialism would presumably provide a context in which individuals could develop freely according to their own desires and abilities. Capitalism, on the other hand, is based on economic competition that inevitably leads to conflict between individuals. It requires that individuals have enough sense of individualism to compete in a free market and thus make the economy function, but it also requires that this surface individualism be supported by a fundamental conformism that leads each individual to participate unquestioningly in a system that is by and large not to his or her advantage. Under apartheid, as *In the Fog of the Seasons' End* graphically shows, the kind of identities available to individuals were especially limited. In this sense, one of the most useful Marxist concepts for understanding La Guma's work is Louis Althusser's notion of "interpellation," or the "hailing of the subject"—the process whereby powerful forces (working in the interest of the prevailing ideology of a given society) form individuals as subjects. For Althusser, we do not form our attitudes so much as they form us, and "the category of the subject is only constitutive of all ideology insofar as all ideology has the function (which defines it) of 'constituting' concrete individuals as subjects" (Althusser 1971, 171).

At stake in the notion of interpellation are the complex and subtle ways through which capitalist society attempts to convince the subordinated classes that the ideas of the ruling (bourgeois) class are right and natural, thus causing the working classes to accept their domination and exploitation willingly. Here, Althusser is influenced by the work of the Italian Marxist Antonio Gramsci, who argued that the European bourgeoisie gained and maintained their power through a complex of political and cultural practices that convinced the more numerous "subaltern" classes to accede willingly to bourgeois authority as natural and proper. The effectiveness of this technique of power, which Gramsci terms "hegemony," resides principally in the ability of the bourgeoisie to obtain the

> "spontaneous" consent given by the great masses of the population to the general direction imposed on social life by the dominant fundamental group; this consent is "historically" caused by the prestige (and consequent confidence) which the dominant group enjoys because of its position and function in the world of production (Gramsci 1971, 12).

If absolutely necessary, this consensual obedience can be supplemented by "the apparatus of state coercive power," that is, by institutions such as the police and the army, which use physical force to impose obedience "on those groups who do not 'consent' either actively or passively. This apparatus is, however, constituted for the whole of society in anticipation of moments of crisis of command and direction when spontaneous consent has failed" (p. 12).

Hegemony is a complex and plural strategy that is by definition never fully successful, making it necessary to keep the police and the military in the background in case of emergency. Such emergencies seldom occur in the metropolitan centers of Europe, but they were more frequent in the colonies, where hegemonic practices of power were always supplemented by brute force, theatrical display, and other techniques held over from the era of feudal–aristocratic rule in Europe. Despite complex cultural interchanges and the Europeanization of certain members of the indigenous elite, most colonial peoples would never mistake the position and attitudes of the British bourgeoisie for their own because of the radical racial and cultural duality of the colonial situation. To put it in Althusserian terms, interpellation occurs when the individual subject is created in the image of official ideology, not when that ideology proclaims the subject an alien (and racially inferior) "other."

Frantz Fanon notes that in a colonial situation, official power depends far more on physical violence than psychological persuasion (Fanon 1968, 38). In this sense, as in many others, the apartheid system closely resembled the earlier colonial systems in Africa, and *In the Fog of the Seasons' End* graphically demonstrates the reliance on physical violence and other coercive practices used by official power in South Africa. Perhaps the most vivid of these demonstrations is La Guma's detailed description of the ruthless torture/murder of Tekwane at the hands of the South African secret police. This murder occurs behind the closed doors of a prison, but La Guma also shows that the authorities are not above committing such atrocities in plain view. In Chapter 9, for example, he describes a brutal and deadly police assault on a peaceful crowd of demonstrators. This description gains power from the fact that it is obviously rooted in the 1960 Sharpeville massacre and other similar events in South African history. At the same time, the incident is recounted in a generalized, rather allegorical fashion that makes it clear that such atrocities were not aberrations in apartheid South Africa, but were the fabric of everyday life. Much as the torture of Tekwane is first described as the experience of an unnamed South African, the victims killed in this attack are identified by designations such as the Washerwoman, the Child, and the Bicycle Messenger. These "typical" names make it clear that in South Africa any nonwhite citizen was in danger at any time of becoming a victim of violence at the hands of a state apparatus that did not stop to make fine distinctions between individuals.

Gramsci's work reminds us that the same might be said for citizens of western Europe and North America, and indeed there are historical instances of police violence against peaceful political demonstrators in such places. But it clear that the level and frequency of such violence were far higher in an apartheid South Africa that continued to rely more on traditional colonial techniques of power than on the more subtle methods of Western industrial countries. La Guma responds to the overt brutality and physical violence of apartheid with a direct call to militant action. This is not to say, however, that La Guma pays no attention to the ideological and cultural practices that were long used to shore up the system of apartheid. In particular, La Guma clearly indicates that the popular culture of global capitalism (largely American in origin) helped create a mind-set in South Africa that perpetuated apartheid. For one thing, La Guma suggests that the images of violence so central to Western popular culture created a decadent attitude that made the brutalities of apartheid seem more thinkable and less monstrous. One motif that runs through the entire book involves newspaper reports of a sensational murder case: an Afrikaner woman in a country town murdered her abusive husband by gradually poisoning him until he was so weak that she was able to over-power and strangle him. On one level, this murder simply illustrates the cru-elty and violence that is central to South African society. On another level, it suggests the possibility of successful resistance to oppression because the woman was eventually able to overpower her stronger husband through per-severance and determined effort. But also important are the prominence the media gives to the case and the fascination it elicits from the populace, which treats it like an event from a soap opera. Attuned to violence through the images conveyed to them by popular culture, most people are not horrified by the story, but merely entertained by it.

Beukes himself sometimes feels that his cloak-and-dagger existence is like something from a film (p. 25). At the same time, he realizes that this film-like nature is an aberration brought about by the unnatural system of apart-heid. But other South Africans are not as adept at seeing beyond the complex entanglement of fiction and reality that characterizes their society. This motif is most obvious in the portrayal of Beukes's friend, Tommy, a decent young man who has little interest in political activism, largely because he is too im-mersed in the escapist world of popular culture. Tommy responds to almost every event in his life by referring to the images and ideas conveyed by (mostly American) film and popular music. Tommy, in short, retreats into the escapist world of popular culture to avoid dealing with the cruel world of reality in South Africa. As the narrator puts it (filtered through Beukes's con-sciousness), reality for Tommy "could be shut out by the blare of dance-bands and the voices of crooners. From this cocoon he emerged only to find the means of subsistence, food and drink. Politics meant nothing to him" (p. 53).

What in the West passes for "high" art (that is, art intended for con-sumption by the ruling classes rather than the working classes) also comes in for criticism in *In the Fog of the Seasons' End*. Realizing that Tommy knows nothing about classical music despite his fascination with Western culture, Beukes remarks, "There's things poor people just don't get to hear" (p. 57). Meanwhile, at one point the South African authorities attempt to demonstrate their enlightened attitude by proposing (in the manner of Marie Antoinette's famous "Let them eat cake") to allow nonwhites occasional access to a new opera house, though they will in fact be unlikely to be able to afford to go there. Beukes dismisses the plan as a ruse, and Elias rejects it as well. Access to an opera house is of very little use to a population that is starving to death: "What a peculiar way of thinking they have," he tells Beukes. "Opera house and no bread" (p. 131).

Indeed, for South Africa's oppressed majority, access to this opera house may not only be of little use, but may also contribute to the problem by creating a diversion from the real problems of their society. This suggestion that the niceties of Western bourgeois aesthetics are irrelevant or even harmful in the crisis context of apartheid South Africa can be read as an allegorization of La Guma's literary project, which dispenses with common Western expectations that art will present pleasant and beautiful images disengaged from the world of politics. Decades of New Critical dominance in American literature studies produced a vision of literature as a realm divorced from history and politics, a vision that is only now beginning to be challenged by newer trends in American criticism. Indeed, as Peter Bürger (1984) has shown, Western notions of the aesthetic inherently tend toward a vision of art as separate from the social world—and as therefore unable to contribute to change in that world. Moreover, Western literature has long been particularly opposed to revolutionary politics. One need only consider the novels of Charles Dickens, sometimes seen as a literary champion of the poor and the downtrodden, to see the central element of horror of revolution that runs through Western literature. In works such as *Barnaby Rudge* and *A Tale of Two Cities*, Dickens depicts popular rebellions in which the participants are shown as crazed and vicious members of lawless mobs.

Most of our modern Western notions of literary aesthetics arose in the nineteenth century, when literature was one of the central tools used by a newly dominant bourgeois class to explain and justify their rise to power in Europe. *In the Fog of the Seasons' End*, however, seeks not to rationalize a revolution from the recent past, but to promote revolution in the future. The book has a fundamentally different purpose from that of most Western literature and therefore necessarily departs in significant ways from Western aesthetic values. Critics such as Adrian Roscoe, who regrets the book's lack of a "rich poetic quality" (Roscoe 1977, 255), or David Rabkin (1973), who laments the book's lack of richly subjective characters, may thus be missing the point, though it should also be said that critics such as Balutansky, who praises the

book's effective use of formal techniques, may be diverting attention from La
Guma's central intention as well (Balutansky 1990).[3] Indeed, critics such as
Leonard Kibera (1976) and Cecil Abrahams (1985), censured by Balutansky
for limiting their analyses to the "scope of La Guma's political concerns," may
actually come the closest to doing justice to the book (Balutansky 1990, 82).

Of course, this is not to say that aesthetic and formal concerns are irrelevant to La Guma's project in *In the Fog of the Seasons' End.* For example, Jan-
Mohamed comments that the fragmented formal structure of the book helps
convey the chaotic nature of life for guerrillas involved in revolutionary activity (JanMohamed 1983, 257).[4] It is important, however, to recognize that
La Guma's use of formal techniques is intended not to set his work apart
from the world of politics and history, but to effect a more intense engagement with that world. In short, La Guma's work, like all literature, depends
on a certain aesthetic dimension for its effects, but the aesthetics of the book
differ significantly from those of Western bourgeois literature. The particular urgency of the political message of *In the Fog of the Seasons' End* marks it
as an African—and especially as a South African—text. Indeed, African revolutionary writers such as Ngugi and Sembène are clearly La Guma's closest literary comrades. Nevertheless, it is valuable for us as Western readers to
realize that La Guma's work has important European antecedents as well.
Many of these are Russians, whose marginality to European history may
have appealed to La Guma. But La Guma's most important Russian influence, Maxim Gorky, is regarded worldwide as one of the great figures of so-
cially-engaged literature, and leftist writers all over the world have identified
Gorky as an important model.[5] This mutual interest in Gorky suggests that
readers who wish to find Western analogues to La Guma's fiction should
search for them not in the canonical "great tradition" of Western bourgeois
literature, but in the works of American proletarian writers such as Mike
Gold and Jack Conroy, or British socialist writers such as Robert Tressell and
Lewis Grassic Gibbon.

These writers' works, like La Guma's, are fundamentally opposed to a
capitalist system that includes bourgeois literature and aesthetics. However,
because of the hegemonic nature of bourgeois power in Europe and America, leftist fiction there is generally oriented toward a deconstruction of ideological practices of manipulation rather than a call for violent revolution.

---

[3] Balutansky does, however, understand the political mission of La Guma's work. She begins
her book with an epigraph quoted from La Guma which rejects the Western notion of "Art
for art's sake" as irrelevant to conditions in apartheid South Africa.

[4] Balutansky makes a similar point about the fragmentation of individual sentences in the book
(Balutansky 1990, 85).

[5] On affinities between Gorky and La Guma, see Chandramohan (1992, 137) and Asein (1978,
75).

Comparing *In the Fog of the Seasons' End* to Tressell's *The Ragged Trousered Philanthropists* (1955, first published in 1914), perhaps the most important modern novel in the British socialist tradition, Robert Green correctly notes that the emphasis on direct political action in La Guma's book differs substantially from the more theoretical and abstract focus of Tressell's book (Green 1979, 88–89). This difference, no doubt, can be attributed to the greater social stability of England relative to a highly volatile South Africa. In South Africa, apartheid adds urgency to political action, and the actual existence of organized armed resistance adds concreteness to the literary theme of revolution by making revolution a genuine historical possibility. Tressell's book focuses on the ideological practices through which the British ruling classes secure the willing obedience of the working classes by convincing them to accept the rightness and naturalness of a capitalist system that leads to fabulous wealth for an elite few and dismal poverty for most workers. Tressell's title refers to the way in which the British working classes, ragged trousers and all, ignore their miserable living and working conditions to labor generously for the benefit of their rich bosses. He attempts to disrupt this process by showing his readers the ways in which British workers are exploited by their capitalist bosses.[6] The system of apartheid in South Africa, despite its fundamentally economic underpinnings, was far less subtle than the capitalist system in England, and few nonwhites in South Africa needed to be convinced that the system was not to their advantage. La Guma can thus dispense with the arguments for an alternative system that are central to Tressell's book. Instead, his task is to exhort the South African populace to take action against a system they already realize is brutally unjust.

Both Tressell and La Guma, in short, employ literary strategies that are designed to counter the specific techniques through which the systems they criticize maintain their power.[7] Tressell's book works primarily at the level of logical argument and persuasion, like the hegemonic practices of capitalist power in England and other industrialized Western countries. *In the Fog of the Seasons' End*, on the other hand, responds to an emergency situation by urging immediate violent opposition to apartheid. However, La Guma's book exceeds those of writers such as Tressell and Gold not only in its negative depiction of the violent workings of official power, but also in its positive suggestion of the possibilities of opposition. Indeed, one of the implications of La

---

[6] American leftist fiction is often even more localized in its task. Thus, Mike Gold's *Jews Without Money* (1984, first published in 1930), probably the most important American proletarian novel, seeks to demonstrate that systemic poverty exists in an America where many people seem to feel that only the lazy and the shiftless can possibly be poor.

[7] It is not surprising, then, that La Guma's book has much more in common with a work such as Maxim Gorky's *Mother* (1972), another classic of European leftist literature, but one that arises from the crisis situation of early-twentieth-century Russia.

Guma's work is that the brutalities of apartheid arise largely out of a sense of weakness on the part of a ruling elite that realizes the fragility of its power. *In the Fog of the Seasons' End* is ultimately far more optimistic than most Western socialist fiction. Not only do the revolutionaries in the book score certain successes against all odds, but the book also ends with the strongly utopian image of children gathered in a sunlit yard and with the strongly hopeful declaration that the system of apartheid has prepared its own downfall (p. 181).

In terms of this novel, at least, Samuel Omo Asein is thus correct when he concludes that "the pervasive note then in La Guma's novels is not that of despair and flight into a protective world of political negativism, but that of hope in the eventual overthrow of the oppressive regime in South Africa" (Asein 1978, 86).[8] Granted, *The Ragged Trousered Philanthropists* ends on a similarly hopeful note, but, more than eighty years later, the revolution foreseen by Tressell has not materialized. La Guma's utopian vision, meanwhile, gains a certain power from the fact that the system of apartheid has now nominally been destroyed. Indeed, the fall of apartheid makes La Guma's work more relevant now than ever, partially for the simple reason that his work can finally be read in South Africa, but mostly because it sounds an important warning against complacency by providing ominous reminders of a past that must never be repeated. From a Fanonian perspective, of course, La Guma's work also urges continued vigilance because the fall of apartheid does not guarantee justice and equality for all South Africans. La Guma's careful association of apartheid with capitalism implies that the destruction of apartheid is only the first step in a revolutionary process that can ultimately succeed only when the class structure of capitalist society has itself been obliterated.

Historical Background
Alex La Guma, like Nadine Gordimer, is a South African writer whose work grows directly out of South African history and in particular out of an opposition to apartheid. The reader should thus consult chapter 7 for historical background to La Guma's work. However, La Guma, as a coloured South African and an active participant in radical opposition to the apartheid regime, occupies a somewhat different position in relation to South African history than Gordimer. For example, while the "Treason Trials" of 1956–1961 involved Gordimer's character Lionel Burger, they involved La Guma directly: he was one of the more than 150 men and women tried (and finally acquitted of) treason for their opposition to apartheid.

---

[8] As Scanlon points out, however, *In the Fog of the Seasons' End* is decidedly more optimistic than some of La Guma's earlier work. As Scanlon puts it, "If La Guma's first novel traces a descent into despair, *In the Fog of the Seasons' End* reveals an upward movement of recovery" (Scanlon 1979, 46).

Biographical Background

Born in Cape Town in 1925, Alex La Guma was the son of Jimmy La Guma, a noted crusader for the civil rights of nonwhites in South Africa. The elder La Guma was a union organizer, coloured secretary of the Cape Branch of the African National Congress, president of the South African Coloured Peoples' Congress, and a member of the central committee of the South African Communist Party. The young Alex followed very much in his father's footsteps. In 1946, at age twenty-one, he organized and led a strike among the workers at a metal box factory where he was employed. The next year, he joined the Young Communist League. In 1948, when the victory of the Boer Nationalist Party led to the beginnings of apartheid as a formal government policy, La Guma became a member of the South African Communist Party and remained so until 1950 when the party was officially banned. La Guma continued his political activities as apartheid was solidified in the next few years, and he was eventually arrested in 1956 on charges of treason.

The ensuing Treason Trials lasted for nearly five years. All of those charged were eventually acquitted, but the trials absorbed the energies and attention of so many antiapartheid leaders that the opposition to apartheid was seriously hampered. Meanwhile, the Sharpeville massacre in 1960 led the government to declare a state of emergency that further curtailed the civil rights of South African citizens. La Guma himself was arrested again in 1961 for his political activities. From this point on he was continually harassed by the government. By 1962, a new Sabotage Act allowed the minister of justice to order anyone placed under house arrest without trial. La Guma was one of the first so detained, and he was officially confined to his house twenty-four hours a day from 1962 until 1966, except for one period in 1963 when he was taken to prison and placed in solitary confinement in an attempt to ensure that he could have no contact with the resistance movement. La Guma was again arrested in 1966, but in September of that year he and his family were granted permanent exit visas that allowed them to move to London in what amounted to political exile.

Once abroad, La Guma continued to crusade for justice in South Africa, traveling widely and giving numerous talks describing the evils of apartheid and promoting the resistance efforts of the ANC and other groups. This project took La Guma around the world, especially to countries sympathetic to his leftist political beliefs. He visited the Soviet Union, Chile (when Allende was president), Vietnam, and Tanzania, where he stayed for a time as writer in residence at the University of Dar es Salaam. He gained a great deal of international prominence during these years. In 1969, for example, he was given India's Lotus Prize for Literature, and in the same year he became the chairman of the ANC's London branch. In 1977, La Guma was elected secretary-general of the Afro-Asian Writers' Association, and in 1978 he moved to Cuba, where he took up residence in Havana as the chief representative of the ANC to the Caribbean and Central and South America. He remained in Cuba until his death (by heart attack) in 1986.

La Guma's political activism was accompanied by (and indeed included) a productive writing career. Beginning in the mid-1950s, he worked as a staff journalist for the progressive Cape Town newspaper *New Age*, for which he managed to write a weekly column until 1962 despite his persecution by the South African authorities. He also began to write fiction during the 1950s, and his first novel, *A Walk in the Night* (1967b), was apparently completed by early in 1960. This book was eventually published in Nigeria in 1962, after considerable difficulty in getting the manuscript out of South Africa. Thus began a career that saw all of La Guma's novels published abroad because they were banned in South Africa. *And a Threefold Cord* (1964) and *The Stone Country* (1967) were originally published in Berlin, while *In the Fog of the Seasons' End* (1972) originally appeared in New York, and *Time of the Butcherbird* (1979) was first published in London.

All of La Guma's fiction is deeply committed to the political opposition to apartheid, though the different novels employ a variety of strategies in their attempt to reveal the abusive and dehumanizing effects of apartheid and to suggest possible alternatives for a better future. *A Walk in the Night* is an extremely violent and essentially naturalistic novel that devotes most of its energy to vivid depictions of the degrading poverty of Cape Town's nonwhite slums and the humiliation of the slums' residents due to the squalor in which they are forced to live and the mistreatment they suffer at the hands of the police and other officials. The plot of the novel, set in the seamy underworld of District Six, the coloured slum of Cape Town, is simple and unfolds within a few hours. The protagonist, Michael Adonis, is a coloured South African who loses his job after his white foreman upbraids him for taking time from work to urinate. Michael is then stopped (without cause) by two white policeman, who insult and humiliate him merely because of his race. Filled with rage, Michael drinks in a pub, then returns to his tenement where he unintentionally kills an old Irishmen in a drunken altercation. Michael escapes, and Willieboy, a young street tough, is blamed for the murder and is eventually killed by a sadistic policeman, Constable Raalt. Michael, meanwhile, has been driven to crime, and he and his new gang are on their way to commit a robbery as Willieboy lies bleeding to death at the end of the novel.

A Walk in the Night is an angry and essentially pessimistic novel in which characters respond to their brutalization by the system with brutality of their own. As La Guma's career developed, however, his delineation of South African society became more sophisticated and his fiction began to include suggestions of more positive modes of resistance. *And a Threefold Cord* con-

tains many of the same suggestions that the characters are at the mercy of
large, impersonal forces, but it is less violent and more subdued than its predecessor. The depiction of the lives of the coloured Pauls family resembles
the striking depictions of poverty that characterized his first novel, though
La Guma's technique in *And a Threefold Cord* is somewhat more symbolic and
less naturalistic than in *A Walk in the Night*. Moreover, the courage and te-
nacity of the Pauls family in the face of its difficulties point toward a greater
sense of hopefulness, especially through the solidarity of oppressed people
working together.

La Guma's third novel, *The Stone Country* is a highly allegorical account
of life in a South African prison that in many ways represents South Africa
as a whole. The book focuses on the experiences of George Adams, a political prisoner who has been incarcerated for distributing political pamphlets
urging resistance to apartheid. Another prominent character is the Casbah
Kid, whose squalid childhood has led him to a life of crime. The Casbah Kid
is thus a character who might have fit very well in La Guma's earlier novels.
Adams, however, possesses a highly evolved political consciousness that represents a clear movement forward in La Guma's development as a political
writer. Though he is not a sophisticated intellectual, Adams's ability to sense
the brutality of apartheid and to articulate the kind of individual dignity that
should be possible in a just society is unmatched by any of the characters in
La Guma's earlier works. And, if conditions in the prison stand in for the
oppressive nature of apartheid society as a whole, George's determination to
work for better conditions in the prison suggests the need for positive political action throughout South Africa.

This aspect of La Guma's career comes to full fruition in *In the Fog of
the Seasons' End*. According to Cecil Abrahams, this book combined with *The
Stone Country* to make La Guma a "major literary figure in African literature"
(Abrahams 1985, 18). La Guma's brief final novel, *Time of the Butcherbird*, is
by far his most symbolic, employing intensely suggestive images in a further
elaboration of La Guma's support for armed rebellion against apartheid. Its
three major characters, a poor black recently released from prison, a rich Afrikaner farmer/politician, and a struggling white English-speaking salesman,
are less individuals than representatives of important groups within South
African society. The black, Shilling Murile, has sworn revenge against the
Afrikaner, Hannes Meulen, for his involvement ten years earlier in the death
of Murile's brother. The English-speaking white, Edward Stopes, has come
to town on a selling trip, and he is something of an "innocent" bystander to
the events of the novel, which have clear implications for the possible future
of South African society. Murile kills Meulen, but in the process kills Stopes
as well, suggesting the ultimate fate of those who support and enforce apartheid and those who simply stand aside and let it continue.

Abdul JanMohamed has suggested that a consistent "marginality" is perhaps the most striking characteristic of La Guma's writing. Neither white nor black, La Guma transcends the simple polar opposition of these two racial groups. Banned from publication in apartheid South Africa, La Guma's work was pushed to the margins of the struggle against apartheid that was its major thrust. Moreover, La Guma's fiction, perhaps because of its overtly leftist political stance, has been less widely accepted in the West than the work of African writers such as Gordimer, Chinua Achebe, Wole Soyinka, or Ngugi wa Thiong'o.[9] As JanMohamed points out, there was little demand for political fiction in the West during the Cold War, when such fiction was vaguely associated with what was seen as the dogmatism of Stalinism. Thus, the only political novels to have a wide readership in the West during the Cold War were those like the fiction of Alexander Solzhenitsyn, which

> revives the legacy of the Cold War by once more valorizing the freedom of Western institutions against the restrictive practices of the Russian "other," or the fiction of V. S. Naipaul, which revives the legacy of colonialism by further valorizing the goodness and civilization of the West against the unredeemable evil and barbarity of the Third World "other" (JanMohamed 1983, 262).

In short, La Guma's fiction, by challenging the Western stereotypes that fed both colonialism and the Cold War, had a doubly difficult time in winning a Western readership. On the other hand, Bernth Lindfors's survey of Anglophone African universities showed that among writers known primarily as novelists, La Guma is surpassed only by Ngugi, Achebe, and Armah in his prominence in the curricula of those universities (Lindfors 1990).[10] La Guma is particularly prominent among African political novelists. He is thus appropriately listed with Sembène and Ngugi as the writers who "naturally come to mind" in the discussion of the development of a revolutionary African aesthetics (Udenta 1993, 9). La Guma's work is also beginning to receive more critical attention in the West, perhaps partially because of the easing of the tensions associated with the Cold War, though much published criticism attempts to divert attention from La Guma's revolutionary politics through discussion of literary form and technique. Book-length studies that show some sensitivity to the political dimension of his work include those by Abrahams (1985), Kathleen Balutansky (1990), and Balasubramanyam Chandramohan 1992). The collection entitled *Memories of Home*, edited by

---

[9] Ngugi's later fiction is also overtly leftist, but his reputation in the West had already been established by earlier works that are not, such as *The River Between* (1965).

[10] La Guma is ranked seventh among all authors in Lindfors's survey, ranking behind these three novelists as well as the dramatists Soyinka and J. P. Clark and the poet Okot p'Bitek (Lindfors 1990).

Cecil Abrahams (1991), also contains useful samples of La Guma's writing and valuable commentaries, including personal reminiscences by La Guma's widow. JanMohamed's chapter on La Guma in *Manichean Aesthetics* (1983) is still probably the best brief survey of his work, while numerous other critical essays discuss more specific aspects of La Guma's various novels.

Further Reading
See the suggestions for further reading at the end of Chapter 7.

Chapter 9

Ngugi wa Thiong'o:
Devil on the Cross

In December, 1977, Ngugi wa Thiong'o was arrested by the Kenyan government and detained without trial (or even official charges) for nearly a year in Kenya's Kamiti Maximum Security Prison, the site of mass hangings of Mau Mau guerrillas for their opposition to British colonial rule in the 1950s. During his stay at Kamiti (which is described in some detail in *Detained* (1981a), Ngugi's prison diary) Ngugi smuggled spare toilet paper into his cell and secretly wrote a novel on it—*Caitaani Mutharaba-ini*, eventually published to brisk sales in Nairobi in 1980. Ngugi's own English translation was published in 1982, as *Devil on the Cross* (1988). The book is an angry and biting satire of neocolonial oppression and corruption in Kenya that clearly represents Ngugi's political position as a champion of Kenya's poor and oppressed. Moreover, it is a particularly successful example of the adaptation of the techniques and conventions of African oral culture to the novel form. *Devil on the Cross* combines a creative use of Gikuyu cultural forms and traditions with references to historical events such as the Mau Mau uprising. The novel makes an important contribution to Ngugi's project of drawing upon the long tradition of Kenyan anticolonial resistance to encourage resistance to oppression in the present day.

At the beginning of *Devil on the Cross*, the narrator explains the value of the book's critical project in a proverbial manner that characterizes his narration throughout: "How can we cover up pits in our courtyard with leaves or grass, saying to ourselves that because our eyes cannot now see the holes, our children can prance about the yard as they like?" (p. 7). It is not productive, the narrator asserts, to ignore the very real problems of postcolonial Kenyan society, so he will not be shy in proclaiming those problems. However, in addition to its searing condemnation of the politicians and rich businessmen who continue to exploit the Kenyan people, *Devil on the Cross* also contains a very strong positive component. In particular, Ngugi offers a declaration of Kenyan cultural autonomy that is designed to help the Kenyan people develop a stronger sense of their own cultural identity, which will allow them to overcome the colonial assertion of Western cultural superiority.

Devil on the Cross draws upon the long heritage of courageous Kenyan resistance to colonial domination. For instance, positive references to the Mau Mau provide examples of the kind of collective action that is again needed to oppose oppression in Kenya (pp. 37–40). Moreover, the text draws in central ways upon indigenous Gikuyu cultural traditions. The narrator introduces himself as the "Prophet of Justice" and the "Gicaandi Player," thus announcing that the text will deal with questions of justice and that it also will be narrated in the mode of the traditional Gikuyu oral storyteller.[1] This narrator recedes into the background as the novel proceeds, but this initial narrative framework remains in place. We Western readers must thus be willing to acknowledge that the text arises from a cultural tradition that differs from our own, and we must strain against the temptation to try to read the book simply as if it were a Western novel. Moreover, it is important to remain aware of the fact that the principal "implied readers" of this book are not Westerners at all and that when we read the book in English, we are reading a translation not only across languages, but also across cultures.

The impact of orality in *Devil on the Cross* goes well beyond mere references to oral tradition. Orality is, in fact, a fundamental aspect of the texture of the book. Ngugi specifically designed it for oral performance to make it more accessible to an audience of Kenyan peasants and workers, many of whom were illiterate. This profound use of Gikuyu oral traditions makes *Devil on the Cross* a crucial turning point in Ngugi's career. The book is also an important departure because it is the first novel that Ngugi wrote in Gikuyu, though he had already established a major reputation as an English-language novelist. Indeed, starting with *Devil on the Cross*, the choice of language becomes central to Ngugi's writing, making him one of the most important figures in the ongoing debate over this issue (Westley 1992). There are several reasons for Ngugi's shift to writing in Gikuyu, but one of the most important involves his attempt to address Kenyan peasants and workers directly. These people are, by and large, not literate in English. Thus, an overt declaration of the intended audience of *Devil on the Cross* is built into the very fabric of the book's language. The book draws extensively upon Gikuyu oral culture, and its narrative is liberally punctuated with proverbs, songs, and other elements normally associated with oral performances rath-

---

[1] The Gicaandi is a traditional instrument often used to accompany the performances of Gikuyu oral narratives. Importantly, the Gicaandi player is associated with popular performances, as opposed to the traditional African griot, who is more a figure of authority.

er than printed novels, establishing a further line of communication with Ngugi's anticipated audience. Critics like Adewoye (1992), Ogunjimi (1984), and Sackey (1991) have emphasized this link to the oral tradition as one of the most important characteristics of *Devil on the Cross.*

On the other hand, Ngugi's book engages in a number of rich dialogues with the Western literary tradition as well. For example, the basic plot of the book parallels that of the bildungsroman, which Barbara Foley calls the "classic form" of the nineteenth-century European bourgeois novel (Foley 1993, 321). The European bildungsroman traditionally tells the story of a young, usually male protagonist who meets certain obstacles and engages in certain conflicts in the course of his development and education. In a similar way, *Devil on the Cross* concerns the education and development of the young woman Wariinga. A long section midway through the book relates her biography in some detail, beginning with her birth in the midst of the "Emergency" of the 1950s, when the British colonial rulers of Kenya imposed extremely repressive measures in their attempt to quell the Mau Mau forces who were waging a guerrilla war against British rule (pp. 138–53). Wariinga's parents are placed in detention camps for suspected complicity with the Mau Mau guerrillas (as were thousands of Kenyans during the Emergency, including Ngugi's parents), so Wariinga is sent to live with an aunt and uncle. As she grows older, Wariinga becomes a good student (especially at mathematics) and a dedicated Christian. She also becomes sexually attractive. Her corrupt uncle offers her as a sexual prize to a rich acquaintance in return for the man's help in securing a bank loan and buying some land. The innocent Wariinga does not even realize that she is being sold like a piece of property. She becomes fascinated by the wealthy lifestyle of the Rich Old Man and is seduced by him; she loses interest in her studies and eventually becomes pregnant. At this point, the Rich Old Man casts her aside, accusing her of infidelity in the most demeaning terms. Wariinga considers first an abortion, then suicide, but she ultimately decides to have the baby and to go on with her life.

At this point, the narrative of Wariinga's life breaks off. However, we already know the rest of her story, because she has related it earlier in the book, casting it in terms of the story of "any girl in Nairobi," thus enhancing her function as a typical representative of Kenyan women (pp. 17–26). After she gives birth to the baby (a girl, named Wambui), she leaves it with her parents, then enrolls in secretarial college to prepare for a career. Afterward, however, she finds that prospective employers expect her to provide sexual favors in addition to typing and office work. She resolutely maintains her integrity, finally acquiring both a job and a new boyfriend, a student who appears to have progressive views about women. Eventually, however, Wariinga's boss (a hypocrite who claims to be a devout Christian) fires her when she continues to refuse his sexual advances. Moreover, now that she has no income, her boyfriend rejects her as well. To make matters worse, she is soon evicted from her rented room. It is at this low point in Wariinga's life that the book actually opens, with Wariinga wandering, forlorn and home-less, so distracted that she nearly falls in front of a bus (p. 12).

She is pulled away from the bus by a young student who gives her a card inviting her to a "Devil's Feast" featuring a competition for thieves and robbers in Ilmorog, her hometown. She decides to attend, and there she meets the poor woman Wangari, who has suffered much of the same gender discrimination as Wariinga. Having lost her small farm to a bank reposses-sion, Wangari has found it impossible to find employment except as a pros-titute. She has therefore been arrested as a vagrant and potential thief, released only because the police suspect that she can lead them to other criminals. Wariinga thus begins to realize that the misfortunes she has expe-rienced go beyond her own life and extend to Kenyan women generally. Wangari is also important because, as a young girl, she supported the Mau Mau guerrillas by carrying guns and bullets to their forest hideouts. Wariin-ga thus becomes aware of the glorious tradition of Kenyan resistance to co-lonial oppression, a tradition that has been virtually extinguished in postcolonial Kenya, where the former Mau Mau guerrillas are treated not as national heroes, but as criminals.

Wariinga's revolutionary consciousness is further raised when she meets the worker Muturi, a former Mau Mau who is now a dedicated socialist working for revolution in Kenya. She also meets the composer Gatuiria, who is trying to help build an indigenous Kenyan cultural tradition. He helps her become aware of the importance of building a new Kenya free of foreign cultural domination. Wariinga goes with her new acquaintances to the Thieves' Competition in Ilmorog. There, she observes various "thieves and robbers," who proudly boast of their wickedness and corruption—as busi-nessmen working in league with foreign companies to exploit the Kenyan people. The oppression of women is quite central to these performances. For example, all of the competitors are men, and the only women who "partici-pate" in the event are scantily clad waitresses who serve drinks to the on-lookers, somewhat in the manner of the "bunnies" in American Playboy Clubs (p. 92). Indeed, one requirement of the competition is that the com-petitors must boast of the number of mistresses they have, just as they must catalog the automobiles they own. The link is clear: women in postcolonial Kenya are treated as possessions on the order of cars; their chief function is to provide pleasure and status for the men who "own" them.

After observing the performance at the Thieves' Competition, Wariin-ga abandons her earlier passive attitude (she had hoped to find happiness through finding a man to love her and take care of her) and goes back to school to finish her engineering degree. By the end of the book she has be-come a competent mechanical engineer and has gained the respect and admiration of her male coworkers. She is engaged to marry Gatuiria, but it is clear that she does not rely on him for her sense of self worth. The new, independent Wariinga thus serves as a powerful positive role model for Kenya as a whole and especially for Kenyan women. Ngugi makes clear, however, that even Wariinga's newfound education and professional competence are not sufficient to ensure that she will be treated with dignity and respect in her society. After all, she still lives in a society dominated by neocolonial capitalism, and the women of Kenya are regarded as little more than prostitutes whose function is to provide sexual services not only to the men of Kenya, but also to the foreign businessmen who come to Kenya in search of easy profits—and easy sex.

Wariinga herself realizes that the problem goes deeper than the use of Kenyan women as bait to lure foreign investors. As she and Gatuiria drive to the home of his rich father for a reception in honor of their impending marriage, she responds to Gatuiria's criticism of the use of Kenyan women as "flowers to decorate the beds of foreign tourists" by reminding him that it is not only foreigners who treat Kenyan women like trinkets and sexual toys, despite the fact that women have played such a central role in the heroic tradition of resistance to colonial domination:

> Even you, the Kenyan men, think that there is no job a woman can do other than cooking your food and massaging your bodies. . . . Why have people forgotten how Kenyan women used to make guns during the Mau Mau war against the British? (p. 245).

When Wariinga and Gatuiria arrive at the reception, Wariinga discovers to her great horror that Gatuiria's father is none other than the Rich Old Man who seduced and then abandoned her in her youth, the father of her child Wambui. When the Rich Old Man recognizes Wariinga, he insists that she not marry his son, as that would be almost a form of incest. He offers instead to resume their former relationship and make her his mistress again. Wariinga suddenly realizes that no Kenyan woman—even one with her education and professional skills—can be free of sexual oppression as long as the country remains in the hands of Rich Old Men like this one. She takes out a gun and shoots the old man dead, thus declaring her intention to embark on a program of violent revolution against the prevailing order. As the book ends, Wariinga's fate is left undetermined, but it is clear that she can never again seek comfort merely in personal achievement. She has now committed herself to the revolutionary transformation of Kenyan society as a whole, and she has done so without the help or support of any man: Gatuiria stays behind with his slain father, unsure which side he should take. By the end of the book, therefore, Wariinga has grown from a frightened, passive, exploited woman, to a proud, defiant woman warrior, committed to the revolutionary emancipation of the Kenyan people.

Wariinga's development, while bearing obvious similarities to the traditional European bildungsroman, deviates from that tradition in important ways. For one thing, Ngugi's novel also draws upon the tradition of the initiation story, a central genre of African oral culture. The book thus resembles texts like Emecheta's *The Joys of Motherhood* in the way it sets up dialogues between European and African versions of the development of individuals. Meanwhile, the very fact that Wariinga is a woman challenges the tradition of the European bildungsroman, whose protagonists are conventionally male. In this way, Ngugi calls attention to the ideological complicity between imperialism and patriarchy. At the same time, he builds upon a symbolic representation of Kenya as feminine and as a victim of rape by her neocolonial oppressors (p. 194). Ngugi's book employs a far less individualistic mode of characterization than is typical of European novels. Wariinga is more a typical representative of oppressed Kenyan women than a distinct individual, and the book in general is less focused on its protagonist than is the typical bildungsroman. Characters like Gatuiria, Muturi, and Wangari play major roles, and to an extent the three combine with Wariinga to constitute a sort of collective protagonist, especially because the characters in *Devil on the Cross* are not so much individuals as types who represent specific groups in Kenyan society. Muturi, for example, clearly stands as a sort of allegorization of the working classes of Kenya. Wangari plays a similar role on the feminine side, and is additionally identified with the Mau Mau tradition. The composer Gatuiria represents important aspects of cultural life in Kenya. On the one hand, he hopes to contribute to the development of a positive Kenyan national identity by a composing a "national oratorio" based on genuinely indigenous musical techniques. On the other hand, his final ambivalence and inability to take effective action against neocolonial oppression marks him as a representative of the generation of Kenyan postcolonial intellectuals who have sometimes mouthed patriotic slogans, but who have seldom acted with conviction to oppose the neocolonial enslavement of most of the Kenyan population. Finally, the status of the various thieves who perform at the Devil's Feast (along with the foreign investors for whom they perform) as allegorical representatives of neocolonialism is abundantly clear.

Eileen Julien (1992) suggests that the bildungsroman tends toward independent individual development, while the African initiation story tends toward the integration of the individual into society. However, the fundamental orientation of the bildungsroman, especially in the British tradition, is also conformist, emphasizing "the reconciliation of the problematic individual" with the society that surrounds him (Lukács 1971b, 132).[2] But *Devil*

---

[2] See Franco Moretti's useful discussion in *The Way of the World* (1987) on the reconciliation to society that is typical of the British (as opposed to the French) bildungsroman.

on the Cross differs dramatically from the British bildungsroman tradition because its protagonist, far from being reconciled to society at the end of the text, has resolved to take arms in an effort to overturn that society and to build a new one. Of course, given the Marxist orientation of Ngugi's thought, Wariinga's turn to revolution at the end of *Devil on the Cross* should not be surprising. Indeed, Ngugi carefully outlines the years of brutal oppression and exploitation that make Wariinga's turn toward revolution entirely understandable.

Devil on the Cross is a didactic work designed to educate Kenyan peasants and workers in the true nature of capitalism, much in the way that proletarian novels of the 1930s sought to educate British and American workers. As Killam points out, *Devil on the Cross* can be seen as a literary enactment of the political and artistic program described in Ngugi's essays and prison diary. Killam notes that the book is aesthetically innovative, but he suggests that this artistic innovation is employed in the service of political statement. "Ngugi is not . . . concerned with finding new ways to be new; he is concerned with finding new ways to be effective" (Killam 1980, 142). In this sense, the best analogue for Ngugi's project in the tradition of Western leftist literature may be the epic theater of Bertolt Brecht, which also employs aesthetic innovation in the interest of Marxist political statement. Indeed, Ngugi greatly admires Brecht as an artist, quoting Brecht's work frequently in his own nonfiction writings. *Devil on the Cross* makes particularly prominent use of some of Brecht's favorite metaphors for the workings of capitalism. Indeed, the central metaphor of *Devil on the Cross* is the very Brechtian notion that capitalism is little more than an organized system of thievery and corruption. The various participants in the Thieves' Competition that is the centerpiece of the book are not criminals in the normal sense (the one "ordinary" thief who shows up for the competition is quickly expelled as unworthy because of the meager level of his crimes) but businessmen who make their wealth by exploiting Kenyan workers.

Ngugi also gets a great deal of symbolic mileage in *Devil on the Cross* from the central Brechtian motifs of prostitution and cannibalism. Prostitutes feature prominently in Brecht's work, where they are used as especially obvious examples of the overt commodification of human beings. Prostitution itself serves in Brecht's work as an image of the way that even the most "personal" of relationships are converted under capitalism into mere economic transactions. *Devil on the Cross* makes frequent reference to the fact that women, the most oppressed sector of postcolonial Kenya, are frequently forced to resort to prostitution (either directly or in more subtle forms) in order to survive. Thus *Devil on the Cross* includes the story of an aged American tourist who comes to Kenya because his wealth can buy the sexual favors of young girls, whom he regards as just another example of the exotic indigenous species (like lions and elephants) that make Kenya so attractive to foreign tourists (pp. 70–71).

Brecht also frequently uses cannibalism as a metaphor for the commodification of human beings under capitalism. Ngugi uses this metaphor throughout *Devil on the Cross* as a symbol of the way foreign business interests and their Kenyan collaborators are literally feeding off of the people of Kenya, though in an African novel the motif has the additional effect of reversing and thus undermining conventional Western stereotypes of Africans as cannibals. Ngugi also links the motifs of prostitution and cannibalism directly together. When Wariinga's uncle offers her to the Rich Old Man, the element of prostitution is clear, but Ngugi also describes the transaction in terms that smack of cannibalism by suggesting that the uncle regards Wariinga as a young chick whose tender flesh will provide "soft food for a toothless old man" (p. 142). Ngugi also uses cannibalism to reinforce his suggestion of a close complicity between Christianity and the colonial and neocolonial oppression of Kenya, a suggestion that is a major element of the book (Balogun 1988). Thus the Devil, who appears to Wariinga in a vision and explains the workings of capitalism, reminds her that a central ritual of Christianity involves eating the body and drinking the blood of Christ, which paves the way for an ideological climate where economic cannibalism is also acceptable (p. 190).

Ngugi's insistence on the class distinction between worker and capitalist shows his acceptance of the Marxist vision of history as class warfare. Muturi's observes that under capitalism there are two kinds of men: "he who lives by his own sweat and he who lives by the sweat of others" (p. 57). On the other hand, Ngugi places special emphasis on the role played by foreign business interests in the neocolonial capitalist system of Kenya. But even here he follows Marx in a fairly direct way: one of Marx's central insights was that capitalism is an inherently global system that by its very nature would expand and extend its dominion over the entire planet—before finally collapsing beneath its own weight.

The international flavor of capitalist domination in Kenya is captured most effectively in Mwireri wa Mukiraai's speech during the Thieves' Competition. Mwireri is an unscrupulous capitalist who has nothing against exploiting the poor of Kenya for his personal gain. His definition of capitalism comes from an insider's perspective: "The system is this: the masses cultivate; a select few . . . harvest. Five rich men grow roots in the flesh of fifty workers and peasants" (p. 166). Mwireri argues, however, that Kenyan capitalists should keep the wealth of Kenya for themselves rather than allowing it to wind up in the pockets of foreign business interests: "Let us steal from among ourselves, so that the wealth of the country remains in the country, and so that in the flesh of ten million poor we can plant the roots of ten national millionaires" (p. 167). But Mwireri's speech is met with great hostility: he is not only shouted off the stage at the competition, but he is also later murdered because his attitude poses a serious threat to the foreign capitalists who dominate the economy. Ngugi's depiction of Mwireri thus serves to draw special attention to this foreign domination. At the same time, Ngugi makes it clear that the poor of Kenya would probably be no better off even if the policy advocated by Mwireri were to be adopted. True liberation in Kenya will require an end not only to foreign domination of the Kenyan economy, but also to capitalism itself.

There are many such instances of Marxist statements in *Devil on the Cross.* Most of them can be enriched by understanding the book's subversive dialogue with the Western literary tradition. But this dialogue is quite complex. It is worth remembering, for example, that Brecht was an important modernist artist and that James Joyce's modernist *A Portrait of the Artist as a Young Man* is the most famous case of an open-ended bildungsroman in modern literature. And *Devil on the Cross* itself includes a number of modernist elements, introducing further complexities into the cultural matrix within which Ngugi's book needs to be approached by Western readers.[3] Ngugi himself has listed numerous Western novelists as important influences on his work, including Conrad, Gogol, Dostoevsky, Tolstoy, Gorky, Sholokhov, Balzac, and Faulkner (Ngugi 1992, 76). This eclectic group shows that Ngugi draws not only upon the great tradition of bourgeois realism, but also on the alternative traditions of modernism and socialist realism. Any account of the book's subversion of the conventions of European bourgeois realism must certainly attend to the book's crucial engagement with Gikuyu and other African oral traditions. But it is worthwhile to consider the contribution of these alternative literary modes as well. Indeed, *Devil on the Cross* incorporates aspects of so many different literary modes that the Western genre it resembles most is probably the Menippean satire described by Mikhail Bakhtin, which combines naturalism with the fantastic and draws upon a variety of other genres, often directly incorporating fragments taken from those genres (Bakhtin 1984a, 118).

Devil on the Cross features a number of such textual insertions: it is, in fact, liberally sprinkled with extracts from other genres, ranging from newspaper advertisements to stories from the Bible to the musical oratorio written by Gatuiria as a celebration of Kenyan culture. There are also numerous embedded tales, as when the various characters describe their personal experiences. One of the most important examples of the incorporation of other genres involves the thieves' speeches in the competition at Ilmorog. Here it is useful to note Bakhtin's suggestion that Menippean satire is closely re-

---

[3] On the impact of modernism on African novelists (including Ngugi), see Nkosi (1981, 53–75).

lated to the classic Greek genres of the diatribe, the soliloquy, and the symposium (Bakhtin 1984a, 119–20). After all, the Thieves' Competition is itself a sort of symposium, and much of the text consists of diatribes against the capitalist manipulations of the thieves and their foreign masters. At the same time, the competition of the thieves clearly participates in important African oral traditions. Their bragging performances resemble certain types of traditional songs, which involve "the motif of the boast and self-adulation." Moreover, Ngugi's very negative depiction of the thieves participates in the African tradition of poetic abuse, which typically "exposes topical scandals, satirizes, or heaps merciless invective on an object of scorn" (Lewis 1979, 112). Similarly, numerous patriotic songs (many associated with the Mau Mau rebellion) are scattered through the text. These songs, together with the frequent quotation of proverbs, emphasize the importance of Gikuyu oral culture as background for the book and set this culture in direct opposition to that of the thieves at Ilmorog.

This rich combination of generic traditions helps to show the real complexity of *Devil on the Cross*. However, Ngugi has explained that his goal in the book was the attainment of a greater simplicity and accessibility; he had realized that the complex technique he used in *Petals of Blood* could only be appreciated by "a reader acquainted with the convention of reading novels, and particularly the modern novel in European languages" (Ngugi 1992, 77). In his use of a relatively simple and straightforward plot and forms of Gikuyu oral narration, Ngugi has created a text that is highly accessible to Kenyan readers with relatively little experience in reading novels, and it is easily understood when read aloud. At the same time, the book presents multiple layers of literary complexity for Western readers who are accustomed to the work of Conrad, Faulkner, and other modern Western novelists. Readers unacquainted with Gikuyu oral culture will miss important dimensions of *Devil on the Cross*; likewise, African readers (or listeners) unacquainted with the Western novel will be unable to appreciate the profundity of Ngugi's dialogue with various forms of the Western literary tradition. The ideal reader of the book, then, is one who is familiar with both African and Western cultural traditions. The real accomplishment of *Devil on the Cross* is that readers unacquainted with one or the other (and maybe even both) can still find the book enjoyable and appreciate its important political message.

Historical Background
Kenya is an East African republic with a population of just over twenty-six million (1992) covering an area of approximately 225,000 square miles— nearly the size of Texas. Moving from east to west, the land consists of a narrow strip of coastal lowlands along the Indian Ocean, a slightly elevated belt of bush-covered plains, a still higher region of scrublands in the north and

fertile grasslands and forests in the south, and finally the mountainous Kenya Highlands in the west, reaching altitudes of thirteen thousand feet in the Yatta Plateau. The western region is marked by a number of spectacular topographical features, including the Great Rift Valley, a dramatic trough that splits the region from north to south. Lake Victoria lies on Kenya's border with Uganda to the west and with Tanzania to the southwest. The capital is Nairobi, a city of approximately one and one half million, located in a highland area near the center of the country. The major coastal port is Mombasa, with over half a million inhabitants. Swahili became the official national language in 1974, though English is also officially recognized and widely used, especially in commerce. Kenya is ethnically quite diverse, with over forty ethnic groups, most of which use their own languages (generally of Bantu or Nilo-Hamitic origin) for much everyday communication. The most prominent among these ethnic groups are the Gikuyu, Kamba, Gusii, Luhya, Luo, and Masai. About eighty percent of the people live in rural areas; most live as farmers or herdsmen in small, dispersed settlements. The majority of Kenyans follow traditional African religious practices, though over half are nominally Christians (thirty-eight percent are Protestant, twenty-six percent Catholic). A number of Muslims live in the Arab-influenced coastal areas, and there are also a small number of Hindus. Approximately fifty percent of the adult population are literate, mostly in English and Swahili.

Kenya is the most industrialized nation in East Africa, and industry is still growing there, especially in the Nairobi area. Chief manufactured products include processed foods, petroleum products, chemicals, cement, and consumer goods. However, many of the industries are foreign owned, and most manufactured goods are still imported from abroad, as is the supply of crude petroleum. Most Kenyans still live by subsistence farming. Even in this predominantly agricultural economy, however, Kenya still imports significant amounts of food to feed its growing population. Kenya's leading agricultural products include corn (the chief subsistence crop) and cash crops such as coffee, tea, sisal, cashews, sugarcane, cotton, and rice. Kenya is the world's leading producer of pyrethrum extract, which is widely used in the manufacture of pesticides. The economy is heavily dependent upon tourism, which is now the nation's largest source of income from abroad. The per capita GNP (1989) is about $380.

The area occupied by modern Kenya may have been inhabited for more than two million years, making it one of the earliest areas of human habitation. It was extensively occupied by farmers and herdsmen as much as 4,000 years ago. By A.D. 100 the area had established a brisk trade with Arabia, and a number of autonomous Arab-dominated city-states were established in the region during the European Middle Ages. The first European visitors arrived from Portugal in 1498, and the Portuguese managed to gain control of most of the coastal regions (including Mombasa) by the end of the sixteenth century. In 1729, however, the Portuguese were expelled from Mombasa and replaced as the leading power on the East African coast by two Arab dynasties—the Busaidi Dynasty (based first in Oman, then, from 1832, on Zanzibar) and the Mazrui Dynasty (based at Mombasa). In 1837 the Busaidi became dominant, wresting control of Mombasa from the Mazrui. The focus of Arab trade remained on the coast, though long-distance caravan travel to Lake Victoria dates to the early nineteenth century.

The European (especially British and German) presence gradually increased through the nineteenth century, and by mid-century European explorers began to map the interior. By 1886 the Germans and British had agreed on areas of influence in East Africa, with most of present-day Kenya going to the British. In 1887 a British association was granted concessionary rights to the Kenyan coast by the sultan of Zanzibar, and in 1888 the association was given a royal charter as the British East Africa Company. However, financial difficulties soon led to a British government takeover of the company, and by 1895 the area was established as the East Africa Protectorate. The period from 1895 to 1901 saw the building of a railway from Mombasa to Kisumu on Lake Victoria to facilitate trade with the interior and Uganda—and to solidify British claims to Kenya in the face of a fear that Germany might attempt to extend its control to the region. By 1903 English settlers had established large-scale farms on land appropriated from the Gikuyu, Masai, and others. Gradually increasing British control led to the renaming of the area as Kenya Colony in 1920. From then through the 1940s, European settlers controlled the Kenyan government and officially owned most of the farmland. Increasing numbers of settlers from India established small trading businesses and took lower government posts during this period.

Kenyans violently resisted British colonial domination from the time of the first official British presence there in the 1890s. Warrior heroes like the Nandi leader Koitalel and the Gikuyu leader Waiyaki led their people in fierce (but doomed) wars against the invading British armies. During the next half century, British control of their Kenyan colony remained firm, though even during this time there was considerable opposition to specific policies. For example, an active labor movement, led by Harry Thuku and others, arose in the 1920s to oppose particularly abusive forms of exploitation of Kenyan workers. However, it was not until after World War II that the Kenyans mounted an effective armed resistance to the continuation of British colonial rule—in the form of the Gikuyu-led Land and Freedom Army, or Mau Mau (a derogatory British designation later defiantly adopted by the resistance fighters). From 1952 to 1956 the Mau Mau waged a fierce guerrilla campaign against the British and their Kenyan agents, though the so-

called Emergency officially lasted until 1960. In this period of virtual mar-
tial law, the British employed a variety of repressive measures in reaction to
the Mau Mau rebellion, which the British depicted as the work of crazed
and bloodthirsty savages in a typical example of colonialist discourse. These
measures included the establishment of a series of concentration camps
where tens of thousands of Kenyans were imprisoned, often without trial.
Conditions in the camps were extremely harsh, and prisoners were frequent
ly tortured. Over five hundred were hanged. To the British, all Gikuyu became suspect: virtually the entire Gikuyu population of Kenya was resettled
into closely guarded villages to prevent them from providing support to the
Mau Mau insurgents. At the same time the Mau Mau territories were heavily bombarded by the British air force.

The Mau Mau were unable to match such firepower. Deprived of food
and ammunition, they gradually lost momentum and energy. On April 26,
1956, the most important Mau Mau leader, Dedan Kimathi, was captured
(then quickly executed), and the movement was essentially broken, though
the repressive security measures of the Emergency would not be lifted for
another four years.[4] The British themselves would never recover from the
Emergency, and Kenyan independence was assured by its end. The long tradition of anticolonial resistance in Kenya (a tradition that is crucial to all of
Ngugi's work) finally culminated on December 12, 1963, when Kenya became officially independent of British rule. Former Mau Mau leaders were
not given a significant role in the new postcolonial government, though the
Mau Mau remained an important presence in the Kenyan imagination. Thus
David William Cohen notes that, since the 1950s,

> what Mau Mau was, what it means, how it was individually and collec-
> tively experienced, whether its ideals and objectives were abandoned or
> carried on, and by whom for what ends have been the most captivating
> questions in Kenyan political life, theater, and literature (Cohen 1994, 60).

Upon independence, the popular leader Jomo Kenyatta, a Gikuyu, became the first prime minister of Kenya; he became president in 1964 (when
Kenya became a republic) and held that office until his death in 1978. Active in the anticolonial resistance since the 1920s (and imprisoned by the
British from 1952 until 1961 as a suspected Mau Mau leader), Kenyatta took
power in a wave of optimism and utopian hope. However, his vehement denial of Mau Mau involvement (and explicit condemnation of the resistance
fighters) was troubling to many, especially when a number of remaining Mau
Mau guerrillas were hunted down and arrested under the new regime. While

---

[4] Ngugi's play *The Trial of Dedan Kimathi* (1977) celebrates Kimathi as a patriot whose goal was
to liberate his people from colonial domination and upon whose efforts the neocolonial struggle should be modeled.

the Kenyan economy experienced periods of improvement under Kenyatta's government, the population remained generally poor, and much of Kenya's wealth remained in the control of foreign investors. Kenyatta's single-party state made gestures toward the establishment of freedom of the press and other civil rights, but his rule was marred by frequent charges of corruption and by the periodic brutal suppression of opposition. This suppression was partially motivated by Cold War pressure from the West, which supplied substantial foreign aid and feared potential communist insurgency in the area. Kenyatta was succeeded by Daniel arap Moi, his hand-picked successor. Moi continued single-party rule and continues in power as of this writing. With the Cold War ostensibly over, Moi has recently received international pressure to ease his suppression of dissent, but recent gestures toward democratization are unconvincing. The 1990s have been marked by significant (sometimes violent) domestic unrest, and the Kenyan economy has experienced radical decline during the decade (Wanyee 1994).

Biographical Background
Ngugi wa Thiong'o was born the son of Gikuyu subsistence farmers in 1938 in Limuru in the Kenyan highlands. His parents separated in about 1946; Ngugi and five siblings were then cared for by their mother, whose hard work inspired Ngugi throughout his career. His childhood in colonial Kenya made him intensely aware of the social and economic distance between native Kenyans and European settlers. He was educated in both mission and independent Gikuyu schools. In 1954 his brother, Wallace Mwangi wa Thiong'o, joined the Mau Mau movement and remained in the forests as a guerrilla until 1956. In 1955 Ngugi's mother was detained by the British and underwent three months of torture and interrogation. In that same year, Ngugi won a place at the prestigious Alliance High School, where he received his secondary education, doing especially well in English and becoming fascinated with literature. He returned home on a school vacation to find his mother incarcerated, his family home and village razed as part of the British project of resettlement during the Emergency.

In 1959, Ngugi entered Makerere University College in Uganda, at that time the most prestigious institution of higher education in East Africa. There he began writing, and by graduation in 1964 he had completed initial versions of what would become his first two novels. He also had a play, *The Black Hermit* (1968), produced at the Ugandan National Theatre in Kampala. In 1964 Ngugi began postgraduate study at Leeds University in England. That same year his novel *Weep Not, Child* (written in 1962) was published. *Weep Not, Child* (1987) reflects the political reality of the Kenya during the late 1940s and 1950s, a period of intense resistance to the British colonial presence in Kenya, especially among the Gikuyu. In particular, the partially autobiographical novel focuses on the tribulations of an impoverished Gikuyu family that is struggling to survive amid political turmoil and harsh material conditions. *The River Between* (written in 1961) was published in 1965. This novel reaches back to the 1920s to depict the impact of British colonialism on traditional Gikuyu culture, somewhat in the way Achebe's *Things Fall Apart* shows the impact of colonialism on Igbo society. Ngugi's book revolves around the largely unsuccessful attempts of the protagonist, Waiyaki, to overcome the rifts in Gikuyu society brought about by colonialism.

    A Grain of Wheat (1986), published in 1967, marked an important departure in Ngugi's career. Dealing with events surrounding the moment of Kenyan independence, it announced the end of Ngugi's focus on the colonial period and the beginning of his increasing concern with the ills of Kenyan society in the era of independence and neocolonialism. During his graduate studies at Leeds, Ngugi's fellow students and his teacher, Marxist literary scholar Arnold Kettle, exposed Ngugi for the first time to the thought of Marx, Engels, Lenin, and other Marxist thinkers. *A Grain of Wheat* clearly shows the influence of Marxist ideas, especially as filtered through the work of Frantz Fanon. Lenin's *Imperialism: The Highest Stage of Capitalism* (1926) was also important in forming Ngugi's new understanding of the complicity between capitalism and imperialism. In *A Grain of Wheat* Ngugi abandons his earlier focus on the individual and begins to turn his attention to the Kenyan people as a collective protagonist. His treatment of individual characters shifts from a concern with their private trials and tribulations to a concern with their relation to "politics—more precisely, characters in the process of creating their own history" (Nkosi 1981, 45).

    A Grain of Wheat is to some extent a transitional novel that still shows remnants of the more conventional bourgeois ideology that informs Ngugi's early work. But *Petals of Blood* (1977) shows the full emergence of Ngugi's Marxist consciousness; it also represents his first unequivocal endorsement of violent resistance to oppression. In its depiction of postcolonial life in the fictional Kenyan town of Ilmorog, the novel focuses on the discrepancy between the reality of postcolonial Kenyan and the ideals for which so many (especially in the Mau Mau movement) fought and died during the struggle for independence. *Petals of Blood* is Ngugi's most formally complex novel, mixing modernist techniques with a detective-story plot and a basic mode of social realism to condemn the evils of neocolonialism in Kenya.

    By 1977 Ngugi had been active for a number of years in various editorial activities and as a member of the English department of the University of Nairobi, which he was instrumental in changing to the Department of Literature, with an increased emphasis on African literature and a de-emphasis of the British tradition. In addition, he had been active for some time in organizing adult education and other cultural activities among the Gikuyu villagers at the Kamiriithu Community Educational and Cultural Centre. His satirical play *Ngaahika Ndeenda* (written in Gikuyu with Ngugi wa Mirii; English translation *I Will Marry When I Want*, 1988) was produced by the center's amateur community theater group in October 1977. The Kenyatta government almost immediately banned the play as a danger to "public security," then razed the center and detained Ngugi. During this imprisonment, Ngugi wrote *Devil on the Cross.* Ngugi was released from detention in December 1978, only to find that he had been stripped of his post at the University of Nairobi. The government continued to harass him, and he and his family received frequent death threats. Ngugi continued to work diligently for freedom in Kenya and to promote his ideas through amateur theatrical productions. In 1982 he was forced into exile to avoid a further detention in Kenya. He has lived in exile ever since and now lives in the United States and teaches at New York University.

Believing that African writers who write in colonial languages are only furthering the continuation of Western cultural imperialism in Africa, Ngugi has recently disavowed writing in English entirely. He now writes even his essays and other discursive pieces in Gikuyu language, and he promotes the use of Gikuyu by editing the Gikuyu-language cultural journal *Mutiiri.* His Gikuyu novel *Matigari* (1986; English translation by Wangui wa Goro, 1989) draws heavily upon traditions of Gikuyu oral narrative to tell the story of its title character. Matagari, a seasoned Mau Mau warrior, emerges from the forests of Mount Kenya several decades after Kenyan independence to discover that very few of the goals of the Mau Mau anticolonial struggle have actually been accomplished. Enraged, Matigari vows to renew the fight for freedom in Kenya. Matigari is probably modeled upon a real-life Mau Mau hero, the famous general Stanley Mathenge, who disappeared with two hundred fighters at the end of the Mau Mau rebellion.[5] On the other hand, Matigari is clearly an allegorical figure who represents the Kenyan people and their spirit of resistance, reemerging after a period of neocolonial slumber.

Ngugi's impressive body of novels, plays, and short stories—see the volume *Secret Lives and Other Stories* (1975)—has made him widely regarded as one of the giants of African literature. His numerous essays and speeches—collected in volumes such as *Homecoming* (1972), *Writers in Politics* (1981b), *Barrel of a Pen* (1983), *Decolonising the Mind* (1992), and *Moving the Centre* (1993)—have made him an important figure in politics and literary criticism as well. Taken together, his novels comprise an alternative history of Kenya that emphasizes its strong

---

[5] Many Kenyans believe to this day that Mathenge and his warriors will emerge from the forests one day and continue to fight for the people suffering under neocolonialist regimes. For a discussion of Mathenge see Maina (1977).

tradition of resistance. They thus serve as a counter to distorted colonialist histories that view Kenya as a timeless land with no history other than the history of British activities there. For Ngugi it is crucial for Kenyans to develop a positive sense of their own history as they attempt to overcome current oppression to build a positive future: "How we look at our yesterday has important bearings on how we look at today and on how we see possibilities for tomorrow. The sort of past we look back to for inspiration in our struggles affects the vision of the future we want to build" (Ngugi 1983, 8).

Ngugi's work has received extensive critical attention. In addition to hundreds of articles in scholarly journals and numerous chapters in books on African literature, there have been a number of book-length studies of Ngugi's work. Early studies, like those of Robson (1979) and Killam (1980), are limited by lack of access to either *Devil on the Cross* or *Matigari*. The slightly later study by Cook and Okenimkpe (1983) includes *Devil on the Cross* and is particularly useful as a general introduction to Ngugi, though it is also too early to cover *Matigari*. More recent studies include those by Jeyifo (1990) and Nwankwo (1992). Particularly useful as a background source is Carol Sicherman's *Ngugi wa Thiong'o: The Making of a Rebel* (1990), which includes extensive historical and biographical documentation of Ngugi's work.

Further Reading

Edgerton, Robert B. 1989. *Mau Mau: An African Crucible*. New York: Ballantine Books.

Itote, Waruhiu. 1967. *"Mau Mau" General*. Nairobi: East African Publishing House.

Kariuki, Josiah Mwangi. 1963. *"Mau Mau" Detainee: The Account by a Kenya African of His Experiences in Detention Camps, 1953–1960*. London: Oxford University Press.

Kenyatta, Jomo. 1962. *Facing Mount Kenya: The Tribal Life of the Gikuyu*. New York: Vintage–Random House.

———. 1968. *Suffering Without Bitterness: The Founding of the Kenya Nation*. Nairobi: East African Publishing House.

Leo, Christopher. 1984. *Land and Class in Kenya*. Toronto: University of Toronto Press.

Maina wa Kinyatti. 1991. *Mau Mau: A Revolution Betrayed*. Jamaica, N.Y.: Mau Mau Research Center.

Maloba, Wunyabari O. 1994. *Mau Mau and Kenya: An Analysis of a Peasant Revolt*. Nairobi: East African Educational Publishers.

Matson, A. T. 1993. *Nandi Resistance to British Rule*. Cambridge: Cambridge University Press.

Maughan-Brown, David. 1985. *Land, Freedom, and Fiction: History and Ideology in Kenya*. London: Zed.

Mazrui, Alamin, and Lupenga Mphande. 1989–90. "The Historical Imperative in African Activist Literature." *Ufahamu* 18.2: 47–58.

Ngara, Emmanuel. 1985. *Art and Ideology in the African Novel: A Study of the Influence of Marxism on African Writing.* London: Heinemann.

Ochieng', William R., ed. 1991. *Themes in Kenyan History.* Nairobi: Heinemann Kenya.

Odinga, Ajuma Oginga. 1967. *Not Yet Uhuru: The Autobiography of Oginga Odinga.* London: Heinemann.

Tignor, Robert L. 1976. *The Colonial Transformation of Kenya: The Kamba, Kikuyu, and Maasai from 1900 to 1939.* Princeton, N.J.: Princeton University Press.

Chapter 10

Tsitsi Dangarembga:
Nervous Conditions

Nervous Conditions (1989a) traces the experiences of its narrator/protagonist, Tambudzai Sigauke, from her entry into a mission school in colonial Zimbabwe, beginning in 1968 at age thirteen, to her admission to a prestigious Catholic-run multiracial colonial academy two years later. In the process of describing Tambudzai's development, Dangarembga addresses a number of important issues related to gender and identity within the context of the patriarchal attitudes that inform both traditional African society and the colonial societies established in Africa by Europeans. As such, the book situates itself firmly in a number of literary traditions, even as Dangarembga presents a fresh new voice in African fiction. As Florence Stratton notes, the female bildungsroman form of *Nervous Conditions* places it in the tradition of African women writers such as Flora Nwapa, Buchi Emecheta, Nafissatou Diallo, and Miriam Were (Stratton 1994, 107). Maggi Phillips (1994) places Dangarembga's book in the same company as the works of Nwapa, Emecheta, Ama Ata Aidoo, and Bessie Head. Of course, the issues raised in *Nervous Conditions* are relevant to the lives of black women in a number of cultural situations. Jacqueline Bardolph (1990) thus places the book in the tradition of writers such as Jamaica Kincaid (from Antigua in the Caribbean), Zoë Wicomb (from South Africa), and Alice Walker (from the United States). *Nervous Conditions* is also a book very much about colonialism, and thus has much in common with the works of numerous postcolonial writers of both genders. Bardolph thus appropriately identifies writers such as Camara Laye, Ngugi wa Thiong'o, Wole Soyinka, George Lamming, and Cheikh Hamidou Kane (all of whom explore childhood experience as an aspect of colonialism) as important predecessors to Dangarembga.

As a bildungsroman, *Nervous Conditions* focuses on the development of its protagonist. However, other characters play important roles as well, and

Tambudzai herself ends her narrative by describing it as "my own story, the story of four women whom I loved, and our men" (p. 204). In addition, Tambudzai's story has a relevance that goes beyond her personal experiences. Through its focus on Tambudzai's education, *Nervous Conditions* explores the phenomenon of cultural imperialism and the impact on African psyches of an entire range of colonial cultural practices that were designed to imbue Africans with a sense of the superiority of European culture and society. Indeed, the changes that Tambudzai undergoes in the course of her education and maturation clearly parallel historical changes that were underway in colonial Zimbabwe (then called Rhodesia). Thus the personal experiences of the protagonist are linked with public events in her society in ways that make her an emblem of her society and also serve as a reminder that individuals always develop within specific historical contexts.

Boehmer notes the combination of public and private perspectives in *Nervous Conditions*, describing the book as "both a post–independence *Bildungsroman* and a retrospective account of Zimbabwe in the 1970s" (Boehmer 1995, 238). Indeed, Tambudzai, in her movement from colonial subjugation to defiant postcolonial independence, comes close to Fredric Jameson's notion of the "national allegory," that is, of the individual character in postcolonial fiction whose experience embodies that of an entire nation as it emerges from colonialism (Jameson 1986). On the other hand, the strongly gendered nature of her situation serves as a powerful reminder that there is no single experience of colonialism and that different colonial subjects may have very different experiences depending upon their gender, social class, or other characteristics. Perhaps, then, Tambudzai is less an example of Jameson's national allegory than of Georg Lukács's "typicality," a concept from which Jameson's is derived, at least in part. Tambudzai is an excellent example of a "typical" character, that is, a character whose "innermost being is determined by objective forces at work in society" (Lukács 1963, 122). Indeed, this mode of characterization (quite common in the African novel) is central to Dangarembga's strategies in the book: numerous characters typify the effects of large social and historical forces on individuals. Dangarembga carefully situates these characters in relation to one another so that they evoke the kinds of relationships between opposing forces that were typical of colonial Zimbabwean society as a whole.

While the work of theorists such as Jameson and Lukács is clearly relevant to *Nervous Conditions*, Frantz Fanon provides the most direct theoretical background to Dangarembga's book, which is very much a Fanonian critique of colonialism and of the radical alienation suffered by colonial subjects as a result of the oppressive and unnatural environment in which they are forced to live.[1] The specific historical context and political perspective of Dangarem-

---

[1] See Zahar (1974) for a discussion of alienation as a key aspect of Fanon's analysis of the colonial condition.

bga's book are made clear from its title, which is taken from Jean-Paul Sartre's introduction to Fanon's *The Wretched of the Earth* (1968).[2] Sartre notes that colonized peoples lead a particularly confusing and contradictory existence because colonial regimes insist that their subjects aspire to European modes of conduct and acculturation; at the same time the regimes declare that these subjects are fundamentally inferior to Europeans and can therefore never hope to fully attain the status of European. Thus, colonial subjects live a complex, split existence, torn between loyalty to their traditional cultures and the desire to participate in the new, modern cultures of their colonial rulers—a desire instilled in them by a variety of colonialist strategies. This situation often leads colonial subjects to accept their own inferiority and thus to cooperate in their own subjugation. For Sartre, then, "the status of 'native' is a nervous condition introduced and maintained by the settler among colonized people *with their consent*" (Sartre 1968, 20). Dangarembga's book explores this process of what might be called psychological, or internal colonization, and the story of Tambudzai's development is largely the story of her gradual recognition of this phenomenon and her decision to rebel against it. At the same time, Tambudzai also comes to rebel against certain patriarchal aspects of her traditional Shona culture. This rebellion introduces a further complexity into the book: it clearly cannot be reduced to a simple good–bad opposition between African traditional and European colonial cultures. Thus, *Nervous Conditions* goes beyond Fanon, whose male-oriented analysis of the colonial condition does not explore gender issues in any substantive way. As Boehmer, puts it, Dangarembga in the book is "feminizing Fanon's findings on colonial cultural alienation" (Boehmer 1995, 228).

Nervous Conditions begins with the very striking statement by Tambudzai that "I was not sorry when my brother died" (p. 1). The early pages of the book explain this lack of mourning at her brother Nhamo's death. She is not sorry partially because he was a rather unpleasant and domineering figure (a sort of patriarchal tyrant in training), but primarily because it is only his death that gives Tambudzai an opportunity to further her education. The family's meager resources had been allocated for Nhamo's education because the education of boys took priority over the education of girls. Dangarembga thus introduces a number of issues related to gender and education very early in the book. The depiction of Tambudzai's thirst for a modern education demonstrates the thoroughness with which Western ideas have penetrated African society by the 1960s. The depiction of Nhamo illustrates the ways in

---

[2] See, for example, Neil Lazarus's interesting argument that, despite obvious differences between the two thinkers, Lukács in fact has a great deal in common with Fanon, especially as "the position he elaborated in the context of proletarian struggle in Europe in the 1910s and 1920s was analogous to that which Fanon would later come to formulate in the context of the national liberation struggle in Algeria" (Lazarus 1990, 16).

which such education does not counter the patriarchal tendencies of traditional African society, but in fact exacerbates them—both because boys have more educational opportunities than girls and because the ideas promulgated in colonial education are saturated with patriarchal attitudes.

The first chapter of the book relates Tambudzai's nostalgic memory of the tranquil and pastoral life in the Shona village of her early childhood. But it also evokes the rapid changes that have already transformed village life within Tambudzai's brief life span: "The river, the trees, the fruit and the fields. This was how it was in the beginning. This is how I remember it in my earliest memories, but it did not stay like that" (p. 3). Tambudzai's fond reminiscences of bathing in the river Nyamarira are immediately followed by a description of the District Council Houses that the colonial government is building near the river. This construction leads to the rapid development nearby of a modern town, where the environment is anything but peaceful and serene. The bathing spot, of course, has to be moved to a less desirable location further up the river. The town exemplifies the intrusion of Western commodities and Western popular culture into African traditional societies, with the inevitable changes that accompany that intrusion. Shops spring up around the Council Houses, selling foodstuffs and cheap Western consumer goods, and providing a focal point for idle youth to loiter and listen to Western popular music. These youth spend their spare change on "Fanta and Coca-Cola and perfume that smelt of vanilla essence, cheap at a tickey a bottle" (p. 4). The town also becomes a bus terminus where travelers can stop for refreshment, a further example of bustling modernity.

From the beginning, however, Dangarembga's treatment of the modernization of Shona society is complex and ambivalent. For example, the shops around the Council Houses may disrupt traditional village life, but they also provide a gathering place that threatens to promote anticolonial solidarity among the young people who meet there. Also, while there is a clear sense of loss in Tambudzai's description of the breakdown of traditional village life, it is also clear that this phenomenon offers important opportunities. From early on, Tambudzai is excited by the notion of Western education. When she is eight, she grows maize that she hopes to sell to pay her way to school. She fails, largely because her brother Nhamo (who finds her dream of education merely silly) pilfers much of the crop for his own use. Her efforts do, however, attract the attention of the local school teacher. He arranges for Tambudzai's initial schooling, which makes it possible for her to capitalize on Nhamo's death and go to the mission school.

The headmaster at the mission school is Tambudzai's English-educated uncle, Babamukuru. The uncle is a member of the colonial bourgeois elite that Fanon sees as mere imitators of their European masters and who, in the postcolonial era, will continue the basic structure of colonial rule in a new

form. Because he returns to Rhodesia to assume a lofty status that is autho-
rized strictly by his Western educational achievements, Babamukuru also
embodies Fanon's warning that "the native intellectual who comes back to
his people by way of cultural achievements behaves in fact like a foreigner"
(Fanon 1968, 223). Indeed, he exemplifies Fanon's description of "native"
intellectuals who develop a "permanent wish for identification with the
bourgeois representatives of the mother country" (p. 178). Babamukuru certainly accepts the superiority of Western culture, and he attempts to convey
that superiority in his professional work. And he shows no signs of the kind
of active opposition to colonial rule that Fanon expects from intellectuals.

Tambudzai is greatly intimidated by her domineering uncle, partially for
the simple reason that he is in a position of patriarchal authority, but also because of the aura of his European education. At the mission school, she lives
in her uncle's household, and he assumes the role of her father. Tambudzai at
first feels proud to live in this household, filled with dazzling modern conve-
niences. She is nearly overwhelmed by them at first; they seem so far beyond
what is available to ordinary Africans. Indeed, in a purely material sense, what
Tambudzai encounters in this household suggests the obvious advantage of
Western culture over her traditional Shona village. Moreover, the difference
between the two styles of life is so striking that Tambudzai feels that she has
become an entirely different person through her move into this new world
(pp. 58–59). There is a certain amount of nostalgia in this sense of transformation, but Tambudzai admits that she is not sorry to leave the difficult life
of her village for the opportunities of a Western education.

These opportunities are not, however, without their problems. Tambudzai's new life creates a gap between her and her family back in the village, and this gap grows wider as her education proceeds. This story, of course,
is a common one around the world. For example, Bardolph notes that Tambudzai can be compared to Thomas Hardy's *Tess of the D'Urbervilles* in the way
that she is "alienated from her background by her years at school and her
good English" (Bardolph 1990, 40). However, the story obviously has a special charge in a colonial situation, as Tambudzai's progressive alienation from
her traditional society occurs through a process of adaptation to the culture
of the colonial rulers. At the mission, Tambudzai shares a room with her cousin, Nyasha. Nyasha and her brother Chido have grown up largely in England
and have been so Westernized that they speak almost entirely in English and
hardly remember their native Shona language. Both children are thus radically estranged from traditional Shona culture. Chido, however, does have a stable cultural position to occupy. He has a good chance of success in colonial
culture if he follows the example of his father.

As a girl, Nyasha stands to profit less from modernization, and thus she
suffers more from her loss of contact with traditional culture. Nyasha has

learned the lessons of British education all too well and has "taken seriously the lessons about oppression and discrimination that she had learnt first-hand in England" (p. 63). She therefore becomes bitter and rebellious when she returns to Rhodesia and finds that in the colonies, the British rhetoric of freedom and equality consists of empty slogans that bear little relation to reality. Inequality is, in fact, the order of the day in Rhodesia, not only in the large gap between the standard of living in the Westernized town and the traditional villages, but also between social classes in the town. Babamuku-ru's servants, for example, enjoy far fewer of the material advantages of mod-ernization than Babamukuru and his family. The class structure of Western capitalist society is literally built into the household: the kitchen and other areas where servants spend their time are far shabbier than the living room and other areas inhabited by the family. Painfully aware of these discrepan-cies, Nyasha finds the relative luxury in which her family lives highly trou-bling. And her attitude comes to play an important role in Tambudzai's developing consciousness.

Through much of the text, Tambudzai is so dazzled by the material op-portunities offered by colonial culture that she is unable to understand the potential disadvantages of colonialism. Growing up in England, Nyasha is less dazzled by Western wealth and more able to mount a critique of colonial-ism. Indeed, she is the focal point of Dangarembga's criticism of colonial culture, a criticism that addresses many of the issues that have long been cen-tral to the African novel. As a student, for example, Nyasha is particularly in-terested in history and in the ways colonialist historiographies have distorted the African past. Finally unable to bear the Eurocentric distortions that she finds in her history book any longer, she flies into a rage, tearing the book to shreds and wrecking her room, filled as it is with Western commodities. "Their history," she screams. "Fucking liars. Their bloody lies" (p. 201).[3] Dan-garembga also makes some important points about Western medicine in her description of a psychiatrist who concludes that Nyasha, who seems on the verge of a nervous breakdown, is merely being difficult because "Africans did not suffer in the way we had described" (p. 201).[4] Nyasha does eventu-ally see a more "human" psychiatrist, who gives her medical treatment that improves her condition to an extent. Her nervous condition, however, like those described by Fanon in the final chapter of *The Wretched of the Earth*

---

[3] As Phillips points out, Nyasha's sense of estrangement from her cultural past makes a major contribution to her nervous instability, as opposed to Tambudzai who remains more thorough-ly rooted in traditional culture even during her Western education (Phillips 1994, 100, 102).

[4] Among other things, Nyasha suffers from anorexia, typically thought of as a Western disease related to the special dynamics of Western families. Moreover, as Bosman notes (quoting the work of Gloria Joseph), even Western feminist analyses of these dynamics have generally elid-ed the experience of black women (Bosman 1990, 95).

(1968), cannot be cured merely by medicine because it arises as much from the historical circumstance of colonialism as from any personal problems.

Nyasha also plays a central role in Dangarembga's exploration of the possibility that the new material wealth brought by colonial capitalism is a mixed blessing even for the upper classes who enjoy its benefits. Tambudzai soon comes to realize that the material splendor she finds in her uncle's house has a cold and impersonal quality that leaves individuals far more alienated from their material environments than they had been in the village. This motif is perhaps clearest in the treatment of food. The villagers of Tambudzai's childhood grow most of their own food as subsistence farmers; they are therefore directly connected to its production in ways that townspeople who buy their food in shops can never be. Food in the modern towns becomes a commodity in the sense defined by Marx—that is, an object produced for sale to others rather than for use by the producer. Food in the village is still appreciated for its own merits. Moreover, food serves an important communal function in the village: the sharing of food represents an important ceremonial activity in which families—and even entire villages—come together. The table in Babamukuru's house is richly laden with a wider variety of food than anyone could hope to have in the village, but meals at this table, however nutritionally rich and well balanced, lack the ceremonial function of those in the village (p. 69).

As Phillips puts it, this description of the food in Babamukuru's household shows that life in this household is "scientifically correct and emotionally emasculated" (Phillips 1994, 101). From a Marxist point of view, of course, this loss is quite predictable and is typical of the process of commodification, which reduces objects to mere markers in the system of market exchange. Commodities are viewed not in terms of their own intrinsic worth or usefulness, but merely for the price they can command when sold. That is, they are viewed in terms of what Marx called "exchange value" rather than "use value." Dangarembga's treatment of food can also be understood in terms of the notion of "reification," to which Lukács pays a great deal of attention, especially in *History and Class Consciousness* (1971a). Reification is the conversion of all aspects of human life (including abstract concepts, social relations, and even humans themselves) into "things." It is clearly related to commodification. However, whereas the notion of commodification emphasizes the participation of commodities in a single, overarching economic system, Lukács's discussion of reification focuses on the flip side of this process: this separation into discrete things implies that human life is radically fragmented, with individuals losing all sense that the different aspects of life fit into a coherent whole. Reification is thus closely related to process of alienation and in particular to the effacement in capitalist society of all traces of the actual production of commodities, which leads to a further separation between the production and consumption of goods. This aspect of reification has become particularly important to Marxist critics in recent years, now that consumers in First World countries like the United States so often buy and use goods that were manufactured in the distant Third World. Reification thus becomes a sort of repression through which citizens of rich countries can enjoy their luxury products without thinking about the lives of the workers who produced those products under the most oppressive of conditions.[5] In the colonial setting, the same phenomenon can occur on the local level. *Nervous Conditions* clearly suggests that Rhodesia's white rulers, as well as upper-class blacks such as Babamukuru, profited from inequities that they had to ignore in order to enjoy their privileged positions.

This process of repression, of course, can never be completely successful, and Marxist critics have noted that citizens of Western nations often enjoy their advantages in rather attenuated ways. Jameson, for example, notes that even sense impressions, including taste, can be greatly diminished in advanced capitalist societies, where "the very activity of sense perception has nowhere to go in a world in which science deals with ideal quantities, and comes to have little enough exchange value in a money economy dominated by considerations of calculation, measurement, profit, and the like" (Jameson 1981, 229). This process leads to the "repression of the culinary senses, of what might be called the gastronomical libido, in Britain and the United States" (p. 228). Nyasha, so painfully aware of the inequities in her colonial society, suffers from this repression in a particularly dramatic way: she is unable to enjoy the privileges that Dangarembga symbolizes with Babamukuru's well-stocked table. Indeed, she eventually rejects food almost entirely, developing a severe form of anorexia that seriously threatens her life. This situation is exacerbated by Babamukuru's domineering attempts to force the girl to eat. Babamukuru, accustomed to being obeyed, takes it as a personal affront that his daughter refuses the food he provides for her, and Nyasha's anorexia can also be read as a form of resistance to his patriarchal authority. It is, in fact, crucial to the message of Dangarembga's book that Nyasha's rebellion is as much a personal statement against her father as a more general statement against colonialism—and as much a statement about the patriarchal oppression of women as about the colonial oppression of Africans. Dangarembga's treatment of gender inequality as an aspect of the pain Nyasha experiences is reinforced by her depiction of Lucia, a woman in Tambudzai's village, who feels as oppressed by traditional culture as Nyasha does by modern colonial culture. Thus, while Phillips is certainly correct that Dangarembga seeks to contribute to the development of a viable Zimbabwean postcolonial cultural identity through the "retrieval of traditional culture,"

---

[5] For a discussion of this phenomenon, see Jameson (1991, 314–15).

Dangarembga also avoids a romanticization of this culture by pointing out some of its weaknesses, particularly regarding the treatment of women (Phillips 1994, 100). Unable to bear children, Lucia is something of an outcast in the children-oriented society of her village. Despite her low social status, however, she is a proud and independent woman who refuses marriage and rebels against the patriarchal structure of her society. She is thus able to carve out a place for herself in that society against all odds, though she also acknowledges the value of Western education, which she dreams of achieving.

Bardolph may be correct that Lucia is too idealized as the paradigm of the "new woman" in Africa (Bardolph 1990, 41–42). On the other hand, Lucia plays an important structural role in the book, suggesting both the oppression and the potential power of women in traditional African society, while at the same time serving as a sort of traditional counterpart to the Westernized Nyasha. All of the women characters in *Nervous Conditions* represent important elements of colonial experience. Tambudzai in many ways exemplifies the colonial subject who, as in Sartre's introduction to Fanon, struggles to come to grips with the effects of two different cultures simultaneously. In contrast, her cousin Nyasha was brought up largely in England and lives in a modern world that is thoroughly dominated by European culture, even after she returns to Rhodesia. Lucia remains in the world of the traditional African village and of traditional African culture. Both Nyasha and Lucia, in fact, are trapped within oppressive patriarchal structures that strictly limit their ability to fulfill their potentials as individuals, though it is significant that Lucia's traditional society nevertheless seems to offer her more opportunities than Nyasha's modern one.

Nervous Conditions makes good use of comparisons and contrasts between the situations of different women characters, and thus makes particularly creative use of the convention of "paired women" that Stratton sees as an important strategy of African women writers from Nwapa, to Emecheta and Mariama Bâ, to Dangarembga herself (Stratton 1994, 97). The convention is, in fact, particularly rich in *Nervous Conditions*, where many of the women characters participate in multiple pairs. For example, if Nyasha is opposed to Lucia, she is also opposed to the more obedient Tambudzai. Lucia, meanwhile, also contrasts with her sister, Tambudzai's strong but quiescent mother, Mainini, while the uneducated Mainini is set against her educated daughter. Nyasha and her mother Maiguru also form a sort of opposed pair in the text, reacting very differently to the domination of the rather pompous Babamukuru. Maiguru, like her husband, has received a master's degree in England. However, while he occupies an important position of authority in the mission school, she is a lowly teacher who is not even paid for her work—her salary goes directly to her husband, who thereby maintains a position of position of economic power that reinforces his authority as head of the family. Maiguru, by and large, accepts his domination in a relatively patient way, though she does occasionally resist when his attempts at dominance go beyond certain bounds; at one point she moves out of the house for several days. Maiguru, in fact, occupies such a subservient position in the family that Tambudzai is shocked to learn that her aunt has the same level of Western education as her uncle. Maiguru and Mainini thus constitute a pair of wives, both dominated by their husbands (who are brothers) in the different cultural circumstances of the town and the village, thus demonstrating that modernization and Western education to not necessarily lead to emancipation for women. As Bardolph puts it, these mothers are "symmetrically opposed":

> Tambudzai's mother, long suffering yet strong, totally entrapped in a back-breaking life and Tambudzai's aunt, Maiguru, a graduate, a "been-to" like her husband, who still keeps silent, accepting the rule of a man whose status and well-publicised bounties partly depend on her own salary (Bardolph 1990, 41).

Of course, these wives necessarily form structural pairs with their husbands, and these siblings/husbands/fathers themselves form a complementary pair. The men represent two different versions of the kind of father figures often found in African novels, especially those that are designed as critiques of patriarchy. Tambudzai's father, Jeremiah, is a relatively weak and ineffectual figure who attempts to maintain control of his household in a traditional manner, even as his traditional society is crumbling around him under the relentless pressure of colonial modernization. Babamukuru, on the other hand, attempts to ride the tide of modernization, parlaying his Western education into a patriarchal power that goes beyond that available to patriarchs in traditional African society. Jeremiah and Babamukuru are not, however, mere stereotypes. They have their positive features as well as their negative ones, their strengths as well as weaknesses, their problems as well as powers.

Dangarembga's portrayal of Babamukuru is particularly complex in this sense. His example provides a clear inspiration to Tambudzai in her quest for an education, even as his dominance makes it very difficult for Tambudzai to develop her own opinions about complex issues. Moreover, by the end of the text, as Tambudzai comes more and more to understand the insidious nature of colonial cultural domination, she also comes to realize that Babamukuru is in some ways the ultimate victim of this domination, even as he works in complicity with it. He has been shaped by powerful forces that are beyond his control, and, however powerful he might seem in his own household, he still occupies a subservient position relative to Rhodesia's white colonizers. Nyasha, wasted and nearing death, recognizes this fact and urges Tambudzai not to blame Babamukuru or Maiguru for her fate (p. 200).

All of the major characters in *Nervous Conditions* represent specific, identifiable forms of colonial experience and are shaped by identifiable historical forces associated with colonialism. Tambudzai, though, functions as a point of convergence of all of these forces. Her growth and maturation lead her by the end of the text to declare her independence from Western cultural domination; thus she can be taken as indicative of the maturation of Zimbabwe as a modern nation, demanding its independence from white colonial and neocolonial rule. We leave her at age fifteen, just beginning work at the prestigious Sacred Heart academy, but she assures us at the end that her subsequent experience—the experience that has enabled her to construct this retrospective narrative—will lead her away from her former reverence for the culture of the West:

> Quietly, unobtrusively, and extremely fitfully, something in my mind began to assert itself, to question things and refuse to be brainwashed, bringing me to this time when I can set down this story (p. 204).

Such passages, which specifically represent a rejection of the values taught to Tambudzai in her colonial education, make the anticolonial orientation of Dangarembga's book clear. On the other hand, Bardolph's description of *Nervous Conditions* as "a committed novel with a clearly feminist approach" is accurate as well, and Dangarembga's vivid descriptions of the special problems encountered by Tambudzai because of her gender are powerful and effective (Bardolph 1990, 43). Indeed, one of the most important achievements of *Nervous Conditions* is its demonstration of the complicity between colonialism and patriarchy, which function not merely as simultaneous forms of parallel oppression, but as inseparable parts of the same phenomenon. The book thus clearly supports Michelle Vizzard's contention that "feminist analysis is *not* an additional extra to projects of anti- or postcolonization, but rather is absolutely integral to them" (Vizzard 1993, 203). Dangarembga's book represents an important contribution not just to African women's literature, but to African literature as a whole and to women's literature around the world.

Historical Background

Zimbabwe has a population of about eleven million (1995 estimate) and covers an area of approximately 150,000 square miles, about one and one-half times that of the United Kingdom. The terrain consists of four main plateau regions. A band of high veld (with an elevation of over four thousand feet) crosses the country from southwest to northeast. A region of middle veld (with an elevation of three to four thousand feet) lies on either side of this band. A highland region runs along the eastern border with Mozambique, reaching a maximum elevation of 8,503 feet at Inyangani. The forests of Zimbabwe produce valuable hardwoods, and the country also has considerable mineral resources, including substantial deposits of gold, nickel, silver, tin, iron, and coal.

Still, the economy of Zimbabwe is primarily agricultural. Tobacco is the most important cash crop, while maize is the principal food crop. Coffee, tea, cotton, groundnuts, sorghum, vegetables, millet, rice, and fruits are also produced. The middle veld includes substantial amounts of ranching land. Zimbabwe's industries produce steel, cement, machinery, textiles, food products, and consumer goods, contributing to an annual per capita gross domestic product of about $800. Most of the country's electricity is generated by a large hydroelectric plant located at Lake Kariba along the Zambian border. Zimbabwe has well-developed road and railway systems and an internal airline system that includes eight airports. Harare (formerly known as Salisbury) is the capital and largest city, with a population of about 700,000. The second largest city is Bulawayo, with a population of just over 400,000.

The population of Zimbabwe consists primarily of black Africans, with small numbers of Asians and other minorities. The number of white inhabitants has steadily declined since independence from British colonial rule to below 200,000. English is the official language of Zimbabwe, but Shona and Ndebele, the languages of the two largest ethnic groups, are widely used as well. About one-fourth of the population is Christians, while another fourth practices traditional African religions. About half the population follows syncretic religions combining elements of Christianity and traditional African religions. Just over half the population is literate, mostly in English.

The modern country of Zimbabwe takes its name from an ancient civilization whose principal city may have been the biblical city of Ophir, where King Solomon had his mines. This city was first occupied by Iron Age people in the third century, though the current impressive ruins (which show a high level of artistic achievement and an advanced standard of living) date to the twelfth to fifteenth centuries. Other Iron Age sites in Zimbabwe date back to the second century. These early civilizations were supplanted by Bantu-speaking peoples who moved into the region in the fifth century. The Portuguese developed relationships with Shona–dominated states in the region in the sixteenth century, trading for gold and other items. Ndebele invaders conquered the Shona in the 1830s and forced them to pay tribute. During the nineteenth century British and Boer traders, hunters, and missionaries gradually moved into the region. In 1889 the British South Africa Company, headed by Cecil Rhodes, obtained a charter to promote trade and European settlement in the region, which they named Rhodesia. By 1890 a group of British and South African pioneers, led by Rhodes's associate Leander Starr Jameson, moved deep into the interior and founded Fort Salisbury on the site of what is now Harare. The Ndebele resisted this intrusion, but were decisively defeated in 1893, clearing the way for domination of the region by Rhodes's company. Revolts by both the Shona and the Ndebele were put down in 1896–1897, leaving the British firmly in control of the region, which became known as Southern Rhodesia. (The area known as Northern Rhodesia occupied the territory that would eventually become Zambia.)

In 1922, European settlers in Southern Rhodesia, who had been agitating for political autonomy for some time, rejected a proposal that they be incorporated into the new Union of South Africa and opted instead to make Rhodesia a self-governing colony under the British Crown. This status became effective in September 1923. In subsequent decades, the colonial government did much to develop the economic infrastructure of Rhodesia, but did little to share the resultant wealth with the African population, which had few political or civil rights under the regime. In 1953, Southern Rhodesia joined Northern Rhodesia and Nyasaland (now Malawi) to form the white-dominated Federation of Rhodesia and Nyasaland, despite African objections to the move. This federation disbanded in 1963 as Zambia and Malawi moved toward independence and indigenous rule. Southern Rhodesia, under the leadership of Ian Smith, moved toward independence from Britain as well, but the new state of Rhodesia remained under the strict control of a white-dominated neocolonial government. Britain refused to acknowledge Smith's 1965 declaration of independence, and the British and Rhodesian governments remained at odds until 1971, when they finally reached an accord that provided for gradually increasing political participation for blacks, though without any guarantee of equal rights under a regime that was in many ways beginning to resemble the apartheid regime in the neighboring country of South Africa.

This situation led to the imposition of United Nations economic sanctions against Rhodesia in an attempt to force the nation toward an equitable treatment of its black majority. Meanwhile, the country's black nationalists, led by Robert Mugabe and Joshua Nkomo, were fighting for their own rights in a campaign of guerrilla war against the white government. Two groups, the Zimbabwe African National Union (ZANU) and the Zimbabwe African People's Union (ZAPU), based in Mozambique and Zambia, respectively, launched a series of assaults that by 1978 forced Smith to reach an agreement with moderate black leaders to establish an interim biracial government, followed by biracial elections in 1979. The elections, however, were tainted by reports of intimidation of voters by government troops and by the fact that Bishop Abel Muzorewa, leader of the coalition that won the election, lost credibility after seeking aid from South Africa. Moreover, the black nationalists (and virtually the entire international community) rejected this settlement as inadequate because it still granted an inordinate amount of political power to the country's small white minority. Finally, all parties reached agreement at a conference in London. British colonial rule was reestablished during a year of transition that led to the birth of the new nation of Zimbabwe, under a black majority government and officially independent of British colonial rule, on April 18, 1980.

Zimbabwe thus became one of the last British colonies in Africa to gain independence. The heroic struggle for self-government in Zimbabwe made the country a key symbol for many black nationalist groups in Africa, and hopes were high that the new nation would provide a stellar example of postcolonial political and economic success. Unfortunately, the years of fighting had left the country economically unstable and torn by deep divisions that were not simple to overcome. ZANU leader Mugabe became the nation's first prime minister, with Nkomo holding a key place in his cabinet. However, tensions arose between the two leaders, with Mugabe's more radical ZANU-PF (Zimbabwe African National Union-Popular Front) party often differing significantly in its policies from Nkomo's more moderate ZAPU party. These disagreements led to Nkomo's ouster in 1982, after which Mugabe gradually consolidated his power and attempted to develop the nation's economy along nominally socialist lines. Mugabe's official espousal of Marxism gained a certain amount of support from socialist governments abroad, but it caused rich Western governments such as Britain and the United States to be hesitant to provide aid to the struggling country. Moreover, the principal foreign support for Mugabe's party came from the Chinese, while Nkomo's party drew most of its foreign support from the more conservative Soviets, leading to further tensions. Further international complications were caused by attempts on the part of the apartheid government in South Africa to destabilize the economy and government of Zimbabwe. In 1987, Zimbabwe established a presidential form of government, with Mugabe as its first president. Factional fighting between forces loyal to Mugabe and those loyal to Nkomo continued. The two leaders merged ZANU-PF and ZAPU in an attempt to end the conflict, and Nkomo returned to the cabinet. Zimbabwe thus became an effectively one-party state. As late as 1996 (when Mugabe was reelected after his main opponent, Muzorewa, withdrew in protest at the last moment), this party still held 147 of the 150 seats in the Zimbabwean Parliament.

In 1991 after the fall of Eastern European communism, ZANU-PF officially abandoned its Marxist stance, but in fact the government of Zimbabwe had been moving away from socialism and toward dictatorship for some time. The official change in policy may have been made in the hope of receiving additional aid from the West, aid that was made particularly necessary in 1992 by a crippling drought. Mugabe declared a national emergency and appealed to the international community for food, money, and medicine to combat the widespread famine and disease that were sweeping the country. Zimbabwe has also been hit particularly hard by the AIDS epidemic that has swept Africa. Critics charged that conditions were worsened by the excessive power and growing corruption of Mugabe's government and suggested that the once-promising country was well on its way to becoming another Kenya, but Mugabe defended his one-party government and pledged to continue to work to improve economic and social conditions in Zimbabwe.

Biographical Background

Tsitsi Dangarembga is one of the brightest new stars to emerge in African literature in the past decade. Born in colonial Zimbabwe in 1960, Dangarembga lived in England between the ages of two and six, lived and studied in Rhodesia until her late teens, and then returned to England to study medicine and psychology at Cambridge University. She returned to Zimbabwe in 1980. Due to her sheltered childhood in a relatively privileged black family, Dangarembga had remained rather oblivious to the political turmoil in her country during her childhood. Back in Zimbabwe, however, she attended the University of Zimbabwe, where she came into contact with socialist and feminist political ideas. She has devoted her energies to socially-committed writing ever since. Suggesting that white Western feminism does not really address her experience, she has identified black American women writers as among her most important literary influences (Dangarembga 1989b, 106). Other important influences include the Americans James Baldwin and Tennessee Williams, the British modernist writer D. H. Lawrence, and the nineteenth-century Russian novelists Leo Tolstoy and Fyodor Dostoevsky. Among African writers, Mariama Bâ has been important for her, as have the male Zimbabwean writers Stanley Nyamfukudza and Dambudzo Marechera.

Though *Nervous Conditions* is Dangarembga's first novel, she is also the author of a 1987 play, *She No Longer Weeps.* This play treats many of the same gender-related themes as the novel, focusing on the experiences of a young urban woman who encounters various problems related to her unwanted pregnancy in the midst of a highly patriarchal environment. The play presents issues of gender and sexuality from a woman's perspective in a frank and open manner and has been a leading work in the emergence of a new wave of women's theater dealing with such themes in Zimbabwe. *Nervous Conditions,* first published in Britain in 1988, has been widely praised by critics and is already beginning to receive substantial critical attention. Named the African region's nominee for the Commonwealth Prize for Literature in 1989, it promises to become one of the most important African novels of the last part of the twentieth century.

Further Reading

Bowman, Larry W. 1973. *Politics in Rhodesia: White Power in an African State.* Cambridge, Mass.: Harvard University Press.

Dixon, Marlene, and Rod Bush, eds. 1983. *Revolution in Southern Africa.* San Francisco: Synthesis Publications.

Kriger, Norma J. 1992. *Zimbabwe's Guerrilla War: Peasant Voices.* Cambridge: Cambridge University Press.

Martin, David. 1982. *The Struggle for Zimbabwe: The Chimurenga War.* London: Faber.

Mathema, Cain. 1994. *ZANU (PF) and Economic Independence.* Harare: Mathema Publications.

Needham, D. E., E. K. Mashingaidze, and N. Bhebe. 1984. *From Iron Age to Independence.* Harlow, Essex: Longman.

Nyangoni, Wellington Winter. 1992. *Underdevelopment, Imperialism, and Neocolonialism in Zimbabwe.* Marlborough, Zimbabwe: Msasa Publications.

Skalnes, Tor. 1995. *The Politics of Economic Reform in Zimbabwe: Continuity and Change in Development.* New York: St. Martin's.

Stoneman, Colin. 1988. *Zimbabwe's Prospects: Class, State, and Capital in Southern Africa.* Basingstoke, England: Macmillan.

Stoneman, Colin, and Lionel Cliffe. 1989. *Zimbabwe: Politics, Economics, and Society.* London: Pinter Publishers.

Wills, Alfred J. 1985. *An Introduction to the History of Central Africa: Zambia, Malawi, and Zimbabwe.* 4th ed. New York: Oxford University Press.

Wiseman, Henry, and Alastair M. Taylor. 1981. *From Rhodesia to Zimbabwe: The Politics of Transition.* New York: Pergamon.

Works Cited

▼▼▼▼▼▼▼▼▼▼▼▼▼

Abel, Elizabeth, Marianne Hirsch, and Elizabeth Langland, eds. 1983. *The Voyage In: Fictions of Female Development*. Hanover, N.H.: University Press of New England.

Abrahams, Cecil A. 1985. *Alex La Guma*. Boston: Twayne.

————, ed. 1991. *Memories of Home: The Writings of Alex La Guma*. Trenton, N.J.: Africa World Press.

Abrahams, Peter. 1943 *Song of the City*. London: Crisp.

————. 1946. *Mine Boy*. New York: Collier.

————. 1948. *The Path of Thunder*. New York: Collier.

————. 1950. *Wild Conquest*. New York: Harper.

————. 1954. *Tell Freedom*. London: Allen and Unwin.

————. 1956. *Wreath for Udomo*. London: Faber and Faber.

————. 1965. *A Night of Their Own*. London: Faber and Faber.

————. 1966. This *Island Now*. London: Faber and Faber.

————. 1985. *The View from Coyaba*. London: Faber and Faber.

Achebe, Chinua. 1964. *Arrow of God*. London: Heinemann.

————. 1972. *Beware, Soul Brother*. Rev. ed. London: Heinemann.

————. 1972. *Girls at War and Other Stories*. London: Heinemann.

————. 1975. *Morning Yet on Creation Day*. London: Heinemann.

————. 1988a. *Anthills of the Savannah*. 1987. New York: Anchor-Doubleday.

————. 1988b. "An Image of Africa: Racism in Conrad's *Heart of Darkness*." In *Heart of Darkness*, by Joseph Conrad. 3rd ed. Ed. Robert Kimbrough. Norton Critical Edition. New York: Norton. 251–62. Originally published in *The Massachusetts Review* 18 (1977): 782–94.

————. 1988c. *Hopes and Impediments: Selected Essays, 1965–87*. London: Heinemann.

————. 1989a. *Arrow of God*. Rev. ed. 1974. New York: Anchor-Doubleday.

————. 1989b. *A Man of the People*. 1966. New York: Anchor-Doubleday.

————. 1990. "An Interview with Chinua Achebe." Interview by Charles Rowell. *Callaloo* 13.1: 86–101.

————. 1991. "Teaching *Things Fall Apart*." In *Approaches to Teaching Achebe's "Things Fall Apart."* Ed. Bernth Lindfors. New York: Modern Language Association. 20–24.

————. 1994a. *No Longer at Ease*. 1960. New York: Anchor-Doubleday.

————. 1994b. *Things Fall Apart*. 1958. New York: Anchor-Doubleday.

Adewoye, Sam A. 1992. "The Strength of the Rhetoric of Oral Tradition in Ngugi wa Thiong'o's *Devil on the Cross*." *Commonwealth Novel in English* 5.1: 11–19.

Ahmad, Aijaz. 1992. *In Theory: Classes, Nations, Literatures*. London: Verso.

Aidoo, Ama Ata. 1969. Introduction to *The Beautyful Ones Are Not Yet Born*, by Ayi Kwei Armah. New York: Collier. vii–xii.

————. 1985. *Someone Talking to Sometime*. Harare: College Press.

————. 1987. *"The Eagle and the Chickens" and Other Stories*. Enugu, Nigeria: Tana.

————. 1988. "To Be an African Woman Writer—An Overview and a Detail." In *Criticism and Ideology: Proceedings of the Second African Writers' Conference, Stockholm 1986*. Ed. Kirsten Holst Petersen. Uppsala: Scandinavian Institute of African Studies. 155–72.

———— 1991. "Changing Her Tune." Interview by Maya Jaggi. *The Guardian* (April 2): 17.

————. 1992. *"An Angry Letter in January" and Other Poems.* Coventry, England: Dangaroo Press.

————. 1993. *Changes: A Love Story.* 1991. New York: Feminist Press at the City University of New York.

————. 1994a. *No Sweetness Here.* 1970. White Plains, N.Y.: Longman.

————. 1994b. *Our Sister Killjoy, or Reflections from a Black-Eyed Squint.* 1977. White Plains, N.Y.: Longman.

————. 1995. *"The Dilemma of a Ghost" and "Anowa": Two Plays.* 1965, 1970. White Plains, N.Y.: Longman.

Allan, Tuzyline Jita. 1995. *Womanist and Feminist Aesthetics.* Athens: Ohio University Press.

Althusser, Louis. 1971. *Lenin and Philosophy and Other Essays.* Trans. Ben Brewster. London: Monthly Review Press. 170–83.

Aluko, Timothy Mofolorunso. *One Man, One Wife.* Lagos: Nigerian Printing and Publishing.

Amadi, Elechi. 1966. *The Concubine.* London: Heinemann.

————. 1986. *Estrangement.* London: Heinemann.

Amadiume, Ifi. 1987. *Male Daughters, Female Husbands: Gender and Sex in an African Society.* London: Zed.

Anderson, Benedict. 1991. *Imagined Communities: Reflections on the Origin and Spread of Nationalism.* 2nd ed. London: Verso.

Andrade, Susan Z. 1990. "Rewriting History, Motherhood, and Rebellion: Naming an African Women's Literary Tradition." *Research in African Literatures* 21.1: 91–110.

Anyidoho, Kofi. 1992. "Literature and African Identity: The Example of Ayi Kwei Armah." In *Critical Perspectives on Ayi Kwei Armah.* Ed. Derek Wright. Washington, D.C.: Three Continents Press. 34–47.

Appiah, Kwame Anthony. 1992. *In My Father's House: Africa in the Philosophy of Culture.* New York: Oxford University Press.

Armah, Ayi Kwei. 1967. "African Socialism: Utopian or Scientific?" *Présence Africaine* 64: 6–30.

————. 1969. *The Beautyful Ones Are Not Yet Born.* London: Heinemann.

————. 1970. *Fragments.* Boston: Houghton Mifflin.

————. 1974. *Why Are We So Blest?* 1972. Nairobi: East African Publishing House.

————. 1978. *The Healers.* Nairobi: East African Publishing House.

————. 1979. *Two Thousand Seasons.* Chicago: Third World Press.

————. 1985a. "One Writer's Education." *West Africa* (August 26): 1752–53.

————. 1985b. "The Teaching of Creative Writing." *West Africa* (May 20): 994–95.

————. 1995. *Osiris Rising.* Popenguine: Per Ankh.

Asein, Samuel Omo. 1978. "The Revolutionary Vision in Alex La Guma's Novels." *Phylon* 39: 74–86.

Awoonor, Kofi. 1972. *This Earth, My Brother.* London: Heinemann.

Bâ, Mariama. 1980. *Une si longue lettre.* Dakar: Nouvelles Éditions Africaines. Trans. Modupé Bodé-Thomas, as *So Long a Letter.* London: Heinemann, 1989.

————. 1984. *Un chant écarlate.* Dakar: Nouvelles Éditions Africaines. Trans. as *Scarlet Song.* Harlow: Longman, 1985.

Bakhtin, Mikhail. 1981. *The Dialogic Imagination.* Ed. Michael Holquist. Trans. Caryl Emerson and Michael Holquist. Austin: University of Texas Press.

————. 1984a. *Problems of Dostoevsky's Poetics.* Trans. and ed. Caryl Emerson. Minneapolis: University of Minnesota Press.

———— 1984b. *Rabelais and His World.* Trans. Helene Iswolsky. Bloomington : Indiana University Press.

————— 1986. *Speech Genres and Other Late Essays.* Trans. Vern W. McGhee. Ed. Caryl Emerson and Michael Holquist. Austin: University of Texas Press.

Balogun, F. Odun. 1988. "Ngugi's *Devil on the Cross:* The Novel as Hagiography of a Marxist." *Ufahamu* 16.2: 76–87.

Balutansky, Kathleen. 1990. *The Novels of Alex La Guma: The Representation of a Political Conflict.* Washington, D.C.: Three Continents Press.

Bamgbose, Ayo. 1974. *The Novels of D. O. Fagunwa.* Benin City, Nigeria: Ethiope Press.

Bandele-Thomas, Biyi. 1991a. *The Man Who Came in from the Back of Beyond.* London: Bellew.

————. 1991b. *The Sympathetic Undertaker and Other Dreams.* London: Bellew.

Bannet, Eve Tavor. 1991. "Rewriting the Social Text: The Female Bildungsroman in Eighteenth-Century England." In *Reflection and Action: Essays on the Bildungsroman.* Ed. James Hardin. Columbia: University of South Carolina Press. 195–227.

Bardolph, Jacqueline. 1990. "'The Tears of Childhood' of Tsitsi Dangarembga." *Commonwealth Essays and Studies* 13.1: 37–47.

Bascom, William R. 1975. *African Dilemma Tales.* The Hague: Mouton.

Bazin, Nancy Topping. 1990. "Venturing into Feminist Consciousness." In *The Tragic Life: Bessie Head and Literature in Southern Africa.* Ed. Cecil Abrahams. Trenton, N.J.: Africa World Press. 45–58.

Ben Jelloun, Tahar. 1987. *La nuit sacrée.* Paris: Éditions du Seuill. Trans. Alan Sheridan, as *The Sacred Night.* London: Quartet, 1989.

Benhedouga, Abdelhamid. 1971. *Rih al-janub.* Tunis: Muassasat Abd al-Karim bin Abd Allah.

Benjamin, Walter. 1955. *Illuminations.* Trans. Harry Zohn. Ed. Hannah Arendt. New York: Harcourt, Brace and World.

Benson, Eugene, and L. W. Conolly, eds. 1994. *Encyclopedia of Post-Colonial Literatures in English.* 2 vols. London: Routledge.

Bernal, Martin. 1987. *Black Athena.* Vol. 1, *The Fabrication of Ancient Greece, 1785–1985.* New Brunswick, N.J.: Rutgers University Press.

Bertoncini, Elena Zubkova. 1987. "An Annotated Bibliography of Swahili Fiction and Drama Published between 1975 and 1984." *Research in African Literatures* 17.1–2: 525–62.

Beti, Mongo. 1956. *Le pauvre Christ de Bomba.* Paris: Laffont. Trans. Gerald Moore, as *The Poor Christ of Bomba.* London: Heinemann, 1971.

————. 1957. *Mission terminée.* Paris: Correa. Trans. Peter Green, as *Mission to Kala.* London: Heinemann, 1978.

————. 1974. *Perpétue et l'habitude du malheur.* Paris: Buchet/Castel. Trans. as *Perpetua and the Habit of Unhappiness.* London: Heinemann, 1978.

————. 1974. *Remember Ruben.* Paris: Union generale d'éditions. Trans. Gerald Moore, as *Remember Ruben.* London: Heinemann, 1980.

Blyden, E. W. 1967. *Christianity, Islam, and the Negro Race.* 1888. London: Edinburgh University Press.

Boehmer, Elleke. 1995. *Colonial and Postcolonial Literature: Migrant Metaphors.* New York: Oxford University Press.

Bois, Marcel. 1992. "Arabic-Language Algerian Literature." *Research in African Literatures* 23.2: 103–111.

Booker, M. Keith. 1994. *The Dystopian Impulse in Modern Literature: Fiction as Social Criticism.* Westport, Conn.: Greenwood Press.

————. 1995. "African Literature and the World System: Dystopian Fiction, Collective Experience, and the Postcolonial Condition." *Research in African Literatures* 26.4: 58–75.

————. 1997. *Colonial Power, Colonial Texts: India in the British Novel.* Ann Arbor: University of Michigan Press.

Bosman, Brenda. 1990. "A Correspondence without Theory: Tsitsi Dangarembga's *Nervous Conditions." Current Writing: Text and Reception in Southern Africa* 2.1: 91–100.

Boyers, Robert. 1984. "Public and Private: On *Burger's Daughter." Salmagundi* 62 (Winter): 62–92.

Brennan, Timothy. 1990. "The National Longing for Form." In *Nation and Narration.* Ed. Homi K. Bhabha. London: Routledge. 44–70.

Brink, André. 1974. *Looking on Darkness.* London: W.H. Allen.

————. 1979. *A Dry White Season.* London: W. H. Allen.

————. 1982. *A Chain of Voices.* London: Faber.

Brink, Andrè, and J.M. Coetzee, eds. 1986. *A Land Apart: A Contemporary South African Reader.* London: Faber and Faber.

Brown, Lloyd W. 1981. *Women Writers in Black Africa.* Westport, Conn.: Greenwood Press.

Bürger, Peter. 1984. *Theory of the Avant-Garde.* Trans. Michael Shaw. Minneapolis: University of Minnesota Press.

Cabral, Amilcar. 1973. *Return to the Source: Selected Speeches.* New York: Monthly Review Press.

Cancel, Robert. 1993. "African–Language Literatures: Perspectives on Culture and Identity." In *A History of Twentieth-Century African Literatures.* Ed. Oyekan Owomoyela. Lincoln: University of Nebraska Press. 285–310.

Carroll, David. 1990. *Chinua Achebe: Novelist, Poet, Critic.* 2nd ed. London: Macmillan.

Cary, Joyce. 1989. *Mister Johnson.* 1939. New York: New Directions.

Chandramohan, Balasubramanyam. 1992. *A Study in Trans-Ethnicity in Modern South Africa: The Writings of Alex La Guma, 1925–1985.* Lewiston, N.Y.: Mellen Research University Press.

Cheney-Coker, Syl. 1990. *The Last Harmattan of Alusine Dunbar.* Portsmouth, NH: Heinemann.

Chetin, Sara. 1993. "Reading from a Distance: Ama Ata Aidoo's *Our Sister Killjoy." In Black Women's Writing.* Ed. Gina Wisker. New York: St. Martin's. 146–59.

Chinodya, Shimmer. 1989. *Harvest of Thorns.* Harare: Baobab.

Chinweizu, Onwuchekwa Jemie, and Ihechukwu Madubuike. 1983. *Toward the Decolonization of African Literature: African Fiction and Poetry and Their Critics.* Washington, D.C.: Howard University Press.

Christian, Barbara. 1985. *Black Feminist Criticism: Perspectives on Black Women Writers.* New York: Pergamon.

Clingman, Stephen. 1986. *The Novels of Nadine Gordimer: History from the Inside.* Johannesburg: Ravan.

Cobham, Rhonda. 1991. "Making Men and History: Achebe and the Politics of Revisionism." In *Approaches to Teaching Achebe's "Things Fall Apart."* Ed. Bernth Lindfors. New York: Modern Language Association. 91–100.

Coetzee, J. M. 1974. *Dusklands.* Johannesburg: Raven.

————. 1977. *In the Heart of the Country.* London: Secker and Warburg.

————. 1980. *Waiting for the Barbarians.* London; Secker and Warburg.

————. 1983. *The Life and Times of Michael K.* New York: Viking.

————. 1986. *Foe.* New York: Viking.

————. 1990. *Age of Iron.* London: Secker and Warburg.

————. 1994. *The Master of Petersburg.* New York: Viking.

Cohen, David William. 1994. *The Combing of History*. Chicago: University of Chicago Press.

Collins, Harold. 1971. "The Ironic Imagery of Armah's *The Beautyful Ones Are Not Yet Born*: The Putrescent Vision." *World Literature Written in English* 20 (November): 37–50.

Conrad, Joseph. 1988. *Heart of Darkness*. 1902. 3rd ed. Ed. Robert Kimbrough. Norton Critical Edition. New York: Norton.

Cook, David, and Michael Okenimkpe. 1983. *Ngugi wa Thiong'o: An Exploration of His Writings*. London: Heinemann.

Cooke, John. 1985. *The Novels of Nadine Gordimer: Private Lives/Public Landscapes*. Baton Rouge: Louisiana State University Press.

Cope, Jack. 1969. *The Dawn Came Twice*. London: Heinemann.

Coquery-Vidrovitch, Catherine. 1988. *Africa: Endurance and Change South of the Sahara*. Trans. David Maisel. Berkeley: University of California Press.

Dadié, Bernard. 1956. *Climbié*. Paris: Seghers.

D'Almeida, Irene Assiba. 1994. *Francophone African Women Writers: Destroying the Emptiness of Silence*. Gainesville: University Press of Florida.

Dangarembga, Tsitsi. 1987. *She No Longer Weeps*. Harare: College Press.

———. 1989a. *Nervous Conditions*. Seattle: Seal Press.

———. 1989b. "Women Write about the Things That Move Them." Interview by Flora Veit-Wild. *Matatu* 3.6:101–108.

Dasenbrock, Reed Way. 1985–86. "Creating a Past: Achebe, Naipaul, Soyinka, Farah." *Salmagundi* 68–69 (Fall–Winter): 312–332.

Dathorne, O. R. 1974. *The Black Mind: A History of African Literature*. Minneapolis: University of Minnesota Press.

Davidson, Basil. 1959. *The Lost Cities of Africa*. Rev. ed. Boston: Little, Brown.

———. 1969. *The African Genius: An Introduction to African Social and Cultural History*. Boston: Little, Brown.

———. 1978. *Let Freedom Come: Africa in Modern History*. Boston: Little, Brown.

———. 1992. *The Black Man's Burden: Africa and the Curse of the Nation-State*. New York: Times Books–Random House.

———. 1994. *The Search for Africa: History, Culture, Politics*. New York: Times Books–Random House.

Davies, Carole Boyce. 1986a. "Feminist Consciousness and African Literary Criticism." Introduction to *Ngambika: Studies of Women in African Literature*. Ed. Carole Boyce Davies and Anne Adams Graves. Trenton, N.J.: Africa World Press. 1–23.

———. 1986b. "Motherhood in the Works of Male and Female Igbo Writers: Achebe, Emecheta, Nwapa and Nzekwu." In *Ngambika: Studies of Women in African Literature*. Ed. Carole Boyce Davies and Anne Adams Graves. Trenton, N.J.: Africa World Press. 241–56.

Déjeux, Jean. 1992. "Francophone Literature in the Maghreb: The Problem and the Possibility." *Research in African Literatures* 23.2: 5–19.

Diallo, Nafissatou. 1975. *De Tilène au plateau: Une enfance dakaroise*. Dakar: Nouvelles Éditions Africaines. Trans. as *A Dakar Childhood*. Harlow: Longman, 1982.

Dickson, Keith A. 1978. *Towards Utopia: A Study of Brecht*. Oxford: Clarendon Press.

Diop, Cheikh Anta. 1974. *The African Origin of Civilization: Myth or Reality*. New York: Lawrence Hill.

Djoleto, Amu. 1967. *The Strange Man*. London: Heinemann.

———. 1975. *Money Galore*. London: Heinemann.

———. 1987. *Hurricane of Dust*. Harlow: Longman.

Dlamanini, Moses. 1984. *Hell Hole, Robben Island: Reminiscences of a Political Prisoner in Africa.* Trenton: Africa World Press.

Ekwensi, Cyprian. 1961. *Jagua Nana.* London: Heinemann.

———. 1963. *Beautiful Feathers.* London: Hutchinson.

Emecheta, Buchi. 1976. *The Bride Price.* New York: Braziller.

———. 1977. *The Slave Girl.* New York: Braziller.

———. 1979. *Titch the Cat.* London: Allison and Busby.

———. 1980. *Nowhere to Play.* London: Allison and Busby.

———. 1982. *Naira Power.* London: Macmillan.

———. 1983a. *Double Yoke.* New York: Braziller.

———. 1983b. *The Moonlight Bride.* New York: Braziller.

———. 1983c. *Second-Class Citizen.* 1974. New York; Braziller.

———. 1983d. *The Wrestling Match.* New York: Braziller.

———. 1985. *The Rape of Shavi.* New York: Braziller.

———. 1988a. "Feminism with a Small *F.*" In *Criticism and Ideology: Proceedings of the Second African Writers' Conference, Stockholm 1986.* Ed. Kirsten Holst Petersen. Uppsala: Scandinavian Institute of African Studies. 173–81.

———. 1988b. *The Joys of Motherhood.* 1979. London: Heinemann.

———. 1990. *The Family.* New York: Braziller.

———. 1994a. *Destination Biafra.* 1982. London: Heinemann.

———. 1994b. *Head Above Water.* 1986. London: Heinemann.

———. 1994c. *In the Ditch.* 1972. London: Heinemann.

———. 1994d. *Kehinde.* London: Heinemann.

Emenyonu, Ernest N. 1990. "Chinua Achebe's *Things Fall Apart:* A Classic Study in Diplomatic Tactlessness." In *Chinua Achebe: A Celebration.* Ed. Kirsten Holst Petersen and Anna Rutherford. Oxford: Heinemann. 83–88.

Ettin, Andrew V. 1993. *Betrayals of the Body Politic: The Literary Commitments of Nadine Gordimer.* Charlottesville: University Press of Virginia.

Fanon, Frantz. 1968. *The Wretched of the Earth.* Trans. Constance Farrington. New York: Grove Press.

Farah, Nuruddin. 1970. *From a Crooked Rib.* London: Heinemann.

———. 1976. *A Naked Needle.* London: Heinemann.

———. 1979. *Sweet and Sour Milk.* London: Allison and Busby.

———. 1981. *Sardines.* London: Allison and Busby.

———. 1983. *Close Sesame.* London: Allison and Busby.

———. 1986. *Maps.* New York: Pantheon.

———. 1992. *Gifts.* London: Serif.

Fishburn, Katherine. 1995. *Reading Buchi Emecheta: Cross-Cultural Conversations.* Westport, Conn.: Greenwood Press.

Foley, Barbara. 1993. *Radical Representations: Politics and Form in U. S. Proletarian Fiction, 1929–1941.* Durham, N.C.: Duke University Press.

Foucault, Michel. 1979. *Discipline and Punish: The Birth of the Prison.* Trans. Alan Sheridan. New York: Vintage–Random House.

Frank, Katherine. 1982. "The Death of the Slave Girl: African Womanhood in the Novels of Buchi Emecheta." *World Literature Written in English* 21.2: 476–97.

Fraser, Robert. 1980. *The Novels of Ayi Kwei Armah: A Study in Polemical Fiction.* London: Heinemann.

Gakwandi, S. A. 1992. "Freedom as Nightmare: Armah's *The Beautyful Ones Are Not Yet Born.*" In *Critical Perspectives on Ayi Kwei Armah.* Ed. Derek Wright. Washington, D.C.: Three Continents Press. 102–15.

Galey, Matthieu. 1968. "Un grand roman africain." *Le Monde* (October 12).

Gates, Henry Louis, Jr. 1984. "Criticism in the Jungle." In *Black Literature and Literary Theory*. Ed. Henry Louis Gates, Jr. London: Methuen. 1–24.

Geesey, Patricia, ed. 1992. Special issue on North African Literature. *Research in African Literatures* 23.2.

Gérard, Albert. 1971. *Four African Literatures: Xhosa, Sotho, Zulu, Amharic*. Berkeley: University of California Press.

———. 1981. *African Language Literatures: An Introduction to the Literary Heritage of Sub-Saharan Africa*. Washington, D.C.: Three Continents Press.

———. 1990. *Contexts of African Literature*. Amsterdam: Rodopi.

Gikandi, Simon. 1987. *Reading the African Novel*. London: James Currey.

———. 1991. *Reading Chinua Achebe: Language and Ideology in Fiction*. London: Heinemann.

Gold, Michael. 1984. *Jews Without Money*. 1930. New York: Carroll and Graf.

Goody, Jack. 1977. *The Domestication of the Savage Mind*. Cambridge: Cambridge University Press.

———. 1987. *The Interface Between the Written and the Oral*. Cambridge: Cambridge University Press.

Gordimer, Nadine. 1949. *Face to Face: Short Stories*. Johannesburg: Silver Leaf.

———. 1953. *The Lying Days*. New York: Simon and Schuster.

———. 1954. *The Soft Voice of the Serpent and Other Stories*. London: Gollancz.

———. 1956. *Six Feet of the Country: Short Stories*. London: Gollancz.

———. 1958. *A World of Strangers*. London: Jonathan Cape.

———. 1960a. *Friday's Footprint and Other Stories*. New York: Viking.

———. 1960b. *Occasion for Loving*. New York: Viking.

———. 1970. *A Guest of Honour*. New York: Viking.

———. 1972. *Livingstone's Companions*. London: Jonathan Cape.

———. 1973. *The Black Interpreters: Notes on African Writing*. Johannesburg: Spro-Cas/ Ravan.

———. 1975. *The Conservationist*. 1974. New York: Penguin.

———. 1980a. *Burger's Daughter*. 1979. New York: Penguin.

———. 1980b. *A Soldier's Embrace: Stories*. London: Jonathan Cape.

———. 1982a. *July's People*. 1981. New York: Penguin.

———. 1982b. *The Late Bourgeois World*. 1966. New York: Penguin.

———. 1983. *Selected Stories*. 1975. New York: Penguin.

———. 1988. *A Sport of Nature*. London: Penguin.

———. 1989. *The Essential Gesture: Writing, Politics, Places*. 1988. New York: Penguin.

———. 1991a. *Jump and Other Stories*. New York: Penguin.

———. 1991b. *My Son's Story*. 1990. New York: Penguin.

———. 1992. *Why Haven't You Written?: Selected Stories, 1950–1972*. New York: Penguin.

———. 1994. *None to Accompany Me*. New York: Farrar, Straus and Giroux.

———. 1995. *Writing and Being*. Cambridge, Mass.: Harvard University Press.

Gorky, Maxim. 1972. *Mother*. Trans. Isidore Schneider. Secaucus, N.J.: Citadel.

———. 1979. *My Universities*. Trans. Ronald Wilks. London: Penguin.

Gramsci, Antonio. 1971. *Selections from the Prison Notebooks*. Ed. Quintin Hoare and Geoffrey Nowell Smith. New York: International Publishers.

Green, Robert. 1979. "Alex La Guma's *In the Fog of the Seasons' End*: The Politics of Subversion." *Umoja* 3.2: 85–93.

Greenblatt, Stephen. 1988. *Shakespearean Negotiations: The Circulation of Social Energy in Renaissance England*. Berkeley: University of California Press.

Greene, Graham. 1934. *It's a Battlefield*. London: Heinemann.

Griffiths, Gareth. 1992. "Structure and Image in Kwei Armah's *The Beautyful Ones Are Not Yet Born.*" In *Critical Perspectives on Ayi Kwei Armah*. Ed. Derek Wright. Washington, D.C.: Three Continents Press. 75–91.

Gurnah, Abdulrazak, ed. 1994. *Essays on African Writing 1: A Re-evaluation*. London: Heinemann.

——. 1995. *Essays on African Writing 2: A Re-evaluation*. London: Heinemann.

Halil, Karen. 1994. "Travelling the 'World Round as Your Navel': Subjectivity in Nadine Gordimer's *Burger's Daughter.*" *Ariel* 25.2: 31–45.

Hamilton, Russell G. 1993. "Portuguese-Language Literature." In *A History of Twentieth-Century African Literatures*. Ed. Oyekan Owomoyela. Lincoln: University of Nebraska Press. 240–84.

Harrow, Kenneth W., ed. 1991. *Faces of Islam in African Literature*. Portsmouth, N.H.: Heinemann.

Head, Bessie. 1969. *When Rain Clouds Gather*. London: Gollancz.

——. 1971. *Maru*. London: Gallancz.

——. 1974. *A Question of Power*. London: Davis-Poynter.

——. 1977. *The Collector of Treasures and Other Botswana Tales*. London: Heinemann.

——. 1981. *Serowe: Village of the Rain Wind*. Oxford: Heinemann.

——. 1984. *A Bewitched Crossroad: An African Saga*. Craighall, South Africa: Donker.

——. 1989. *Tales of Tenderness and Power*. Johannesburg: Donker.

Head, Dominic. 1995. *Nadine Gordimer*. Cambridge: Cambridge University Press.

Hegel, G. W. F. 1956. *The Philosophy of History*. Trans. J. Sibree. New York: Dover.

Hernadi, Paul. 1972. "Dual-Perspective: Free Indirect Discourse and Related Techniques." *Comparative Literature* 24: 32–43.

Hill-Lubin, Mildred A. 1982. "The Relationship of African-Americans and Africans: A Recurring Theme in the Works of Ata Aidoo." *Présence Africaine* 124: 190–201.

——. 1989. "The Storyteller and the Audience in the Works of Ama Ata Aidoo." *Neohelicon* 16.2: 221–45.

Holquist, Michael. 1984. Prologue to *Rabelais and His World*, by Mikhail Bakhtin. Bloomington: Indiana University Press. xiii–xxiii.

Honwana, Luís Bernardo. 1964. *Nós matamos o Cão-Tinhoso*. Laurenco Marques, Mozambique: Composto e impresso na Sociedado de Impressa de Mocambique. Trans. Dorothy Guedes, as *We Killed Mangy-Dog*. London: Heinemann, 1969.

Horkheimer, Max, and Theodor W. Adorno. 1972. *Dialectic of Enlightenment*. Trans. John Cumming. New York: Seabird Press.

Hove, Chenjerai. 1988. *Bones*. Harare: Baobab.

——. 1991. *Shadows*. Harare: Baobab.

Innes, C. L. 1990. *Chinua Achebe*. Cambridge: Cambridge University Press.

——. 1992. "Mothers or Sisters? Identity, Discourse and Audience in the Writing of Ama Ata Aidoo and Mariama Bâ." In *Motherlands: Black Women's Writing from Africa, the Caribbean, and South Asia*. Ed. Susheila Nasta. New Brunswick, N.J.: Rutgers University Press. 129–51.

Innes, C. L., and Bernth Lindfors, eds. 1978. *Critical Perspectives on Chinua Achebe*. Washington, D.C.: Three Continents Press.

Irele, Abiola. 1978. "The Tragic Conflict in the Novels of Chinua Achebe." In *Critical Perspectives on Chinua Achebe*. Ed. C. L. Innes and Bernth Lindfors. Washington, D.C.: Three Continents Press. 10–21.

——. 1990. *The African Experience in Literature and Ideology*. Bloomington: Indiana University Press.

————. 1993. "Narrative, History, and the African Imagination." *Narrative* 1.2: 156–72.
Iyasere, Solomon O. 1978. "Narrative Techniques in *Things Fall Apart.*" In *Critical Perspectives on Chinua Achebe.* Ed. C. L. Innes and Bernth Lindfors. Washington, D.C.: Three Continents Press. 92–110.
Iyayi, Festus. 1979. *Violence.* Harlow: Longman.
————. 1982. *The Contract.* Harlow: Longman.
————. 1986. *Heroes.* Harlow: Longman.
Jacobson, Dan. 1960. *The Evidence of Love.* London: Weidenfeld and Nicolson.
Jad, Ali B. 1983. *Form and Technique in the Egyptian Novel, 1912–1971.* Oxford: Ithaca Press.
Jahn, Janheinz. 1968. *Neo-African Literature: A History of Black Writing.* Trans. Oliver Coburn and Ursula Lehrburger. New York: Grove Press.
James, C. L. R. 1977. *Nkrumah and the Ghana Revolution.* London: Allison and Busby.
Jameson, Fredric. 1981. *The Political Unconscious: Narrative as a Socially Symbolic Act.* Ithaca, N.Y.: Cornell University Press.
————. 1986. "Third-World Literature in the Era of Multinational Capitalism." *Social Text* 15: 65–88.
————. 1991. *Postmodernism, or, The Cultural Logic of Late Capitalism.* Durham, N.C.: Duke University Press.
————. 1992. *Signatures of the Visible.* New York: Routledge.
JanMohamed, Abdul R. 1983. *Manichean Aesthetics: The Politics of Literature in Colonial Africa.* Amherst: University of Massachusetts Press.
————. 1984. "Sophisticated Primitivism: The Syncretism of Oral and Literate Modes in Achebe's *Things Fall Apart.*" *Ariel* 15.4: 19–39.
Jeyifo, Biodun. 1990. *Ngugi wa Thiong'o.* London: Pluto.
————. 1991. "For Chinua Achebe: The Resilience and the Predicament of Obierika." In *Chinua Achebe: A Celebration.* Oxford: Heinemann. 51–70.
Jordan, A. C. 1940. *Ingqumbo yeminyanya.* Lovedale, South Africa: Lovedale Press.
Julien, Eileen. 1992. *African Novels and the Question of Orality.* Bloomington: Indiana University Press.
Juraga, Dubravka, and M. Keith Booker. 1993. "Literature, Power, and Oppression in Stalinist Russia and Catholic Ireland: Danilo Kiš's Use of Joyce in *A Tomb for Boris Davidovich.*" *South Atlantic Review* 58.4: 39–58.
Kane, Hamidou. 1961. *L'aventure ambiguë.* Paris: Julliard. Trans. Katherine Woods, as *Ambiguous Adventure.* New York: Walker and Company. 1963.
Kaye, Jacqueline. 1992. *Maghreb: New Writing from North Africa.* York, England: Talus.
Kershner, R. B., Jr. 1986. "Degeneration: The Explanatory Nightmare." *Georgia Review* 40: 416–44.
Kettle, Arnold. 1951. *An Introduction to the English Novel.* Vol. 1. London: Hutchinson.
Kibera, Leonard. 1970. *Voices in the Dark.* Nairobi: East African Publishing House.
————. 1976. "A Critical Appreciation of Alex La Guma's *In the Fog of the Seasons' End.*" *Busara* 8.1: 59–66.
————. 1992. "Pessimism and the African Novelist: Ayi Kwei Armah's *The Beautyful Ones Are Not Yet Born.*" In *Critical Perspectives on Ayi Kwei Armah.* Ed. Derek Wright. Washington, D.C.: Three Continents Press. 92–101.
Kibera, Leonard, and Sam Kahiga. 1968. *Potent Ash.* Nairobi: East African Publishing House.
Killam, G. D. 1977. *The Writings of Chinua Achebe.* London: Heinemann.
————. 1980. *An Introduction to the Writings of Ngugi.* London: Heinemann.
King, Bruce, ed. 1993. *The Later Fiction of Nadine Gordimer.* London: Macmillan.

Kourouma, Ahmadou. 1968. *Les soleils des indépendances*. Montreal: Presses de l'Université de Montreal. Trans. Adrian Adams, as *The Suns of Independence*. London: Heinemann, 1981.

———. 1990. *Monnè, outrages et défis*. Paris: Éditions du Seuil. Trans. Nidra Poller, as *Monnew*. San Francisco: Mercury House, 1993.

Kristeva, Julia. 1980. *Desire in Language: A Semiotic Approach to Literature and Art*. Trans. Thomas Gora, Alice Jardine, and Leon S. Roudiez. Ed. Leon S. Roudiez. New York: Columbia University Press.

La Guma, Alex. 1964. *And a Threefold Cord*. Berlin: Seven Seas.

———. 1967a. *The Stone Country*. Berlin: Seven Seas.

———. 1967b. *A Walk in the Night*. Evanston, Ill.: Northwestern University Press.

———. 1972. *In the Fog of the Seasons' End*. London: Heinemann.

———. 1979. *Time of the Butcherbird*. London: Heinemann.

Landrum, Roger L. 1970. "Chinua Achebe and the Aristotelian Concept of Tragedy." *Black Academy Review* 1: 22–30.

Lang, George. 1987. "Text, Identity, and Difference: Yambo Ouologuem's *Le Devoir de Violence* and Ayi Kwei Armah's *Two Thousand Seasons*." *Comparative Literature Studies* 24.4: 387–402.

Larson, Charles. 1972. *The Emergence of African Fiction*. Rev. ed. Bloomington: Indiana University Press.

Laye, Camara. 1953. *L'enfant noir*. Paris: Plon. Trans. James Kirkup and Ernest Jones, as *The Dark Child*. New York: Farrar, Straus and Giroux, 1954.

———. 1966. *Dramouss*. Paris: Plon. Trans. as , *A Dream of Africa*. London: Colins, 1968.

Lazarus, Neil. 1990. *Resistance in Postcolonial African Fiction*. New Haven, Conn.: Yale University Press.

Leeuwenburg, Rina. 1985. "Nadine Gordimer's *Burger's Daughter*: Why Does Rosa Go Back?" *New Literature Review* 14: 23–31.

Lenin, Vladimir Ilich. 1926. *Imperialism: The Highest Stage of Capitalism*. In *"Imperialism" and "The State and Revolution."* New York: Vanguard.

Lessing, Doris. 1952. *Martha Quest*. London: Michael Joseph.

———. 1954. *A Proper Marriage*. London: Michael Joseph.

———. 1958. *A Ripple from the Storm*. London: Michael Joseph.

———. 1965. *Landlocked*. London: MacGibbon and Kee.

Lewis, Maureen Warner. 1979. "The African Impact on Language and Literature in the English-Speaking Caribbean." In *Africa and the Caribbean: The Legacies of a Link*. Ed. Margaret E. Crahan and Franklin W. Knight. Baltimore: Johns Hopkins University Press. 101–23.

Liking, Werewere. 1983. *Elle sera de jaspe et de corail*. Paris: Éditions l'Harmattan.

Lindfors, Bernth. 1990. "The Teaching of African Literatures in Anglophone African Universities: An Instructive Canon." *Matatu* 7: 41–55.

———, ed. 1991. *Approaches to Teaching Achebe's "Things Fall Apart."* New York: Modern Language Association.

Lopes, Henri. 1982. *Le pleurer-rire*. Paris: Présence Africaine. Trans. Gerald Moore, as *The Laughing Cry*. London: Readers International, 1987.

Lukács, Georg. 1963. *The Meaning of Contemporary Realism*. Trans. John Mander and Necker Mander. London: Merlin Press.

———. 1971a. *History and Class Consciousness: Studies in Marxist Dialectics*. Trans. Rodney Livingstone. Cambridge, Mass.: MIT Press.

———. 1971b. *The Theory of the Novel*. Trans. Anna Bostock. Cambridge, Mass., MIT Press.

————. 1983. *The Historical Novel.* Trans. Hannah Mitchell and Stanley Mitchell. Lincoln: University of Nebraska Press.

Lyons, R. H. 1975. *To Wash an Aethiop White.* New York: Teachers College Press.

Macgoye, Marjorie Oludhe. 1986. *Coming to Birth.* London: Heinemann.

————. 1987. *Street Life.* Nairobi: Heinemann.

Mahfouz, Naguib. 1956. *Bayn al-qasrayn.* Cairo: Maktabat Misr. Trans. William Maynard Hutchins and Olive E. Kenny, as *Palace Walk.* New York: Doubleday, 1990.

————. 1957. *Qasr al-shawq.* Cairo: Maktabat Misr. Trans. William Maynard Hutchins, Lorne M. Kenny, and Olive E. Kenny, as *Palace of Desire.* New York: Doubleday, 1991.

————. 1958. *Al-sukkariyah.* Cairo: Maktabat Misr. Trans. William Maynard Hutchins and Angele Botros Samaan, as *Sugar Street.* New York: Doubleday, 1992.

Maillu, David. 1973. *My Dear Bottle.* Nairobi: Comb.

————. 1974. *After 4:30.* Nairobi: Comb.

Maina, Paul. 1977. *Six Maumau Generals.* Nairobi: Gazelle Books.

Mandel, Ernest. 1975. *Late Capitalism.* Trans. Joris De Bres. London: NLB.

Mangua, Charles. 1971. *Son of Woman.* Nairobi: East African Publishing House.

————. 1972. *A Tail in the Mouth.* Nairobi: East African Publishing House.

Maran, René. 1921. *Batouala.* Paris: A. Michel. Trans. Barbara Beck and Alexandre Mboukou, as *Batauala.* London: Heinemann, 1973.

Marechera, Dambudzo. 1978. *The House of Hunger.* New York: Pantheon.

————. 1980. *Black Sunlight.* London: Heinemann.

Marx, Karl, and Friedrich Engels. 1978. *The Marx-Engels Reader.* 2nd ed. Ed. Robert C. Tucker. New York: Norton.

Mazrui, Ali A. 1971. *The Trial of Christopher Okigbo.* London: Heinemann.

————. 1986. *The Africans: A Triple Heritage.* Boston: Little, Brown.

McHale, Brian. 1979. "Modernist Reading, Post-Modern Text: The Case of *Gravity's Rainbow.*" *Poetics Today* 1: 85–110.

McLynn, Frank. 1992. *Hearts of Darkness: The European Exploration of Africa.* New York: Carroll and Graf.

Memmi, Albert. 1965. *The Colonizer and the Colonized.* New York: Orion Press.

Miller, Christopher. 1985. *Blank Darkness: Africanist Discourse in French.* Chicago: University of Chicago Press.

————. 1990. *Theories of Africans: Francophone Literature and Anthropology in Africa.* Chicago: University of Chicago Press.

Mitchison, Naomi. 1973. *A Life for Africa: The Story of Bram Fischer.* London: Merlin Press.

Mofolo, Thomas. *Chaka.* 1981. Trans. Daniel Kunene. London: Heinemann.

Moretti, Franco. 1987. *The Way of the World: The Bildungsroman in European Culture.* London: Verso.

Mortimer, Mildred P. 1990. *Journeys through the French African Novel.* London: James Currey.

Moser, Gerald M. 1967. "African Literature in Portuguese: The First Written, the Last Discovered." *African Forum* 2.4: 78–96.

Moses, Michael Valdez. 1995. *The Novel and the Globalization of Culture.* New York: Oxford University Press.

Mphahlele, Es'kia. 1959. *Down Second Avenue.* London: Faber and Faber.

————. 1961. *The Living and the Dead.* Ibadan, Nigeria: Ministry of Education.

————. 1962. *The African Image.* London: Faber and Faber.

————. 1967. *In Corner B.* Nairobi: East African Publishing House.

———. 1971. *The Wanderers*. New York: MacMillan.

———. 1972. *Voices in the Whirlwind*. New York: Hilland Wang.

———. 1979. *Chirundu*. Johannesburg: Raven.

———. 1981. *The Unbroken Song*. Johannesburg: Raven.

———. 1988. *Renewal Time*. Columbia, Louisiana: Readers International.

Mudimbe, V. Y. 1973. *Entre les eaux*. Paris: Présence Africaine. Trans. Stephen Becker, as *Between Tides*. New York: Simon and Schuster, 1991.

———. 1976. *Le bel immonde*. Paris: Présence Africaine. Trans. Marjolijn de Jager, as *Before the Birth of the Moon*. New York: Simon and Schuster, 1989.

———. 1979. *L'écart*. Paris: Présence Africaine. Trans. Marjolijn de Jager, as *The Rift*. Minneapolis: University of Minneapolis Press, 1993.

———. 1988. *The Invention of Africa: Gnosis, Philosophy, and the Order of Knowledge*. Bloomington: Indiana University Press.

Mulaisho, Dominic. 1971. *The Tongue of the Dumb*. London: Heinemann.

Munonye, John. 1966. *The Only Son*. London: Heinemann.

Mwangi, Meja. 1974. *Carcase for Hounds*. London: Heinemann.

———. 1975. *Taste of Death*. Nairobi: East African Publishing House.

———. 1976. *Kill Me Quick!* London: Heinemann.

———. 1976. *Going Down River Road*. London: Heinemann.

———. 1979. *The Cockroach Dance*. Nairobi: Longman.

———. *Weapon of Hunger*. Nairobi: Longman.

Nazareth, Peter. 1972. *In a Brown Mantle*. Nairobi: East African Literature Bureau.

Ndawo, Henry Masila. 1952. *uHambo lukaGqoboka*. Lovedale, South Africa: Lovedale Press. First published 1909.

Newman, Judie. 1988. *Nadine Gordimer*. London: Routledge.

Ngara, Emmanuel. 1985. *Art and Ideology in the African Novel: A Study of the Influence of Marxism on African Writing*. London: Heinemann.

———, ed. 1995. *New Writing from Southern Africa: Authors Who Have Become Prominent since 1980*. London: Heinemann.

Ngaté, Jonathan. 1988. *Francophone African Fiction: Reading a Literary Tradition*. Trenton, N.J.: Africa World Press.

Ngugi wa Thiong'o. 1964. *Weep Not, Child*. London: Heinemann.

———. 1965. *The River Between*. London: Heinemann.

———. 1967. *A Grain of Wheat*. London: Heinemann.

———. 1968. *The Black Hermit*. London: Heinemann.

———. 1972. *Homecoming: Essays on African and Caribbean Literature, Culture, and Politics*. New York: Lawrence Hill.

———. 1975. *Secret Lives and Other Stories*. London: Heinemann.

———. 1977. *Petals of Blood*. London: Heinemann.

———. 1980. *Caitaani mutharaba-ini*. Nairobi: Heinemann. Trans. Ngugi wa Thiong'o, as *Devil on the Cross*. London: Heinemann, 1982.

———. 1981a. *Detained: A Writer's Prison Diary*. London: Heinemann.

———. 1981b. *Writers in Politics*. London: Heinemann.

———. 1983. *Barrel of a Pen: Resistance to Repression in Neo-Colonial Kenya*. Trenton, N.J.: Africa World Press.

———. 1986. *Matigari ma Njiruugi*. Nairobi: Heinemann. Trans. Wangui wa Goro, as *Matigiri*. London: Heinemann, 1989.

———. 1992. *Decolonising the Mind: The Politics of Language in African Literature*. London: James Currey.

———. 1993. *Moving the Centre: The Struggle for Cultural Freedoms*. London: James Currey.

Ngugi wa Thiong'o and Micere Githae Mugo. 1977. *The Trial of Dedan Kimathi*. London: Heinemann.

Ngugi wa Thiong'o and Ngugi wa Mirii. 1988. *I Will Marry When I Want*. Trans. by the authors. London: Heinemann.

Njau, Rebeka. 1975. *Ripples in the Pool*. Nairobi: Transafrica.

Njoku, Benedict Chiaka. 1984. *The Four Novels of Chinua Achebe*. New York: Peter Lang.

Nkosi, Lewis. 1983. 1981. *Tasks and Masks: Themes and Styles of African Literature*. Harlow, Essex: Longman.

——. *Mating Birds*. Nairobi: East African Publishing House.

Nkrumah, Kwame. 1970. *Class Struggle in Africa*. New York: International Publishers.

Nwankwo, Chimalum. 1986. "The Feminist Impulse and Social Realism in Ama Ata Aidoo's *No Sweetness Here* and *Our Sister Killjoy*." In *Ngambika: Studies of Women in African Literature*. Ed. Carole Boyce Davies and Anne Adams Graves. Trenton, N.J.: Africa World Press. 151–59.

——. 1992. *The Works of Ngugi wa Thiong'o: Towards the Kingdom of Woman and Man*. Okeja: Longman Nigeria.

Nwankwo, Nkem. 1964. *Danda*. London: Heinemann.

——. 1975. *My Mercedes Is Bigger Than Yours*. London: Deutsch.

Nwapa, Flora. 1966. *Efuru*. London: Heinemann.

——. 1970. *Idu*. London: Heinemann.

——. *Never Again*. Enugu, Nigeria: Nwamife.

——. 1981. *One Is Enough*. Enugu, Nigeria: Tana.

——. 1986. *Women Are Different*. Trenton: Africa World Press.

Obiechina, Emmanuel. 1975. *Culture, Tradition and Society in the West African Novel*. Cambridge: Cambridge University Press.

——. 1990. *Language and Theme: Essays on African Literature*. Washington, D.C.: Howard University Press.

——. 1993. "Narrative Proverbs in the African Novel." *Research in African Literatures* 24.4: 123–40.

Odamtten, Vincent O. 1994. *The Art of Ama Ata Aidoo: Polylectics and Reading Against Neocolonialism*. Gainesville: University Press of Florida.

Ogot, Grace. 1966. *The Promised Land*. Nairobi East African Publishing House.

——. 1968. *Land Without Thunder*. Nairobi East African Publishing House.

——. 1976. *The Other Woman*. Nairobi: Transafrica.

——. 1980a. *The Island of Tears*. Nairobi: Uzima.

——. 1980b. *The Graduate*. Nairobi: Uzima.

——. 1981a. *Ber Wat*. Kisimu, Kenya: Anyange.

——. 1981b. *Aloo Kod Apul-Apul*. Kisumu, Kenya: Anyange.

——. 1983a. *Miaha*. Nairobi: Heinemann. Trans. as *The Strange Bride*. Nairobi: Heinemann, 1989.

——. 1983b. *Simbi Nyaima*. Kisumu, Kenya: Anyange.

Ogundipe-Leslie, Molara. 1973. Review of *The Emergence of African Fiction*, by Charles R. Larson. *Okike* 4: 81–89.

——. 1987. "The Female Writer and Her Commitment." In *Women in African Literature Today*. Ed. Eldred Durosimi Jones, Eustace Palmer, and Marjorie Jones. Trenton, N.J.: Africa World Press. 5–13.

Ogunjimi, Bayo. 1984. "Language, Oral Tradition and Social Vision in Ngugi's *Devil on the Cross*." *Ufahamu* 14.1: 56–70.

Ogunyemi, Chikwenye Okonjo. 1996. *African Wo/Man Palava: The Nigerian Novel by Women*. Chicago: University of Chicago Press.

Ojinmah, Umelo. 1991. *Chinua Achebe: New Perspectives*. Ibadan: Spectrum.

Okara, Gabriel. 1964. *The Voice*. London: Deutsch.

Okpaku, Joseph. 1970. "Culture and Criticism: African Critical Standards for African Literature and the Arts." In *New African Literature and the Arts*. Ed. Joseph Okpaku. New York: Crowell. 13–23.

Okri, Ben. 1980. *Flowers and Shadows*. Harlow: Longman.

———. 1981. *The Landscapes Within*. Harlow: Longman.

———. 1986. *Incidents and the Shrine*. London: Heinemann.

———. 1988. *Stars of the New Curfew*. London: Secker and Warburg.

———. 1991. *The Famished Road*. London: Jonathan Cape.

———. 1993. New York: Doubleday. *Songs of Enchantment*.

Olaniyan, Richard, ed. 1982. *African History and Culture*. Lagos: Longman.

Omotoso, Kole. 1972. *The Combat*. London: Heinemann.

Ong, Walter J. 1982. *Orality and Literacy: The Technologizing of the Word*. London: Methuen.

Osinya, Alumidi. 1977. *Field Marshal Abdulla Salim Fisi, or How the Hyena Got His!* Nairobi: Joe.

Ouologuem, Yambo. 1968. *Le devoir de violence*. Paris: Éditions du Seuil. Trans. Ralph Manheim, as *Bound to Violence*. London: Secker and Warburg, 1971.

Owomoyela, Oyekan, ed. 1993. *A History of Twentieth-Century African Literatures*. Lincoln: University of Nebraska Press.

Owusu, Kofi. 1990. "Canons Under Siege: Blackness, Femaleness, and Ama Ata Aidoo's *Our Sister Killjoy*." *Callaloo* 13.2: 341–63.

Oyono, Ferdinand. 1956a. *Le vieux nègre et la médaille*. Paris: Julliard. Trans. as *The Old Man and the Medal*. London: Heinemann, 1967.

———. 1956b. *Une vie de boy*. Paris: Julliard. Trans. John Reed, as *Houseboy*. London: Heinemann, 1967.

Pakenham, Thomas. 1991. *The Scramble for Africa: The White Man's Conquest of the Dark Continent from 1876 to 1912*. New York: Random House.

Palmer, Eustace. 1972. *An Introduction to the African Novel*. New York: Africana.

———. 1983. "The Feminine Point of View: Buchi Emecheta's *The Joys of Motherhood*." *African Literature Today* 13: 38–55.

Parrinder, Patrick. 1992. "*Heart of Darkness*: Geography as Apocalypse." In *Fin de Siècle/Fin du Globe* Ed. John Stokes. New York: St. Martin's. 85–101.

Paton, Alan. 1948. *Cry, the Beloved Country*. New York: Scribner.

p'Bitek, Okot. 1953. *Lak Tar Miyo Kinyero wi Lobo*. Kampala: Eagle.

———. 1966. *Song of Lawino*. Nairobi: East African Publishing House.

———. 1970a. *Song of Ocol*. Nairobi: East African Publishing House.

———. 1970b. *African Religions in Western Scholarship*. Nairobi: Kenya Literature Bureau.

———. 1971. *Two Songs: Song of Prisoner and Song of Malaya*. Nairobi: East African Publishing House.

———. 1974. *The Horn of My Love*. London: Heinemann.

———. 1986. *Artist, the Ruler*. Nairobi: Heinemann.

Peck, Richard. 1989. "One Foot before the Other into an Unknown Future: The Dialectic in Nadine Gordimer's *Burger's Daughter*." *World Literature Written in English* 29.1: 26–43.

Pepetela. 1980. *Mayombe*. Lisboa: Edicoes 70. Trans. Michael Wolfers, as *Mayombe*. London: Heinemann, 1983.

Peters, Jonathan. 1993. "English-Language Fiction from West Africa." In *A History of*

Twentieth-Century African Literatures. Ed. Oyekan Owomoyela. Lincoln: University of Nebraska Press. 9–48.

Petersen, Kirsten Holst, and Anna Rutherford, eds. 1990. *Chinua Achebe: A Celebration.* Oxford: Heinemann.

Phillips, Maggi. 1994. "Engaging Dreams: Alternative Perspectives on Flora Nwapa, Buchi Emecheta, Ama Ata Aidoo, Bessie Head, and Tsitsi Dangarembga's Writing." *Research in African Literatures* 25.4: 89–103.

Priebe, Richard. 1976. "Demonic Imagery and the Apocalyptic Vision in the Novels of Ayi Kwei Armah." *Yale French Studies* 53: 102–36.

Quayson, Ato. 1994. "Realism, Criticism, and the Disguises of Both: A Reading of Chinua Achebe's *Things Fall Apart* with an Evaluation of the Criticism Relating to It." *Research in African Literatures* 25.4: 117–36.

Rabkin, David. 1973. "La Guma and Reality in South Africa." *Journal of Commonwealth Literature* 8.1: 54–61.

Ravenscroft, Arthur. 1969. *Chinua Achebe.* Ed. Ian Scott-Kilvert. London: Longman.

Riemenschneider, Dieter, and Frank Schulze-Engler, eds. 1993. *African Literatures in the Eighties.* Amsterdam: Rodopi.

Rive, Richard. 1964. *Emergency.* London: Faber and Faber.

———. 1986. *"Buckingham Palace," District Six.* London: Heinemann.

———. 1990. *Emergency Continued.* London: Readers International.

Robson, Clifford B. 1979. *Ngugi wa Thiong'o.* London: Macmillan.

Rodney, Walter. 1972. *How Europe Underdeveloped Africa.* Dar es Salaam: Tanzania Publishing House.

Rooney, Caroline. 1992. "'Dangerous Knowledge' and the Poetics of Survival: A Reading of *Our Sister Killjoy* and *A Question of Power.*" In *Motherlands: Black Women's Writing from Africa, the Caribbean, and South Asia.* Ed. Susheila Nasta. New Brunswick, N.J.: Rutgers University Press. 99–126.

Roscoe, Adrian. 1977. *Uhuru's Fire: African Literature East to South.* Cambridge: Cambridge University Press.

Rui, Manuel. 1977. *Sim camarada!* Lisboa: Edicoes 70. Trans. as *Yes, Comrade!* Minneapolis: University of Minnesota Press, 1993.

Rushdie, Salman. 1982. "The Empire Writes Back with a Vengeance." *Times* (London) (July 3): 8.

Sackey, Edward. 1991. "Oral Tradition and the African Novel." *Modern Fiction Studies* 37.3: 389–407.

Said, Edward. 1979. *Orientalism.* New York: Vintage–Random House.

———. 1993. *Culture and Imperialism.* New York: Knopf.

Salih, Tayeb. 1969. *Mawsim al-hijrah il'a al-shamal.* Cairo: Dar al-Hilal. Trans. Denys Johnson Davies, as *Season of Migration to the North.* Portsmouth, NH: Heinemann.

Sartre, Jean-Paul. 1968. Preface to *The Wretched of the Earth*, by Frantz Fanon. New York: Grove Press. 7–31.

Scanlon, Paul A. 1979. "Alex La Guma's Novels of Protest: The Growth of the Revolutionary." *Okike* 16: 39–47.

Schipper, Mineke. 1989. *Beyond the Boundaries: African Literature and Literary Theory.* London: Allison and Busby.

Schreiner, Olive. 1883. *Story of an African Farm.* New York: American Publishers.

Schwarz-Bart, André. 1959. *Le dernier des justes.* Paris: Éditions du Seuil. Trans. Stephen Becker, as *The Last of the Just.* London: Secker and Warburg, 1961.

Sellin, Eric. 1976. "The Unknown Voice of Yambo Ouologuem." *Yale French Studies* 53: 151–57.

Sembène, Ousmane. 1956. *Le docker noir*. Paris: Nouvelles Éditions Debresse. Trans. Ros Schwartz, as *Black Docker*. London: Heinemann, 1987.

———. 1957. *Ô pays, mon beau peuple!* Paris: Le Livre Contemporain.

———. 1960. *Les bouts de bois de Dieu*. Paris: Le Livre Contemporain. Trans. Francis Price, as *God's Bits of Wood*. New York: Doubleday, 1962.

———. 1962. *Voltaïque*. Paris; Présence Africaine. Trans. as *Tribal Scars and Other Stories*. Washington, D.C.: Inscape, 1975.

———. 1965a. *Referendum*. Paris: Présence Africaine.

———. 1965b. *Vehi-Ciosane ou Blanche-Genèse, suivi du Le Mandat*. Paris: Présence Africaine. Trans. Clive Wake, as *The Money Order, with White Genesis*. Oxford: Heinemann, 1972.

———. 1973. *Xala*. Paris: Présence Africaine. Trans. Clive Wake, as *Xala*. Chicago: Lawrence Hill, 1976.

———. 1981. *Le dernier de l'empire*. Paris: L'Harmattan. Trans. Adrian Adams, as *The Last of the Empire*. Oxford: Heinemann, 1983.

———. 1987 *Niiwam, suivi de Taaw*. Paris: Présence Africaine. Trans. Gioia Eisman, et al., as *Niiwam and Taaw*. Oxford: Heinemann, 1991.

Sepamla, Sipho. 1979. *The Root Is One*. London: R. Collings.

———. 1981. *A Ride on the Whirlwind*. Johannesburg: Donker.

———. 1986. *Third Generation*. Johannesburg: Skotaville.

———. 1989. *A Scattered Survival*. Braa,fontein, South Africa: Skotaville.

Serote, Mongane. 1981. *To Every Birth Its Blood*. Johannesburg, Raven.

Seruma, Eneriko. 1970. *The Experience*. Nairobi: East African Publishing House.

———. 1971. *The Heart Seller*. Nairobi: East African Publishing House.

Sicherman, Carol M. 1990. *Ngugi wa Thiong'o, The Making of a Rebel: A Source Book in Kenyan Literature and Resistance*. London: Hans Zell.

Smith, Rowland, ed. 1990. *Critical Essays on Nadine Gordimer*. Boston: G. K. Hall.

Sow Fall, Aminata. 1976. *Le revenant*. Dakar: Nouvelles Éditions Africaines.

———. 1979. *La grève des bàttu*. Dakar: Nouvelles Éditions Africaines. Trans. Dorothy S. Blair, as *The Beggars' Strike*. Harlow: Longman, 1981.

———. 1984. *L'appel des arène*. Abidjan: Nouvelles Éditions Africaines.

———. 1987. *Ex-père de la nation*. Paris: L'Harmattan.

———. 1993. *Le jujubier du patriarche*. Dakar: Éditions Khoudia.

Soyinka, Wole. 1965. *The Interpreters*. London: Deutsch.

———. 1973. *Season of Anomy*. London: Collings.

Steady, Filomina Chioma. 1981. *The Black Woman Crossculturally*. Cambridge, Mass.: Schenkman.

Stratton, Florence. 1994. *Contemporary African Literature and the Politics of Gender*. London: Routledge.

Sundquist, Eric J. 1993. *To Wake the Nations: Race in the Making of American Literature*. Cambridge, Mass.: Belknap–Harvard University Press.

Taiwo, Oladele. 1976. *Culture and the Nigerian Novel*. New York: St. Martin's.

Tomlinson, John. 1991. *Cultural Imperialism: A Critical Introduction*. Baltimore: Johns Hopkins University Press.

Tressell, Robert. 1955. *The Ragged-Trousered Philanthropists*. 1914. London: Lawrence and Wishart.

Tuma, Hama. 1993. *The Case of the Socialist Witchdoctor and Other Stories*. Oxford: Heinemann.

Turner, Margaret E. 1990. "Achebe, Hegel, and the New Colonialism." In *Chinua*

Achebe: A Celebration. Ed. Kirsten Holst Petersen and Anna Rutherford. Oxford: Heinemann. 31–40.

Tutuola, Amos. 1952. *The Palm-Wine Drinkard and his Dead Palm-Wine Tapster in the dead's Town.* London: Faber and Faber.

Udenta, Udenta O. 1993. *Revolutionary Aesthetics and the African Literary Process.* Enugu, Nigeria: Fourth Dimension.

Umeh, Marie, ed. 1995. *Emerging Perspectives on Buchi Emecheta.* Trenton, N.J.: Africa World Press.

Van Allen, Judith. 1976. "'Aba Riots' or Igbo 'Women's War'?: Ideology, Stratification, and the Invisibility of Women." In *Women in Africa: Studies in Social and Economic Change.* Ed. Nancy J. Hafkin and Edna G. Bay. Stanford, Calif.: Stanford University Press. 59–85.

Vassanji, M. G. 1989. *The Gunny Sack.* Oxford: Heinemann.

Vizzard, Michelle. 1993. "'Of Mimicry and Women': Hysteria and Anticolonial Feminism in Tsitsi Dangarembga's *Nervous Conditions.*" *Span* 36: 202–210.

Wachira, Godwin. 1968. *Ordeal in the Forest.* Nairobi: East African Publishing House.

Waciuma, Charity. 1969. *Daughter of Mumbi.* Nairobi: East African Publishing House.

Wagner, Kathrin M. 1994. *Rereading Nadine Gordimer.* Bloomington: Indiana University Press.

Walsh, William. 1970. *A Manifold Voice: Studies in Commonwealth Literature.* New York: Barnes and Noble.

Wanyee, Patricia. 1994. "Kenya: Moi Tightens His Grip." *NewsNotes* 19.6: 10–11.

Warwick, Peter. 1983. *Black People and the South African War, 1899–1902.* Cambridge: Cambridge University Press.

Watt, Ian. 1957. *The Rise of the Novel: Studies in Defoe, Richardson, and Fielding.* Berkeley: University of California Press.

Weinstock, Donald, and Cathy Ramadan. 1978. "Symbolic Structure in *Things Fall Apart.*" In *Critical Perspectives on Chinua Achebe.* Ed. C. L. Innes and Bernth Lindfors. Washington, D.C.: Three Continents Press. 126–34.

Wesseling, H. L. 1996. *Divide and Rule: The Partition of Africa, 1880–1914.* Trans. Arnold J. Pomerans. Westport, Conn.: Praeger.

Westley, David. 1992. "Choice of Language and African Literature: A Bibliographic Essay." *Research in African Literatures* 23.1: 159–71.

Wiesel, Elie. 1987. "Night." Trans. Stella Rodway. In *The Night Trilogy.* New York: Hill and Wang. 5–119.

Williams, Eric. 1944. *Capitalism and Slavery.* New York: Putnam.

Williams, Raymond. 1977. *Marxism and Literature.* New York: Oxford University Press.

Wolf, Eric R. 1982. *Europe and the People without History.* Berkeley: University of California Press.

Wolitz, Seth I. 1973. "L'art du plagiat, ou une brève défense de Ouologuem." *Research in African Literatures* 4.1: 130–34.

Wren, Robert M. 1980. *Achebe's World: The Historical and Cultural Context of the Novels of Chinua Achebe.* Washington, D.C.: Three Continents Press.

Wright, Derek. 1989. *Ayi Kwei Armah's Africa: The Sources of His Fiction.* London: Hans Zell.

———. 1990. "Ayi Kwei Armah and the Significance of His Novels and Histories." *International Fiction Review* 17.1: 29–40.

———. 1992a. "'Dystropia' in the African Novel: A Critique of Armah's Language in *The Beautyful Ones Are Not Yet Born.*" *Commonwealth Novel in English* 5.2: 26–38.

————, ed. 1992b. *Critical Perspectives on Ayi Kwei Armah.* Washington, D.C.: Three Continents Press.

Xitu, Uanhenga. 1978. *Manana.* Lisboa: Edicoes 70. First published 1974.

Zahar, Renate. 1974. *Frantz Fanon: Colonialism and Alienation.* New York: Monthly Review Press.

Zwelonke, D. M. 1973. *Robben Island.* London: Heinemann.

Index

▼▼▼▼▼▼